TRINIDAD CARNIVAL

TRINIDAD CARNIVAL

THE CULTURAL POLITICS OF A TRANSNATIONAL FESTIVAL

Edited by Garth L. Green and Philip W. Scher

INDIANA UNIVERSITY PRESS
Bloomington and Indianapolis

This book is a publication of

Indiana University Press
601 North Morton Street
Bloomington, Indiana 47404-3797 USA

http://iupress.indiana.edu

Telephone orders 800-842-6796
Fax orders 812-855-7931
Orders by e-mail iuporder@indiana.edu

The paper used in this publication meets the minimum requirements of American National Standard for Information Sciences—Permanence of Paper for Printed Library Materials, ANSI Z39.48-1984.

Manufactured in the United States of America

Library of Congress Cataloging-in-Publication Data

Trinidad carnival : the cultural politics of a transnational festival / edited by Garth L. Green and Philip W. Scher.
p. cm.
Includes bibliographical references and index.
ISBN-13: 978-0-253-34823-4 (cloth : alk. paper)
ISBN-13: 978-0-253-21883-4 (pbk. : alk. paper) 1. Carnival—Trinidad and Tobago. 2. Carnival—West Indies. 3. Trinidadians—Foreign countries—Ethnic identity. 4. West Indians—Foreign countries—Ethnic identity. 5. Trinidad and Tobago—Social life and customs. 6. West Indies—Social life and customs. I. Green, Garth L. II. Scher, Philip W., 1965-
GT4229.T7T74 2007
394.250972983—dc22

2006028100

1 2 3 4 5 12 11 10 09 08 07

For Constance, Julia and Marston
PWS

For Sharon and Alexander
GLG

CONTENTS

Acknowledgments

This book began an embarrassingly long time ago, in 1996, as a fortieth-year celebration of the 1956 *Caribbean Quarterly* special issue devoted to Trinidad Carnival. Ten years later it neatly became a fiftieth anniversary special. There is certainly no one who writes about the Carnival who does not, first and foremost, open that special issue and then, immediately follow with Errol Hill's 1972 tour de force, *The Trinidad Carnival: Mandate for a National Theatre*. It is to the authors of these important and pioneering works that we give special thanks and remembrance.

Philip W. Scher would like to thank my generous mentors in Caribbean studies, folklore, and anthropology, specifically Roger D. Abrahams, Kevin Yelvington, and David Scott, who, in ways they may not even know, have inspired, challenged, and shaped my thinking about the region. Arjun Appadurai, Sandra T. Barnes, Webb Keane, Richard Grinker, Richard Bauman, Charles Briggs, Frances Henry, Jeff Henry, Robert K. Lee, Jason Griffiths, Cito Velasquez, Grace and Winston Carr, Christopher Cozier, Sankar and Betty Baldeosimgh, and Garry Chin.

Garth L. Green would like to thank my teachers the late William Roseberry, Rayna Rapp, Deborah Poole, Brackette Williams, Virginia Dominguez, and Richard G. Fox for providing the right mix of encouragement and freedom to discover my own way of doing anthropology. I am especially appreciative of the support Kevin Yelvington and David Scott provided throughout the long gestation of this project. I would like to express my great appreciation to those people in Trinidad who were so generous with their time, patience, friendship and, of course, hospitality: Robert K. Lee, Kathryn Chan, Brian Kong, Grace and Winston Carr, Desmond and Elinor Dharamjit, Lynette Hutchinson, and Abigail Hadeed. At the University of the West Indies I would like to thank Gordon Rohlehr for serving as my Fulbright sponsor as well as Rawle Gibbons, Ramesh Desosaran, and Bridget Brereton. A special thanks to Pat Bishop for "making sure I didn't get it wrong." I hope that I have met her expectations. Finally, I would also like to thank Cito Velasquez, Peter Minshall, and Todd Gulick for teaching me how to make mas.

The editors have greatly appreciated the patient and thorough work of our sponsoring editor at Indiana University Press, Dee Mortensen, and the other editors and folks who worked on the book: Miki Bird, Greg Domber, Beth Marsh, Jennifer Maceyko, and our copyeditor, Joyce Rappaport. If anything is wrong, it's our fault.

TRINIDAD CARNIVAL

Introduction: Trinidad Carnival in Global Context

Garth L. Green and Philip W. Scher

This collection seeks to detail the transformations that have occurred within Trinidad and the wider Caribbean diasporic community, illustrating how these changes have been manifested through the Carnival and its "offspring" events, festivals created by transplanted Trinidadians in their new homelands of Canada, Aruba, New York, and England. As is the case with many developing countries, Trinidad has felt the effects of the reorganization of international capitalism in the form of economic restructuring, currency flotation, divestment of state-owned industries, retrenchment in the public sector, rising unemployment, and an increase in violent crime and the drug trade. Within this matrix of uncertainty, Carnival serves as a battleground in which the guardians of national morality and social welfare portray themselves as combating the allied forces of venality, sin, and depravity. These factors are often encapsulated as various foreign threats that include the drug trade from South America, the crass materialism of the United States, and, from the perspective of some Trinidadians, the vulgarity and violence of Jamaican popular culture. Other narratives of the "state of the nation" characterize the Carnival as a social problem of its own that no longer represents the creativity, resourcefulness, and resiliency of Trinidadian culture. The Carnival itself has become a reflection of the entire society, nation, and culture.

While this study may be seen as a contribution to a growing literature on globalization, we contend that the Carnival in Trinidad, and the others considered in the pages of this volume, are historical products. They result from the movement of people, ideas, and objects made possible by modern transportation and communications systems as well as by shifts in labor markets, the increasing ease of the movement of capital, and an emergent cultural hybridity. Yet as Kevin Yelvington (2001), Michel-Rolph Trouillot (1992), and others have argued, the Caribbean has long been a product of global forces. The current context of the Carnival emerges out of the development of Trinidadian society from early colonization by Spain, the creation of a slave society and economy based on sugar production, the aftermath of emancipation, successive waves of immigration and emigration, the changing economic fortunes of Caribbean states, struggles for independence, and post-independence nation building. The historical and social contexts of the Carnival suggest a number of themes that have persisted to the present and influence how the Carnival is represented today: class, ethnic, racial, and religious conflict; the perceived threat of working-class violence and lewdness; the squandering of resources; and a lack of respect for civil authorities and social hierarchies.

This volume contains essays that examine the social, political, economic, and cultural implications of the Trinidad Carnival and its "offspring" as well as the interactions among them. Within anthropology, the increased attention to the complex and methodologically challenging task of tracing social and cultural relationships and processes over time and space without regard to some notion of geographical, political, or even cultural boundaries has led to a renewed interest in the Caribbean as an area of research (Yelvington 2001). To properly understand Caribbean carnivals, both in Trinidad and around the world, it is necessary to place them within the broader context of cultural politics. Key to such a project is understanding the ways local and global histories are interwoven. The Carnival in Trinidad and those in England, the United States, Canada, and other parts of the Caribbean are aspects of the processes of cultural change in the "metropole" and in the "periphery." Yet, to prioritize either of these locations is to lose sight of the active and ongoing relationships that the so-called core and peripheral locations have had for centuries.[1] The histories of the festivals under consideration in the essays in this volume possess similar contours as a result of similar, sometimes the same, processes. The particular configuration that any Carnival may take and the role it may play in the lives of those who participate in it and those who do not depends upon the particular conjunctions of class, gender, ethnicity, and generation as well as the broader structures of community and nation found in each locale. In the essays chosen for inclusion here, Carnivals are situated within migration patterns, diverse forms of colonialist discourse, forms of cultural resistance, and desires for cultural recognition.

The Trinidad Carnival is a product of such local and global histories—Spanish, British, and French colonialism; the plantation system, slavery, indentured servitude, the international markets for sugar, cocoa, and oil; and anticolonial agitation, decolonization, and the vicissitudes of state and nation formation after independence. Caribana, Brooklyn Carnival, and Aruba Carnival are products of more recent trends and movements. They are made possible by transformations in international labor markets, increased ease of international travel and communication, and restructurings of economic formations in Great Britain, the United States, Canada, and the Caribbean.

We see Carnival as integral to the cultural politics of Trinidad and Tobago. It is this centrality that places it at the core of efforts of West Indian migrants to draw upon the carnival form and its history in emerging local cultural politics of identity. The idea of cultural politics we develop in this introduction relies upon political economy approaches within anthropology that compel one to consider the place of "class, capitalism, and power" (Roseberry 1988) in the constitution of localized subjects, yet can also account for subjects who may occupy multiple localities, as can be argued in the case of the transnational communities considered in these essays. We cannot separate our analysis of cultural identity, cultural practices, and cultural change from an analysis of work, power, and politics. The authors here focus in different ways and with varying emphases on changes in forms, participants, and the cultural valuations of both through transformations in the social, political, cultural, and economic worlds of Great Britain, Canada, the United States, and the Caribbean. The key factors informing these analyses include shifting labor markets and immigration policies; struggles for political recognition, economic autonomy, and cultural legitimacy; the ebbs and flows of Trinidad and Tobago's oil industry; and the desire to create alternative forms of economic development. We locate the social and cultural phenomena of the Carnival within an analysis of the conditions of existence of those who make it, watch it, experience it, and talk about it within particular historically constituted structures of power and representation that influence those activities (Roseberry 1988).

The Trinidad Carnival and its constituent artistic forms—calypso, steel pan, soca, and masquerade—have been sources of trenchant social and political commentaries and the subject of considerable controversy throughout its history from its origins in colonial Trinidad, during the period of struggle against colonial rule, and in the aftermath of the formation of an independent state. The middle and ruling classes of Trinidad have stridently denounced the Carnival since the early 1840s following the complete emancipation of the slaves in 1838; consequently, Carnival has been subjected to government intervention and scrutiny (Crowley 1956; Pearse 1956; Brereton 1975; de Verteuil 1984; Trotman 1984; Liverpool 1993; Cowley 1996). The government has sought to appropriate the festival as a symbol of the nation and in doing so to establish the government's legitimacy to rule as representative of "the people" since the advent of full internal self-rule in 1956 and with greater urgency since independence from Great Britain in 1962.

The history of Carnival and Trinidadian society from the 1780s through World War II centers on the dialectical play of accommodation and conflict between a European elite class composed of British administrators and import–export merchants and a French Creole plantocracy, on one hand, and an emergent black and colored middle class that claimed to speak on the behalf of the working classes, on the other (Trotman 1986; Rohlehr 1990). Less prominent in these early conflicts were poor rural laborers from India and their descendants who came to Trinidad through the system of indentured labor. In the later years of the nineteenth century, the generally positive attitude of the black and colored middle classes toward the Carnival as the basis of a national culture complemented agitation for constitutional reform away from Crown Colony government, economic reorganization away from the plantation system, and greater electoral representation. Carnival became a battleground in which a uniquely Trinidadian culture established itself in contrast to the dominant British culture of the elites. These emergent middle classes offered financial and other forms of support to the working classes who participated in the Carnival, yet in exchange for that support, they meddled in the type and content of masquerades and demanded more "proper" behavior by revelers. For example, the sexually suggestive and sometimes threatening styles of masquerade that dominated the Carnivals of the mid-1800s alarmed the predominantly British, Protestant middle class that controlled the newspapers in Trinidad. From the late 1800s to World War II, the colored middle class attempted to clean up the Carnival by eliminating violence and lewdness through sponsored competitions that encouraged good behavior and rewarded inoffensive costumes that imitated European characters. The cultural politics of the Carnival in the colonial state reached a peak in the late 1880s. This period of intense political activity on the part of an emergent colored middle class called for greater local control over government affairs. The Carnival became the focus of a cultural nationalism that sought to assert the existence of a Trinidadian nation, one that, so the proponents argued, should rule themselves. The middle-class political leaders seeking to consolidate their political power and exert their vision of national culture sought the political support of the working classes, themselves seeking both recognition of their cultural achievements and the autonomy to develop their forms of song, masquerade, and music as they saw fit. The dynamic between accommodation and confrontation that characterized the Carnival in the early twentieth century persists today.

Following World War II and the development of ethnic-based political parties after the ultimate failure of more class-based efforts to mobilize the working population to greater self-rule, the nationalist and anticolonial movement led by the predominantly Afro-Trinidadian middle class portrayed the Carnival as the centerpiece of a national culture. After limited home rule was granted in 1956, the newly elected government of Premier Eric Williams and his People's National Movement (PNM) party took administrative control of the Carnival from a variety of private groups and created the Carnival Development Commission (CDC). During this period, middle-class nationalists bestowed greater respectability on the Carnival and the Carnival arts. At this time, pan, or the steelband movement, a product of the Afro-Trinidadian working classes, became less identified with criminal elements and received greater support and sponsorship from influential figures in politics and the arts; calypsonians received greater recognition from record producers and political figures; and masqueraders enjoyed increased attention and recognition from government.

After Trinidad gained independence from Great Britain in 1962, the Carnival continued to change as conditions of life in Trinidad changed: the steelbands faded as the prime source of music accompanying masqueraders on the streets; recorded music and brass bands on trucks became more common as masqueraders demanded greater volume; the forms of masquerade people played shifted as the large steelbands, which were popular among working-class Trinidadians during the 1950s, diminished in prominence; and smaller historical or fantasy bands more popular with various segments of the middle class became renowned for their meticulously detailed construction and brilliant costuming. This period came to be known as the Golden Age of Masquerade, and masmen George Bailey, Harold Saldenha, and Carlyle Chang became synonymous with a new Carnival aesthetic that served as the standard of excellence for future generations of designers. However, economic problems throughout the 1960s led to large-scale emigration to the United States and Great Britain by working class Trinidadians of both African and Indian descent, reducing the numbers of men who were the main supporters of the steelbands and masbands.

The political and social problems that marked the late 1960s and early 1970s—labor unrest, Black Power demonstrations, and military mutiny—were not overcome through government policy or electoral transformations but through increasing oil revenues in 1974 after the rise of the price of oil following the Arab oil embargo. The oil boom brought about tremendous increases in personal and public wealth. Concomitant social changes created a new sector of the middle class that flocked to the Carnival in unprecedented numbers. These social and economic changes in the local environment in which the Carnival took place hastened greater experimentation in materials. The masquerade bands became more lavish as people were willing and able to spend more money on the Carnival. A new aesthetic grew out of the changing social position of the masqueraders and the designers of the bands themselves. The bust that came with the dramatic decline in oil prices in 1981 posed further challenges to the people of Trinidad and Tobago.

The boom-bust years also allowed the development of greater economic independence for women, continuing a trend that began during and intensified after World War II. Part of that economic independence translated into greater prominence in the Carnival. Bandleaders now estimate that women compose 70–80 percent of the masqueraders in the bands. The Carnival of 1988 signaled their full arrival with the first appearance of the band *Savage Saga. Savage* became a model Carnival experience for the rising middle class. Attractive young women were its main clientele; it offered the best musical bands to provide music for masqueraders on the road Carnival Monday and Tuesday; it boasted of nearly three thousand members wearing costumes of no notable distinction; and promised its members an enjoyable and care-free experience. In a sense, this is the Carnival as pure enterprise and as leisure activity.

APPROACHES TO THE STUDY OF TRINIDAD CARNIVAL

Social scientists, historians, and other writers have analyzed the Trinidad Carnival from a variety of perspectives, often examining how social and political context affects the ways in which Carnival occurs (E. Hill 1972; Liverpool 1993; Van Koningsbruggen 1997) as well as the dynamics of race, gender, and class that characterize Carnival (Alonso 1990; Lee 1991). The most illuminating analyses of the Trinidad Carnival take the greatest care to identify and trace the social transformations that affect the festival and identify the social location of key actors involved in cultural debates. Such studies socially ground controversies and clearly identify the stakes involved in the debate over the festival's form, practice, and meaning (Pearse 1956; Brereton 1979; Trotman 1986; Rohlehr 1990). Less successful studies appear to be more interested in promoting a particular nationalist agenda or restating a long-held grievance than directly encountering the apparently contradictory aspects of Carnival head-on. Rather than question the categories of analysis and interpretation they use to discuss the Carnival, they assume those categories as historical givens. As Stallybrass and White (1986:19) have suggested, nostalgia, uncritical populism, and licensed complicity are common errors in cultural nationalist or biased analyses of carnivals.

One common way of understanding both the Carnival in Trinidad and Tobago and others is to see them as the "collective expression of the perceptions, meanings, aspirations, and struggles engendered by the material conditions of social life and informed by the cultural traditions of the group" (Lee 1991:417).

For Lee and others (Buff 1997; Liverpool 2001) the history of Carnival indicates changes in the structure of social relations from the time of slavery to the present in Trinidad and Tobago. The history of Carnival may be narrated through the significant social transformations in the history of Trinidad: emancipation; the development of the black and colored middle class; the growth of anticolonial nationalist agitation; and the formation of national culture following independence.

Another common approach to the analysis of both Trinidad and Tobago and overseas Carnivals examines controversies over the nature of Trinidad's cultural heritage that arise during the Carnival season (Juteram 1989; Cohen 1993; Gallaugher 1995; Segal 1995; Green 1999). Common themes in these works explore conflicts concerning exactly whose culture is presented as *the* national culture. Some of the controversies and tensions explored include calypso and the representation of different ethnic groups and women; the behavior of women on the streets; and the response of police and other authorities to the festival. In these studies, Carnival is an important platform in which cultural conflicts are expressed. Controversies about culture during Carnival indicate debates among Trinidadians or Caribbean immigrants about the nature of their community and its internal relationships as well as the relationship of the immigrant community to the larger society in which it lives.

Since Trinidad achieved independence in 1962, Carnival has become increasingly commercialized, politicized, professionalized, and intellectualized. The state, especially the post-independence state, has taken a greater role in the event and to some this is yet another opportunity for the political leadership to legitimate the power structure, promote a false image of social harmony, and dispense patronage so as to preserve their positions of power and control (Stewart 1986). It is a tool of political patronage, cynical racial manipulation, and commercial opportunism. To others, the Carnival remains the medium through which hegemony may be countered, wherein racial, gender, and class stereotypes, stigmas, and hierarchies may be challenged, questioned, and subverted; and wherein new social worlds free from such forms of oppression, worlds radically different from the one that spawned the Carnival, may be imagined and experienced, if only for a few moments or days (Liverpool 1993; Cowley 1993).

We emphasize the futility of reducing the carnivals to any singular kind of entity with universally realized qualities and attributes. What development bureaucrats, corporate sponsors, political functionaries, culture ministers, pan enthusiasts, mas players, calypsonians, folks on the street, and scholars may speak of when they say *Carnival*, may be quite different from one another. We suggest that what any one of these figures may argue is the "true essence" of the Carnival must be situated within any number of political, economic, and cultural projects. The invocation of "the Carnival" calls forth idealized images of resistance, the assertion of identity, and of national pride and struggle that resonate in myriad ways for different peoples, each engaged in located struggles for economic autonomy, cultural integrity and respect, and political power. The work of anthropologists, ethnomusicologists, and art historians presented here demonstrates the polysemic nature of the carnival as a social, cultural, political, and economic phenomenon. The event is composed of numerous events and activities, none of which may be said to be of greater importance than another. In fact, it is important for the careful reader to consider just what the implications are of highlighting one element or kind of Carnival experience over another (Green 1999, 2005).

Both of us have found ourselves protesting to snickering colleagues, friends, and relatives that we were not just studying a parade, that it was much more than that. But what is "it?" One Trinidadian friend described the Carnival to Green, early in his fieldwork, as a "state of mind," and perhaps this is what Nurse (1996) is alluding to when he suggests that cultural industries succeed or fail to the degree that they allow consumers to partake of the cultural values embedded within the practices or events on offer. Yet what is the nature of participation in England? Different regions of Trinidad? Brooklyn? Aruba? How do these forms of participation differ? How does the meaning of that participation differ among different subjects? How does the local context of power and meaning influence the ways in which participants think of their experience and themselves? To participate in the Carnival is not so much to see oneself in costume, to feel the heat of the sun and the welcome breeze in the middle of the day, to hear the sounds of the pan in the distance on a cool night, to lime (casually socialize) in the panyard, to hear and share in the laughter of a raucous audience in a calypso tent after a particularly clever or wicked bit of innuendo. It is more than just painting your face or the sight of thousands of fellow revelers on Jouvert morning. It is more than the visceral pounding from the sound systems in the streets and on the trucks. It is more than the heavy scent of contact cement and the burn of a glue gun at 3 o'clock in the morning. It is more than the sting of cheap rum, the ache in one's feet, and the scratchy throat and nasal congestion from the Sahara dust kicked up at the Savannah. It is more than any one type of costume, no matter how traditional, pretty, glamorous, creative, or skimpy. It is more than a set of performative formulas trotted out for the "heritage" festival or ossified cultural artifacts lifelessly placed behind thick scratched sheets of Plexiglas in a folklore museum. It is the chance that these experiences may occur, but that none of them must occur in order for the experience to be meaningful to the person who has it. We suggest that reductionist analyses of Carnivals will always miss something of importance. That is the full, always emergent, life of these events as they change in accordance with the needs, desires, and longings of those who make it. The Carnival is a framework of possibilities that has a rich history of choices made by those who have taken part in it over time, but the choices of the past do not constrain the choices that may be made today or tomorrow despite what administrators, organizers, commentators, and scholars may say. As Pat Bishop, a prominent choir director and conductor of pan orchestras, has argued, "The Carnival thrives on novelty and coming different" (Bishop 1994).

For some, Carnival is a "money spinner," a generator of foreign exchange. For others, it is an integrated part of the festival calendar and an important contributor to tourism; for others still, it is a cultural come-on to potential investors; and for yet others it is an assertion of identity, cultural creativity and genius of the grassroots in defiance of oppressive colonial, postcolonial, and other dominant regimes, middle-class propriety, vulgarity, and hypocrisy. It is at once a national treasure, an especially Afro-Trinidadian affair that perplexes or offends some Hindus, Muslims, and Pentecostal Christians in Trinidad and to uninformed observers in Brooklyn and Toronto nothing more than an ethnic parade and food festival. It is a Las Vegas spectacular, a kinetic sculpture, street theater, a great fete, a bacchanal, a cultural goldmine just waiting for benevolent entrepreneurial exploitation for the good of the country and community.

Whatever the Carnivals may be in their many incarnations, they are the products of unique histories, manifestations of social tensions, barometers of cultural change, and crucibles for creating, discovering, and asserting identities. The Carnivals encompass contradictory ideas and practices. People in position to assert their visions of what the Carnivals are seek to extinguish or at best minimize alternative interpretations and activities by rewarding those representations and practices that conform with their vision and by punishing or condemning those that do not.

The central elements of the event are few—pan, calypso, soca, and mas. Pan takes many forms. Calypso takes many forms. Soca takes many forms. Mas takes many forms. None of these arts and performative forms is static. New forms emerge and older ones remain or diminish in importance only to be resurrected. There is no "right" or "authentic" form. There is no "best" form that everyone should adopt and to which everyone should conform, although there are surely struggles about such forms. There is no one configuration of forms and practices that can be said to "best" represent who Trinidadians—of whatever sort—may consider themselves to be—or may wish to be considered as by various "others"—tourists, international business, cultural critics.

What we have found to be the most enduring feature of the Carnival, wherever it may be, is its persistent elusiveness, its unwillingness to be constrained by any effort to codify it once and for all. One often reads of Carnival as a form of resistance or as a steam valve or as the allowable expression of discontent permitted by the powerful within certain limits. One may also find interpretations of Carnival as a key feature of some primordial identity suddenly threatened by commercialism, political patronage, and corruption. It is both full of profound meaning and profoundly meaningless. What accounts for this diversity of views and the denial of this diversity by many scholars?

We suggest that it is the political agendas informing scholarship and a woeful lack of theoretical reflection that explain the too frequent dismissal of ambiguity and contradiction in the Carnivals. The Carnival is subject to numerous forms or reductionist analysis. That is to say that many scholars are eager to demonstrate just how Carnival is a form of resistance (and that's all) (Liverpool 1993) or hopelessly distorted by political manipulation and commercialism (Lewis 1968; John Stewart 1983) or an assertion of identity that should be good for development (Nurse 1996, 1999). We prefer to look at the accommodations and negotiations that arise out of the sometimes complementary and sometimes conflicting motivations and interests between and among participants, officials, and entrepreneurs, between locals, foreigners and expatriates, and between men and women. We have sought to add a degree of theoretical framing and self-reflexivity to the analysis of Carnivals and the Carnival arts through the essays we have chosen for inclusion. De Freitas addresses this issue most directly in her reflections upon the different ways in which Trinidadians responded to her as both scholar and masquerader.

We are most concerned here with how regimes of representation, migration patterns, settlement patterns, local political cultures, and community forms flow together in particular spaces at particular times to create these many Carnivals and to change them. The Carnivals of the diaspora are not merely waiting for news and innovation from the "mothership"; the traditions of the past are modified in the context of particular struggles, which, consequently, create changing impressions on just what the past was.

STUDIES OF CARNIVALS OF THE CARIBBEAN DIASPORA

Scholarship on other carnivals begun by expatriate Trinidadians in the Caribbean, North America, and Great Britain has increased considerably in recent years with the growing enthusiasm for transnationalism and diaspora studies (Manning 1978, 1984, 1990; Cohen 1980, 1993; Abrahams 1983; Pryce 1985; Kasinitz and Freidenberg-Herbstein 1987; Mahabir 1988/1989; Payne 1990; Kasinitz 1992; Buff 1997; Razak 1998; Scher 1998, 2003; Edmondson, 1999). These works concentrate on the political significance of these celebrations,

their implications for community formation, and their influence on the construction, maintenance, and assertion of identity.

Throughout the twentieth century, Trinidadians have migrated to the United Kingdom, throughout the West Indies (as students in Jamaica and as workers in Aruba), and North America. Trinidadians came to the United States in the 1920s and in even greater numbers during the 1960s. Large numbers of Trinidadians immigrated to Great Britain following World War II. Many calypsonians spent a good number of years in England before returning to Trinidad.[2] Trinidadian immigrants created Carnivals in New York and Notting Hill; mas designers would follow them in what eventually became a year-round circuit of Carnivals. Masquerade band designers responded to the demands of these communities to assist and advise in the administration of bands and in the design of costumes and would travel to these places to oversee costume production. Other bandleaders shipped costumes or pieces of costumes from Trinidad where they would be fully assembled in mas camps in the importing country. This small export industry grew gradually and developed without any assistance from the government or any of the Carnival administrative organizations. In the early 1990s, the National Carnival Commission (NCC) began to recognize that this commerce had developed and could be significant. It began to assert greater control over what had already been established by the producers themselves without the interference of marketing geniuses and business planners.

Frank Manning's (1978) discussion of Carnival in Antigua in the context of tourism development suggests that Carnival is a site in which foreign cultural forms and ideas are reinterpreted within indigenous systems of meaning as part of the process of "cultural revitalization." Razak takes a similar approach in her study of Carnival in Aruba, which was founded by Trinidadian workers but has been reconfigured by Arubians to be relevant to the construction of Arubian national identity.[3] Manning contends that Carnival is a collective public performance that eludes and evades the efforts of state ministries and tourism entrepreneurs to control it.

Cohen (1980, 1993) and Kasinitz (1992) consider the political conflicts surrounding the founding and planning of a West Indian Carnival in Notting Hill Gate, England, and Brooklyn, New York, respectively. Both Cohen and Kasinitz explore the economic and social connections among those who conceived of and organized the events. Tensions in both places arose among various groups of West Indians as they sought representation and control. In addition to the struggles within the West Indian community in London and Brooklyn, the organizers encountered resistance from the local police force. Their work demonstrates how Carnival becomes a highly charged political issue as subordinated social groups struggle among themselves over the content and form of their public representation as part of a larger struggle for legitimacy and status within the social order in which they are subordinated. Yet even as new political and social contexts faced West Indians abroad in the 1960s and 1970s, developments in the Carnival in Trinidad were rapidly changing. Understanding these developments, specifically in relation to the entrance of Trinidad into a changing global economy, is vital for understanding the shape and form of the exported Carnivals.

THE DECLINE OF TRADITIONAL AND HISTORICAL MAS

In the 1970s, the characters associated with masculine assertions of language and aggression including Robber, Bat, Dragon, Devils of various types, Pierrot Grenade, Sailor, and other forms of military mas disappeared from the streets. These characters re-emerged in the pretty mas and the Children's masquerade competition where they stand for "Trinidadian history and culture." In 1981, each section of Wayne Berkeley's *Masquerade* depicted an early twentieth-century or late nineteenth-century "traditional" Carnival masquerade such as Dame Lorraine, Pierrot, Midnight Robber, Bat, or Moko Jumbie. This trend of Carnival as the theme for Carnival bands became quite common and aroused some early criticism. In discussing the 1982 Carnival, Anthony (1989:429) decries the stylization of old-time masquerade characters in the big bands as "the genuine having to give way to the new fads of line and design."

Numerous explanations have been offered for the decline of "traditional mas." One Trinidadian scholar (Allong 1984) offers a psycho-political explanation, arguing that with self-government and the emergence of standard political avenues for the expression of dissent, it was therefore no longer socially necessary to assert defiance through masquerade. She suggests that since the black urban working classes had found their champion in Eric Williams, they no longer aspired to middle-class linguistic and cultural norms. The lifting of the colonial yoke provided increased social mobility and decreased the need for the imagined power realized temporarily through a masquerade. This explanation is a logical outgrowth of the idea that Carnival is a "steam-valve."

One significant factor in the decline in historical masquerades may be the intense nationalist fervor that came with independence. Trinidadians began to take pride in their cultural forms and accomplishments instead of looking to the great civilizations and empires of the past. Bands began to choose folklore, natural wonders, and local historical events as the themes for their presentations. The increasing frequency of local themes for bands provides evidence of the changing nature of masquerade and of the increasing awareness of the need to take greater pride in Trinidad and Tobago's history. The 1975 declaration of veteran masman Irving McWilliams that "we possess sufficient material to project our own ideas" and Wayne Berkeley's pronouncement that "the days of historical mas are over, with original imaginative production, the sky is the limit" (*Express,* January 19, 1975) typifies the cultural pride of the early 1970s during which masquerades moved from those based on European history to more local themes. In 1970, McWilliams came out with one of the first bands on a local theme, *The Wonders of Buccoo Reef,* which, with 1,400 members, was one of the largest bands ever. Most masquerade bands were still rather small by comparison rarely exceeding a few hundred people. McWilliams brought out bands with local themes throughout the 1970s including *Anansi Stories* (1972), *Mama Dis Is Mas* (1974), and *Know Your Country* (1978), attracting large numbers of masqueraders (usually around 3,500 people). His band reached its peak in 1980 with the then unprecedented 4,500 masqueraders for *D Rains Came.* Other local themes included Albert Bailey's *Our Joy of Craft* in 1973, Stephen Lee Heung's *We Kinda People,* and Edmond Hart's *Whey Whey,* both in 1975.

THE OIL BOOM

Changes in masquerade themes, calypso subjects, and composition arose in response to changes in the greater sociopolitical and economic environment of Trinidad. The "oil boom" refers to the dramatic shifts in the fortunes of Trinidad and Tobago due to the tremendous increase in the price of oil after OPEC, the Organization of Petroleum Exporting Countries, exerted greater control over the international price of crude oil in 1973. Until 1970, oil prices hovered around $1.80/barrel.[4] In 1973, prices began at $2.59/bbl and rose to $11.65 by January of 1974, to $12.38 in late 1975, and to a phenomenal $40/bbl in 1981 (Alleyne 1988:23). Trinidad's oil-based economy resulted in state revenues that raised the standard of living and the cost of labor thereby increasing the cost of other industrial products, unfortunately making them less competitive in the export market (Alleyne 1988:24). Trinidadian development planners discovered that dependence on oil did not necessarily generate self-sustaining industrial growth, even though it provided the resources for building infrastructure such as ports, roads, airports, and even educational, health, and welfare programs.

In 1974, the effects of the Arab oil embargo and the subsequent rise in the price of crude oil led to unprecedented wealth in Trinidad and Tobago. The economic expansion assumed an unusual contour because of the political context of national sovereignty that Trinidad now enjoyed. In 1973, legislation restricted the degree of foreign ownership of Trinidadian businesses. Then the nationalization of the oil industry in August 1974 greatly enhanced government revenues and foreign exchange earnings as profits increased at a dizzying pace. In early 1975, oil production rose to an unprecedented 200,000 barrels a day and the economy grew at the rate of 5 percent per year (Cross 1980:16). When the government nationalized the sugar industry in 1977, it then controlled both levels of employment and the reallocation of profits in the two most important industries in the country. Even so, the decline in the sugar industry continued after nationalization since the new company no longer enjoyed the protective tariffs of its British-owned predecessor. Oil continued to fuel the growth of the economy. In the year before nationalization, the revenue from the export of crude oil was TT $265,226,300. Six years later, in 1982, the revenue had increased tenfold to TT $2,679,250,500 (Central Statistical Office 1984:164–165).

The expansion of the oil industry opened up areas of the more agricultural southern part of Trinidad, established a network of roads, and encouraged migration to towns and villages as people sought work in the oil industry and its various support services (Alleyne 1988:20). The expansion of the marine fields during the 1960s dramatically changed the nature of the industry in Trinidad since marine drilling does not require as many workers and provides greater productivity at less cost than land drilling. By 1977, marine production accounted for nearly 81 percent of total oil production and Amoco controlled nearly 75 percent of that (Alleyne 1988:21). Oil production reached a peak in 1978 with 83.8 million barrels and then began a decline that has not stopped.

Eric Williams, the long-serving prime minister, wanted to make Trinidad a major industrial power in the Caribbean by using oil wealth to create a nucleus of related industries with forward and backward linkages, including oil refining and the production of iron, steel, liquid ammonia, methanol, urea, and fertilizer. The cost for establishing these industries was quite high and resulted in enormous public debt. The government developed an energy-based industrial sector, extended and improved the economic and social infrastructure (water, telephone, electricity, roads, housing, education, and health), invested in agriculture, manufacturing, and tourism to diversify the economy, and exerted much more control in all sectors of the economy through equity holdings in significant sectors. However, the rapid growth in personal and national income led to increased demand for imports. Inflation rose at nearly 11 percent a year. The boom continued until 1981 when, despite rising international prices for oil, production declined with a consequent reduction in government revenue. When the price of oil began to decline worldwide in 1983, revenues dropped dramatically. By 1985, despite the decline in government revenue from oil, public expenditures continued to increase and public debt rose in response. The budget surpluses enjoyed from 1974 to 1984 turned into a deficit in 1985. Subsidies to agriculture, manufacturing, electricity, water, transport, and communication all declined by nearly 30 percent (Ryan 1988:574–575).[5] During the boom, low-interest government loans for housing construction and small businesses as well as a large number of joint government–private enterprises created thousands of new jobs. According to the Annual Statistical Digest, in 1981 the government provided nearly 43 percent of all employment outside of farming and small establishments (Central Statistical Office 1984:87). Construction and its associated industries—hardware, transport, and the building supplies—boomed. Jobs were numerous and well paid. Migration from rural to urban areas intensified especially among Indo-Trinidadians who turned away from agriculture in favor of better paying jobs in industry or the trades. Many Indo-Trinidadians started private businesses such as small shops, hardware and building suppliers, transport, taxi services, and entered skilled trades such as carpentry, welding, construction, electricians, and car repair (Klass 1991:56). Consumption rose among all groups in Trinidad with people buying televisions, automobiles, imported foods, and clothing, and engaging in frequent international travel (Klass 1991: 56–57).

The decline in the price of oil in the early 1980s adversely affected Trinidad and Tobago's economy. Between 1982 and 1996, unemployment rose to 25 percent, foreign reserves were substantially reduced, living standards declined, costs increased, poverty became more widespread, and, as the attempted coup by the Jamaat al-Muslimeen in July 1990 demonstrated, political unrest intensified. In 1985, the National Alliance for Reconstruction (NAR), a coalition of opposition parties, defeated the PNM, which had been in power since 1956. Large numbers of Trinidadians continued to migrate away from the country, even as wealth poured into the society in limited sectors. While some became accustomed to an increased standard of living, others were flocking to the metropolitan centers of North America and Europe and swelling the ranks of an already substantial community.

THE EXPANSION OF PRETTY MAS

The Carnival of the boom years is marked by unprecedented elaboration of design, ingenious experimentation with materials, and tremendous increases in the numbers of people playing mas, especially women and non-African Trinidadians. During this time, formally educated middle-class artists changed aesthetic standards through their use of new materials and application of their wide-ranging knowledge of theatrical design on Carnival costuming and performance. The materials they introduced were expensive and often imported with the result that people raised their expectations of a certain level of craftsmanship. The work of Peter Minshall[6] and Wayne Berkeley exemplify the emergence of two new trends in Carnival aesthetics during the boom years, and they have continued to remain tremendously influential.

Ever since Minshall designed his first Trinidadian masquerade band, *Paradise Lost,* for Stephen Lee Heung in 1976, his work has been an unusual synthesis of the structural principles of traditional masquerade forms, the technical sophistication and experimentation in materials of modern theater, and the allegorical complexity of performance art. Critics have attacked his work for being too abstract, too monochromatic, and too self-conscious. However, his bands won the People's Choice award nine times before the award was discontinued in 1987; he also received the Band of the Year Award seven times. Minshall's avoidance of fantasy themes and his refusal to treat mas as merely color, extravagance, and hedonism has been attacked by some commentators because they feel he only reminded everyone of the tensions of everyday life in a highly stylized form rather than offering them some kind of relief. Middle-class commentators on Carnival tend to see mas as a time for fantasy and for blowing off steam, not as a time for the lower classes to assert their cultural forms and attack the hypocrisy and pretensions of the middle classes. The same commentators also attack the prevalence of "wine and jam" songs in calypso and pine for the time when calypsonians constructed songs with clever innuendoes or political commentaries.

Wayne Berkeley is the same age as Minshall and trained in England at the same school, London Polytechnic. He came to the Carnival after designing successful Carnival Queen costumes in the 1960s. He designed his first masquerade band, Bobby Ammon's *Secrets of the Sky,* in 1967. He then began to design bands for Stephen Lee Heung, gained a reputation for elegant design and quality craftsmanship, and won many band of the year titles. In the early 1980s, he withdrew from Carnival for eight years, citing creative exhaustion. He returned in the late 1980s, began his own band organization, and then won Band of the Year an unprecedented five times in a row.

These two designers appeal to two main factions of the middle classes in Trinidad, although Minshall appeals to a much wider social spectrum. Their sense of theater differs, as does their understanding of the place of Carnival in the Trinidadian imagination. Furthermore, each represents the growing shift in class, educational experience, and cosmopolitanism of masquerade designers. These new "masmen" found themselves not only bringing in new styles and influences, but also catering to a new and growing audience: women. The growing numbers of women on the road during Carnival in Trinidad had resounding consequences in the overall development of the festival and generated new debates about the role of Carnival in the national consciousness, especially as women were perceived to be engaged inordinately in "lewd" behaviors in public.

WOMEN IN MAS

The "indecent" behavior of masqueraders has always been an issue of great public debate. In the 1800s, critics focused on the behavior of the working classes and fretted about the possible negative effects of this behavior on the middle class. In the late nineteenth century, the Carnival came to be known as the *jamette* Carnival, after those citizens of the underworld, petty criminals, prostitutes, thieves, pimps, who were called *jamettes*. The middle and upper classes in this period perceived Carnival as a dangerous and licentious affair that threatened to drive commerce and capital from the shores of Trinidad. At the heart of this "unsavory spectacle" were tough warrior women who sang songs of praise for their stickfighting men, drank, and formed gangs that sometimes wore matching, multicolored costumes. Critics of the festival during this time reserved special opprobrium for those fellow members of the middle and upper classes who condescended to play mas on the streets alongside the rabble. By the 1970s and 1980s, although the middle classes were now thoroughly integrated into the Carnival parades, there were still deep reservations about what role women should play. These debates marked a deep and abiding concern about sexuality and display in the Carnival now that young middle-class women were the performers.[7]

The coming to prominence of women in the Carnival is tied to the economic and social expansion of Trinidadian society following World War II. Writing in the mid-1950s, Barbara Powrie attributes the increasing presence of women in the Carnival of the streets to their economic emancipation through wartime employment, which allowed them greater social freedom. Even then Powrie could say that these new emancipated women "are less inclined to fear the accusation of sexual promiscuity when they have been seen in male company (1956:103)." Middle-class attitudes had changed greatly after the war. Before the war, "few parents would consent to their daughters being 'interfered'[8] with by male revelers, especially those from lower class bands" (Powrie 1956: 99). By the mid-1950s, "street bands contain a fair proportion of women and there is now no rooted objection to women taking part in such a band" (Powrie 1956:102).

Commentators began to remark on the increasing presence of women in the mas bands in the early 1980s, according to Anthony (1989:424). But even earlier, in the late 1960s and the early 1970s, bandleaders such as Edmond Hart and Irving McWilliams had very large numbers of women in their bands. Very large jouvert bands, such as Victor Rique's, often had 3,000 members and were divided into sections like those of the large pretty mas bands. Rique's 1983 offering, *Los Danceros,* boasted 3,000 people, mostly women, and was one of the first bands with such a large percentage of women. That same year Edmond Hart's presentation, *Antony and Cleopatra,* had 3,200 members, more than 90 percent of them women. By 1988 and the first appearance of the FunLovers Association presentation, *Savage,* the takeover seemed complete. Their 1989 presentation, *Brasilia,* sold out in six weeks and boasted an estimated 4,000 members.

The scanty costumes of "skimpy mas,"[9] as it came to be called, and the intense wining before the television cameras in 1988 prompted explosions of commentary. Skimpy mas has been an issue of growing concern in the last fifteen years. Without doubt, for the hand-wringing critics, the Carnival appears to be a parade of flesh and the behavior of women has become especially problematic. The costumes are felt to have become more revealing each year. Juteram (1989), Miller (1991), and others have speculated that this may be a form of sexual liberation and a defiant expression of women's sexuality in the face of a dominating male presence or a form of sexual exploitation and manipulation of women by male designers to satisfy the prurient pleasure of men.[10]

Women's behavior is under greater scrutiny and subject to more intense public commentary during and after the Carnival than men's because of the ideology surrounding the wife–mother role and the idea that women are vessels of the nation's purity. During and following the 1988 Carnival, newspapers were flooded with comments on the behavior of women. The great wining controversy prompted the publication of a special magazine, *Women in Mas'* (Baptiste 1988), that featured a number of articles exploring the meaning and implications of the rising numbers of women in mas. Concern over the behavior of these women reached such a fever pitch that by 1988:

> hundreds of women . . . made an obscene spectacle of themselves on the streets and . . . before the cameras of Trinidad and Tobago Television. . . . The lewdness . . . marked the nadir in feminine behaviour at Carnival. . . . Band after band filtered across the stage . . . with the women displaying their barest form. (*Express,* February 28, 1988:8)

THE NEW NATIONAL CARNIVAL COMMISSION

Interest in the economic potential of the Carnival in Trinidad and Tobago has been growing since 1980. There have been a few attempts to ascertain its contribution to the national economy, but most figures are inconclusive or speculative. The National Carnival Commission suggests that the Carnival generates US $50–66 million over a two-month period (Nurse 1996:6). Given the great potential contribution of the Carnival to the economy, administrators and businesspeople are interested in making the Carnival and its related art forms "money spinners."[11] The tremendous success of Trinidadian-style Carnivals in North America and Great Britain serves as a model to those Trinidadians who wish to make the Carnival an international commercial success. The Carnival, once a vulgar and sometimes obscene lower-class affair with which no respectable person would care to be associated, became, during the movement for independence in the late 1950s, a demonstration of the "genius of the people." In the early 1990s, it became a potential growth-market and profitable enterprise.

The administrative framework within which the Carnival takes place has altered to facilitate this greater interest in its economic potential. The National Carnival Commission controls the administration of the Carnival. The National Carnival Commission Act of 1991 reorganized the NCC into a semiautonomous corporation, allowing it to raise monies and enter into contracts and partnerships without the prior approval of Parliament. The Act charged the NCC with the goal of self-sufficiency and decreased its government subsidy, although it remained substantial. The broad goal of the NCC is to make the Carnival a viable national, cultural, and commercial enterprise. It is expected to do this by providing the managerial and material infrastructure for the presentation and marketing of the cultural products of Carnival and by facilitating ongoing research as well as the preservation and permanent display of Carnival products created each year. The Act confers upon the NCC the power, authority, and responsibility to regulate and coordinate all Carnival activities; develop and review rules and regulations for Carnival activities; promote and enhance the production and marketing of Carnival products and services; and develop a marketing strategy to optimize the contribution of the Carnival to the national economy through the sale and provision of Carnival goods and services domestically and for export as well as through linkages with the tourism industry.

In the early 1990s, Alfred Aguiton, the head of an advertising agency, led the NCC's drive to operate the Carnival more efficiently and profitably and to make the Carnival the centerpiece of a new cultural tourism. Proponents of the cultural tourism initiative contended that it would bring more visitors to Trinidad and Tobago and solidify an identity for the country in the minds of potential international investors. Culture—that is, a national culture distinctly associated with Trinidad and Tobago and comprising pan, calypso, soca, chutney, and masquerade—is seen as a source for economic growth and development within the government's economic plan.

The NCC imposed more and more restrictions and regulations on the festival in efforts to improve its administrative practices. Seeking to expand the opportunities for exposure and audiences, the NCC conducted a series of staged performances consisting of weeks of elimination-competitions culminating with the crowning of the Carnival King and Queen on Dimanche Gras. To encourage more participation and to reward those participants, the NCC gave awards in twenty costume categories, three band categories determined by membership size, twenty-six individual costume categories, and eight skills and design categories. Perhaps most importantly given the battles for rights and monies that were to come, the NCC also controlled media rights to the festival and negotiated contracts for national, regional, and international telecasts (Green 2005).

Contestants receive cash prizes, appearance fees, and transportation costs. The NCC also subsidized the costs for constructing the viewing stands at the Queen's Park Savannah and along the parade route, utilities, and other infrastructural and support services. The NCC also set standards of vulgarity, obscenity, and lewdness and demanded that participants comply with its regulations on all aspects of presentation. Violators of the rules of conduct would be disqualified, denied prize monies, appearance fees, and access to the national media. In the eyes of many commentators (Deosaran 1978; Johnson 1984; Stewart 1986), the interventions of the NCC and its predecessor led to the Carnival becoming increasingly uniform, repetitive, and commercialized. They argued that the Carnival failed to speak to the changing social experience of the majority of Trinidadians.

The 1991 charter of the NCC emphasized the need for it to become self-supporting. One aspect of this process has been to decentralize Carnival events and yield authority to the professional organizations. This reduces the overall production costs for the NCC and allows the performers to reap the financial benefits (or suffer the financial losses) many believe have accrued to the NCC over the years.

During the 1970s, the organizations representing creative contributors to the Carnival—masquerade bandleaders (the Carnival Bandleaders Association and later the National Carnival Bands Association; NCBA), calypsonians (Trinidad and Tobago Unified Calypsonians Association; TTUCA), and steelbands (Pan Trinbago)—sought to gain greater control over their presence in the Carnival. Stuempfle (1995) exhaustively documents the struggle of the steelband movement to gain first the support of the middle classes and then the authority to run their own affairs. In 1979, controversy and violence marred the Carnival when Pan Trinbago and the government argued over appearance fees. Ultimately, Panorama, the national steelband competition that occurs during the Carnival season, was canceled, and firebombs were set off at the official competition sites sanctioned by the administrative body running the Carnival at that time, the Carnival Development Commission (CDC). Separating the Panorama from the Dimanche Gras show in 1976 and placing it on the Saturday before Carnival was an important event in the independence of the steelband movement from control by the CDC. By 2001, Panorama came fully under the control of Pan Trinbago. Part of the change is due to the new mission of the NCC and the reduction of its government subsidy, but it is mostly the result of strong lobbying and demands by Pan Trinbago for control of what it sees as the premier event of steelband.

The struggle has continued, however, with a great number of conflicts arising between the CDC, and later the NCC, and these professional organizations despite what appear to be their mutual interests. In addition, these organizations also have deep divisions within them that tend to perpetuate the conflicts. Profound and divisive conflicts among the masquerade bands have arisen over such issues as the allocation of prize monies, judging criteria and procedures, and congestion on the road.

CULTURE AND COMMERCE

The NCC Charter of 1991 emphasizes the role of the NCC in encouraging the commercial potential of the Carnival. Since the late nineteenth century, Carnival has always involved a commercial element. Yet in the thirty years since the oil boom of the mid-1970s and subsequent bust of the early 1980s that forced dramatic economic restructuring, interest has grown in developing the cultural sector of the economy by offering new products, services, and exports to create new jobs and increase foreign exchange earnings (Nurse 1996:5).

The perceived potential of the "culture industries" in Trinidad and Tobago are the local effects of larger global trends involving technological restructuring, economic liberalization, and the emergence of multicultural aesthetics. Cultural entrepreneurs have been encouraged by the changing demographic profile of Carnival participants at home and abroad because more and more people who would identify themselves as members of the middle class now partake of the Carnival festivities in Trinidad. By the late 1980s, many new masquerade bands emerged and catered to these groups. These bands find their clientele in the clerical workers and mid-level administrators whose numbers increased with the growth of government services and the expansion of the banking and insurance industries. The new bands offer their clients an experience that differs dramatically from that offered by the older bands that were established on local community ties.

The growing visibility and popularity of the Carnivals inspired, organized, and carried out by expatriate Trinidadians in metropolitan centers including London, Brooklyn, and Toronto only intensified the desire to increase the international exposure of the Carnival. These festivals and numerous others in North America and Great Britain were enhanced by the Caribbean diaspora of the 1960s, which is an outgrowth of shifts in the organization of global capital. Development officers in Trinidad and Tobago believe that overseas Carnivals provide entree into foreign markets and contribute to the emergence of a new export sector in the culture industries. These festivals have provided year-round opportunities for calypsonians, soca performers, musicians, designers, and craft-workers from Trinidad and Tobago. Following the Carnival season in Trinidad, which usually ends in late February, there is regular work overseas from April to October.

The success of these foreign festivals has aroused both hope and resentment in Trinidad among Carnival administrators, artists, and the population as a whole. The Notting Hill Carnival in England attracts two million people and is the largest festival in Europe, while Caribana in Toronto and the West Indian American festival on Labor Day in Brooklyn attract similar numbers. Conservative estimates from Caribana suggest a $180 million contribution to the tourism economy; also, a 1992 study of the West Indian American Festival finds a $70 million influx from visitors (Nurse 1996:6). While these groups are enthusiastic about the worldwide spread of "their" culture, they wonder how foreigners so strongly support what is, to them, just a shadow of the real Carnival.

Trinidadians fervently believe that their Carnival is "a better product" than that found overseas and therefore attribute the success of foreign Carnivals to more effective and aggressive administrative organization and marketing. It is particularly galling to Trinidadians that the popularity of the overseas festivals has not been translated into anything of tangible value for Trinidadians in Trinidad save for the handful of designers or bandleaders who have been able to ply their trade in the overseas events.

Scholars, columnists, and some masmen have condemned the commodification of the current Carnival that is exemplified by the assembly-line production of indistinguishable costumes bought and sold in a market transaction. The failure of masqueraders to be involved in the making of their costumes serves as a grim indicator of the loss of the true Carnival spirit. The essence of the criticism is that the Carnival has degenerated into a hedonistic spectacle, that community involvement has declined, and that masqueraders (Trinidadians) have forgotten the esoteric skills involved in costume production and masquerade performance. Another aspect of the criticism contends that the nation's youth do not respect or understand the Carnival. Those who long for the Carnival of old lament the cultural amnesia that afflicts Trinidadians and denigrates indigenous traditions. These criticisms point to anxieties about the maintenance of cultural authenticity, control over cultural identity, and international recognition as the political, cultural, and economic context within which the Carnival is organized, administered, and experienced changes.

The national response of the NCC and other interested parties (such as hotels) to these crises of authenticity and recognition has been to promote, preserve, and re-present "old-time" Carnival elements through school programs, museum displays, and special showcases of "traditional" costume forms, performative styles, and calypsos. With reference to the international sphere, business persons, culture brokers, and state officials have sought to assume stricter control over the marketing, promotion, and merchandising of the Carnival, to increase the presence of Trinidad in Carnivals abroad, and to create more Carnival-related events outside the Carnival season.

It is in this contemporary climate that our volume seeks to make a contribution toward understanding the broad scope of such international cultural forms. We are not so concerned with issues of commodification per se. We see these discussions as symptomatic of a larger problematic; namely that an ideology of Carnival as national culture is itself shaped by global and transnational forces, and that these resulting ideologies themselves necessarily shape the Carnival as they become increasingly institutionalized both in the Caribbean and abroad. We therefore are interested in tracing some of these forces to show how specific Carnivals, specific masqueraders, and specific Carnival controversies are in motion, are well-traveled and circulate throughout the population not just of Trinidadians, but of Caribbean people everywhere, defining their Caribbeanness while helping to change those definitions as new contexts arise.

NOTES

1. In a recent essay, Nurse (1999) suggests that the Carnival is an example of culture from the formerly colonized world affecting that of the former colonizing countries. Yet he does not consider the extent to which the Carnival in Trinidad is not and has not been solely a product of local history in Trinidad.

2. Bryce-Laporte and Mortimer (1983) provide a general overview of West Indian immigration to the United States. Cohen (1993) discusses West Indian immigration to England throughout the 1950s and 1960s while Gmelch (1992) provides a more personal view of the experience of immigration in the words of migrants themselves.

3. Razak uses *Arubian* to describe citizens of Aruba as well as an adjective following Papiamento usage in Aruba.

4. All figures are given in U.S. dollars.

5. Ryan includes a reprint of the Central Statistical Office report, "The National Income of Trinidad and Tobago, 1966–1985 (M. Rampersad, L. C. Pujadas 1987), from which these figures are taken.

6. Peter Minshall is a Euro-Trinidadian who, although born in Guyana, grew up in Trinidad and became involved in the Carnival at a very early age. He has also served as

an artistic director of the opening ceremonies of the 1992 Summer Olympics in Barcelona, the opening ceremonies of the 1994 World Cup Soccer Tournament, and the opening and closing ceremonies of the 1996 Summer Olympics in Atlanta.

7. There is a widely held belief that Carnival babies are a common offspring of the intensified atmosphere of sexuality during the Carnival season. A comparison of the average number of births for September to December with that of the rest of the year reveals a 20 percent increase in live births during the nine months following the Carnival season from January to March, thus lending some credence to the "myth" of the Carnival baby.

8. According to Powrie (1956:99–100), "interfered with" refers to a Carnival custom involving "little more than the touching or pinching of the more outstanding part of the female body."

9. Skimpy mas is costuming that reveals more than covers. It refers to the lack of elaborate costumes and calls forth images of the Brazilian Carnival dominated by thongs and bikinis.

10. In his essay on auto-eroticism and wining, Daniel Miller (1991) examines the issue of women's suggestive dancing before the television cameras during the 1988 Carnival. He suggests that the extreme form of sexual expression is an assertion of women's independence from men.

11. Although it may sound more intriguing than the American English moneymaker, "money spinner" is a common term in British English and refers to the capacity of any event or object to generate profit, income, and, in the case of the Carnival, foreign exchange. By referring to the Carnival as a money spinner, people express the hope that it can be the center of a tourism industry, more specifically a cultural tourism industry.

1. The Invention of Traditional Mas and the Politics of Gender

Pamela R. Franco

Since the 1960s, women's participation in Trinidad's pre-Lenten Carnival has steadily increased.[1] By 2005, however, the festival came to a crossroads. For the first time in its recorded history, women are very visible in the historically male enclaves of calypso and steelband, and are also the numerical majority in the street parade on Carnival Monday and Tuesday. Women's dominance of the street parade has resulted in significant changes to the overall aesthetic of the festival. In performance, for example, women prefer the highly sexualized dance, *wining*,[2] instead of the traditional characterization or playing someone other than themselves, a hallmark of performance theory and masquerade systems. In dress, they generally opt for costumes that emphasize and display their semiclad bodies.[3] Without moorings or "roots" to which one could anchor this novel masquerade style, critics, culture brokers, and scholars turned in the late 1980s to the familiar, the male-centered traditional mas,[4] hoping that it would help them to make sense of this new phenomenon.

Thus in 1988, there was a concerted effort to revive and reposition traditional mas characters. Two new events, Viey la Cou (the old yard) and the Ole Time mas parade, were added to the schedule of Carnival activities. Almost immediately, the use of traditional characters was enveloped in a cultural nationalist discourse. "We don't want to lose our rich Carnival heritage [the traditional characters] which is being denied us with every passing Carnival more and more," declared a writer in *Express* (February 5, 1988). The fact was that with "every passing Carnival" there was a steady increase of female maskers; at the same time, the number of traditional characters was decreasing. Consequently, the former was at the center of the festival, and the latter was relegated to its

Traditional characters, Devil, Fancy Indians, and Fancy Sailor at Viey La Cou, 1996. Photograph by Pamela R. Franco.

margins. Interpreting this sequence of events as a case of cause and effect, the organizers of the new performances sought to rectify what they perceived to be a problem. They presented Viey la Cou and the Ole Time mas parade as effective solutions. Selecting "*authentic* characters . . . play[ed] by the actual persons who performed years ago" (*Express,* February 5, 1988), they hoped to reinscribe the festival with its "roots," its authentic self. To accomplish this goal, the organizers tacitly valorized such mas characters as the Midnight Robber, the Moko Jumbie, and the *Jab Jab*[5] by re-presenting them as the standard or canon of mas. Instead of clarifying the extant situation of female dominance, this strategy of reclamation, coupled with cultural nationalist rhetoric, created a dichotomous situation, pitting the male-dominated traditional characters on one side and the contemporary women's mas on the opposite side.

Today this binary continues to be at the center of many popular debates, specifically those on authenticity in mas. The model of authenticity that is often invoked is heavily indebted to the 1956 *Caribbean Quarterly* (*CQ*) special issue that was dedicated to Trinidad Carnival. The brainchild of British anthropologist Andrew Pearse and Trinidadian folklorist Andrew Carr, it was the first scholarly analysis of Carnival. The titles of its articles included "Carnival in

Nineteenth-Century Trinidad," "Traditional Masques in Trinidad Carnival," "Carnival in New Orleans," and "The Changing Attitude of the Coloured Middle Class towards Carnival." Additional essays on three male characters, the Midnight Robber, the Dragon, and the Pierrot Grenade, as well as Mitto Sampson's "Calypso Legends of the Nineteenth Century" completed the special issue. The uncritical repetition (Hill 1972; Stewart 1984) of the content and assertions of these articles helped to establish certain mas characters as traditional and their performance styles as standard. In addition, they facilitated the construction of a mas hierarchy in which the traditional characters are elevated to the level of the "real" or "authentic." But the equating of the traditional with the authentic is problematic. As constructed, the category of traditional mas is a highly gendered and racialized conceptualization of Carnival. It does not totally represent the reality and breadth of the festival. Instead, it indicates the authors' applied methodologies and the political climate of the 1950s, which the late Daniel Crowley posited as a critical trajectory in selecting the characters that would eventually comprise the category of traditional mas. He explained, "Nationalism, it was all around us . . . You couldn't miss it."[6] Not only is this statement very illuminating, but it also makes sense. Many qualities of the 1950s anticolonial–nationalist movement are echoed in Crowley's imagining of the traditional characters. Both sought to reconceptualize and reposition blacks, or Afro-Trinidadians, in the island's cultural and political landscapes. In sum, the cultural and political were intertwined.

In the late twentieth century, the revival of male-centered traditional characters does not help us "make sense" of the contemporary mas. Instead, it has created significant problems for female maskers. They include the positing of femininity as a sign of inauthenticity, the evaluation of women's mas through their reproductive role as mothers, and the interpretation of women's mas style as a form of "emasculation." In this chapter, I discuss how the specific methodologies that were applied in a 1950s nationalist climate aided the construction of the traditional mas as male-centered. I will also examine the consequences of this gendered construction on the contemporary mas. The aim is twofold: (1) to show that the category of the traditional mas, as created by Daniel Crowley, privileges gender (male) and race (African), and (2) to illustrate its inadequacy as an explanatory paradigm for "making sense" of the female-dominated contemporary Carnival.

INVENTION OF TRADITIONAL MAS

The 1956 special issue of the *CQ* in 1956 presented the first scholarly analysis of Trinidad's premier festival. Diverse topics provided the reader with a history of Carnival's origins, its principal characters, and performance styles. However, it is the first two articles, Andrew Pearse's "Carnival in Nineteenth-Century Trinidad" and Daniel Crowley's "Traditional Masques of Trinidad Carnival,"[7] that are critical to our understanding of how the category of traditional mas was invented or constructed. New traditions are invented through conscious selection of symbols that are connected to a reinterpreted past, and are used to serve contemporary goals or situations (Hobsbawm 1983). New traditions are most likely to be created "in response to novel situations . . . [or] when a rapid transformation of society weakens or destroys the social patterns for which 'old' traditions had been designed" (Hobsbawm 1983:2–4). In essence, new situations require new traditions. In the twentieth century, nation building and nationalist movements have necessitated the creation of new traditions as a way of defining the nation as an "imagined community" and to give "permanence and solidity to a [new] political form" (Brennan 1993:47–49). In similar fashion, in 1950s Trinidad, the nationalist movement required cultural icons that expressed not only the changes and new face of the nation but also represented the cohesiveness of the national community. Carnival, as the most prominent of all cultural forms, quickly became the icon par excellence because, presumably, it was a very public display of nationalist ideology. It was in this nationalist climate that the traditional characters were imagined and created. So, to fully understand the rationale behind their construction there are three major elements, essential to the process of inventing new traditions, to be considered: (1) the characters' connections to a historical past, real or fictitious, (2) the privileging of a specific community or group, and (3) the period in which the new tradition was constructed. The following discussion will reveal the intertextual link between the traditional mas and the new nation.

In his article, Andrew Pearse located the origins of the public or street festival in the dynamic and racialized politics of slavery, as well as in the resistance of the black underclass to the Victorian code of moral ethics. He categorized his article around a tripartite slavery–emancipation model: (1) pre-emancipation (1783–1833), (2) post-emancipation (ca. 1834–1860), and (3) the Jamette Carnival (ca. 1860–1890).[8] In the pre-emancipation Carnival, whites, primarily the English and French, were the dominant participants.[9] The French organized "concerts, balls, dinners, hunting parties, and fetes champetres[10] [during] the Carnival season, which lasted from Christmas to Ash Wednesday"(Pearse 1956:7). For the English, Christmas was the season "of rowdy merrymaking and licence" (Pearse 1956:13), and at Carnival, they organized "fancy dress" balls under the patronage of the governor. The "coloured middle class"[11] also celebrated the season by hosting private masquerade balls. Until 1826, however, they were required to obtain permission to host any evening activity that included music and dancing (Pearse 1956:11).[12] In all three cases, there was some form of public or street processioning, with many whites opting for participation within the confines of their carriages. At Christmas, slaves had "considerable freedom for dancing, pageantry, parades and traditional good strife between plantation bands" (Pearse 1956:11). They performed under the master's watchful gaze. Slaves, however, rarely paraded in the street Carnival. Thus, in Pearse's pre-emancipation Carnival, the principal event was the private masquerade ball. Although freed citizens of different ethnic groups hosted this event, they did so in their separate spheres.

In the post-emancipation Carnival, the former slaves' participation increased, resulting in significant changes to both the festival's structure and its contents.[13] After 1838, many ex-slaves fled the plantations and relocated to the capital city of Port of Spain. In Carnival, they introduced an "Africanized" style of performance—a multimedia affair that included singing, dancing, mime, theatrical reenactments, and a percussive style of music. They also introduced the *Canboulay,*[14] which Trinidadian playwright Errol Hill (1972: 23–31) would later identify as the festival's "ritual beginning." In Pearse's post-emancipation Carnival, the premier disguises were the all-male characters: the Highlander, the Pulchinello, Pirates, Turks, and Death (Day 1852). Presumably, a growing black presence in the streets, combined with a loud, percussive musical performance forced "the white elite of the society to with[draw] from public participation" (Pearse 1956:21). This action cleared the path for blacks to introduce their masquerade style. For Pearse, it is the black (male) presence in the streets coupled with the multimedia, percussive performance style that precipitated the changes that would eventually lead to the restructuring of the festival.

The Jamette Carnival, which highlighted such mas characters as the *Pissenlit*[15] and Stickfighter, shifted the focus away from the private masquerade balls to the public or street festival. Allegedly, these masquerades did not permit "our mothers, wives, and sisters to walk the streets and promenades without having their senses shocked by sights and sound in the fullest sense of the word 'disgusting'" (Pearse 1956:31). Although newspapers described the jamette mas as "disgusting," Pearse reinterpreted it as oppositional to the established values and norms of the superstructure, which he defined as "the interwoven, administrative, legal, economic and religious institutions stemming from the colonising power" (Pearse 1956:39). In all probability, nineteenth-century, working-class blacks, the chief participants of Jamette Carnival, also may have perceived their performances to be oppositional, or in direct contrast, to the Victorian code of moral ethics. Unlike the colored middle class, they were less inclined to aspire to the white community's sense of morality and to adopt their cultural practices (Brereton 1979:152–175). Black's unwillingness to adhere to the mainstream value system resulted in frequent misunderstandings and confrontations with the local authorities, finally culminating in the 1881 Canboulay Riots.[16] In the Jamette Carnival, Pearse crystallized an image of blacks as racialized protagonists.

By pinpointing a specific historical moment or event, in this case slavery–emancipation, Pearse effectively established a new origin for the modern festival, one that overshadowed the French Creole's claim of introducing the pre-Lenten festival to the island in the late eighteenth century. To legitimize this new claim, Pearse needed to identify "a past with which it [the modern festival] [was] continuous and in whose terms it [was] explicable" (Toren 1988:697). His slavery–emancipation frame was most effective because not only did it connect the contemporary festival to a major historical event in the past, but it also positioned blacks at the center of the activities. But, as Paul Gilroy (1992:198) notes, when and where "new beginnings have been identified . . . new modes of recollection are . . . necessary." In other words, Pearse's relocation of Carnival's origins in a slavery–emancipation paradigm required a new episteme, one in which blacks were reconstituted as protagonists. Thus, his rewriting of the extant slavery narrative privileged the instrumentality of black males in the postemancipation shift from the private masquerade balls (white/Europe/elite) to the street or public festival (black/Africa/folk). By doing this, Pearse, in 1956, effectively marginalized the European's (i.e., colonial's) and, to a lesser degree, black women's contributions to Trinidad Carnival.

While Andrew Pearse located the origins of the festival in slavery and represented black males as the festival's principal maskers, North American anthropologist Daniel Crowley, in his article "Traditional Masques of Carnival," identified and foregrounded those characters that best exemplified Pearse's originary model of black male agency. Crowley organized his article in a typological fashion, using such categories as "Rare and Extinct," "Sailor and Military," "Indians and Other Warriors," "Historical," and "Clowns," to name a few. In the "Rare and Extinct" category, for example, he brought together a group of disparate characters who had once been popular but either were absent or at the periphery of the 1955 Carnival, when he conducted his research. They included Negre Jardin or "Garden Nigger," the Stickfighter, the Pissenlit or "bedwetter," and Jamet bands, all subscribed to, almost exclusively, by black male maskers. Their performance styles varied from the combative Stickfighter to the sexual play of the Pissenlit.

A brief review of Crowley's cast of traditional mas reveals a gender focus and a performance aesthetic based on a combination of stylized choreography, eloquent speeches, and dramatic reenactments. For example, the disguises of the male-dominated Sailor and Military bands extended from the very simple

Wild Indian, ca. 1957. From the author's collection.

to the fancy sailor. Their performances ranged from throwing powder on each other and on spectators to mock militaristic maneuvers. Their dances, which were determined by each character's "occupation," emphasized stylized, intricate footwork.[17] Similarly, the Indian mas (more accurately Hollywood-inspired representations of Native Americans) was also categorized in two genres, the Wild and the Fancy. The former generally meant representations of such "warlike" groups as the Apaches, Seminoles, and Sioux, and the latter was an elaborate depiction of Native American costume. In performance, the Indians spoke an invented Indian language. Likewise, the Midnight Robber recited boastful and self-aggrandizing speeches. The most sumptuous costumes were found in the Historical, Fancy Dress, and Original bands. Generally, their themes were adaptations of events and stories, culled from European or Middle and Far Eastern history, Greek mythology, and the Bible. They showcased beautiful, voluminous costumes, pageantry and a non-percussive musical style.[18] Perormances were dramatic reenactments of carefully chosen historical events that were acted out in front of the judges. Although the membership of these bands was heterogeneous, men constituted at least two-thirds of the maskers and held the principal roles. Finally, such characters as the Clown, Burroquite or Sumari,[19] and Maypole dancers[20] completed Crowley's list of "traditional masques." Unlike the mas of previously mentioned categories, many of these characters were prominent at Carnivals in outlying towns and villages. With the exception of Sumari, black male maskers were the principal performers. In sum, Crowley's overall emphasis on certain Carnival characters inscribed a model of traditional mas in which black male maskers were the preeminent actors, and stylized dance, orality, and theatrical dramas were the preferred performance aesthetics.

The foregrounding of male maskers and their performance styles was not arbitrary. Pearse and Crowley's imagining of the origin of the festival and the traditional mas is indebted to three major factors: (1) the authors' knowledge of and dependence on Melville Herskovits's theory of acculturation,[21] (2) the application of a West African masquerade model, and (3) the political climate in which the *CQ* special issue was conceived and published. As I will demonstrate, these factors together determined the gender and racial profiles of the traditional or Ole Time mas.

Briefly, Herskovits (Pearse 1956:10) defined acculturation as the study of "those phenomenon which result when groups of individuals having different cultures come into continuous first-hand contact, with subsequent changes in the original cultural patterns of either or both groups." Among Africans in the New World, the degree of acculturation was determined by many variables, including the demographic ratio of one cultural group to another, climate and topography, the frequency and points of contact or interaction with Europeans, and whether or not these contacts took place in a rural or urban setting (Pearse 1956:10). Herskovits termed the new forms that resulted from acculturation *Africanisms* because, despite varying degrees of transformation, many of the cultural elements were "traceable to an African origin" (Holloway 1991:ix). In the 1950s, Crowley, Herskovits's student, and Pearse, a visiting colleague at Northwestern University, would have understood *Africanism* in a very similar manner, as an endpoint or product that, at some level, revealed specific elements that were traceable to Africa.

In Carnival, Africanisms were realized in the syncretic mas forms that either showed recognizable signs of the cultures in contact or, in a more covert manner, made reference to shared philosophies. For example, in his account of the nineteenth-century Carnival, Pearse (1956:24) acknowledged the syncretic nature of the early masquerades when he wrote that "we can distinguish the persisting elements of both Europe and Creole provenance." Creole, here, is a synonym for black or African. Similarly, Crowley also foregrounded the characters whose costumes and/or performances were illustrative of acculturation. The Moko Jumbie, or West African stilt walker, was a perfect example of this process. He "wore a long full skirt and a jacket or 'eton' of brightly-coloured satin or velvet . . . his hat was fashioned into an 'Admiral's' hat with long peaks in front and back" (Crowley 1956:50). Here was a West African masquerade figure dressed in a sumptuous European-styled costume and wearing an admiral's hat!

The Historical band, with its European themes and costumes, illustrated a less overt form of syncretism. "This hierarchy [Kings, Queens, High Priests, High Priestess, etc.] not only provides a masque for every taste and pocketbook, but also faithfully reflects the African and the Crown Colony [England] societies" (Crowley 1956:84). While the external trappings and themes of the Historical mas overtly indexes European history, the underlying content of court tradition makes reference to parallelism in African and European social structure. In this example, shared social ideologies, experienced by two different cultural groups, underpin the European costume and historical referents.

While Crowley's choice of Carnival characters underscored the syncretic nature of much of the traditional mas, it was the application of a West African system of masquerading that facilitated the privileging of a multimedia performance style and the foregrounding of male maskers. Briefly, in West Africa, with rare exception, masquerades are performed almost exclusively by men.[22] For example, the Yoruba ancestral mask, Egungun, and Gelede, a mask to honor women, are performed by initiated adult males. In the latter, using layers of cloth, men transform their bodies into that of a pregnant female, revealing the fact that, if or when necessary, they would cross-dress to play female roles. Varying combinations of singing, miming, virtuosity in dancing, and the percussive rhythms of the drums enhance maskers' performances. Women, children, and foreigners constitute the audience. Despite their marginalization, women are essential to the overall performance "since the efficaciousness of the mask requires its legitimation by those supposedly unaware that it is an illusion and who accept their own exclusion from the secret of its meaning" (Kasfir 1998: 18). In other words, the success of a West African masquerade is dependent on the audience's willingness to "believe" and play along with the illusion of transformation. Similarly, the success of the traditional mas performances was due, in part, to the audience's very active participation and their acceptance of the character on its own terms. Also, the ole time characters were performed, almost exclusively, by male maskers; their disguises were of a persona other than themselves; their performances often consisting of a combination of dance, mime, song, and verbal virtuosity. When necessary, they cross-dressed. Crowley's academic training with Africanist scholars William Bascom and Melville Herskovits insured that Africa would be a principal trajectory for his analysis. Thus, it is feasible to suggest that the masquerade model that informed his construction of traditional mas was a West African one.[23]

The emphasis on Africa—acculturation, Africanisms, African masquerading systems—was complemented by the political climate in which the special issue was written and published. It was during a period of intense political upheaval in Trinidad and Tobago, the region, and the world. For example, in 1955, the Reverend Martin Luther King, then leader of the Montgomery Improvement Association, led the Montgomery Bus Boycott, which catapulted the North American Civil Rights movement into high gear. In 1957, Ghana, led by Dr. Kwame Nkrumah, was the first African nation to attain its independence from Britain. In that same year, Haitians elected François "Papa Doc" Duvalier, as President. And in 1959, Fidel Castro carried out a successful revolution in Cuba. In the post–World War II West Indies, leaders sought to mobilize citizens in attempts to establish regional unity. The creation of the West Indies Federation, and later independence, would create a novel nationalist environment for which many of the "old" (colonial) traditions were no longer applicable or relevant. This shift necessitated the construction of new traditions that were appropriate to the presiding political climate.

One such tradition was Eric Williams's program to educate the masses in Trinidad and Tobago. However, in true du Boisian style, Williams believed that people had to be led by the intellectual class.[24] He thus created the University of Woodford Square, actually a park in the center of the commercial district, and installed himself as its sole "professor." It was here that Williams "lectured" to his "students," mainly the black working class, on the legacy of slavery and colonialism. He linked the inferior status of blacks to these two phenomena (Oxaal 1968). Reportedly, his first "lecture" on June 21, 1955 drew a crowd of 20,000 "students" (Cudjoe 1993:58). These public lectures garnered name recognition and a substantial following for Williams. In October 1956, his political party, the People's National Movement (PNM), won the general election, giving Trinidad and Tobago its first-elected black Chief Minister and government. In 1957, on the heels of this auspicious event, Williams, through his minister of education and culture, announced the appointment of a committee to consider the future development of Carnival "along national lines" (*Trinidad Guardian*, January 3, 1957) with the government as its new patron.

But Carnival in the 1950s was a dichotomous affair. The majority of its participants were black. However, their portrayals or themes were overwhelmingly based on non-African and non-Caribbean historical narratives. In 1957, the first Carnival following the PNM's victory, the festival's organizers introduced a new competition category. The Band of the Year award was a very public acknowledgment of the superiority of one mas band over all others. This award also bestowed prestige on the winner. That year, George Bailey won the coveted prize with his band's portrayal *Back to Africa*, a title that conjured up an image of Africa as the ancestral land. Prior to 1957, Carnival representations of Africa had frequently been based on a spurious Western and Hollywood perception of the African continent as primitive and uncivilized. For example, some of the popular mas bands had been *Ju-Ju Warriors, South African Zulus, African Congo Warriors*, and *Heroes of the Dark Continent.*[25] In 1947, the winners of the Best Warriors Carnival competition category were (1) Uganda, (2) Tanganyika, and (3) Tribal Ju-Ju (Anthony 1989:181). These early depictions reinforced the Western imagining of a savage and wild continent. A decade later, Bailey attempted to counter the pejorative visualization of Africa. Historian Michael Anthony (1989: 263) described the band's impact.

> Bailey's band *Back to Africa* made a stunning and immediate impact, and straightaway changed the then current viewpoint towards African masquerade. People had been accustomed to seeing the fierce-looking Zulu, the prancing Watusi, and the crocodile-loving Zambesi. They had never seen an elaborate, elegant, dignified, and at the same time wondrously colourful display of African masquerade, and they had never dreamt that any African masquerade could reach such heights of splendour so as to challenge the classic styles of Greece and Rome.

To reclaim Africa, Bailey framed the continent in the visual and structural idiom of the historical mas bands. The maskers were organized around a hierarchy of principal characters, and many costumes showcased European-style capes and trains made from velvet and satin. For example, "the King of the Band . . . Oba Adele the First was a magnificently-dressed character, with a cape about fifteen yards long, held up by maidens, and with burnished rhinestones studding his crown (Anthony 1989:264)." Compare this description with the king of Harold Saldenha's *Imperial Rome* (1955): "The King of this band, Valman Jones, was spectacular as Nero Caesar. Dressed in royal purple and gold, he was wearing a cape about fifteen yards long" (Anthony 1989:248). Overall, Bailey's depiction of Africa veered somewhat from the stereotypical images of "the fierce-looking Zulu, the prancing Watusi, and the crocodile-loving Zambesi" to

Masqueraders from Harold Saldenah's *Holy War,* 1958. From the author's collection.

include a novel view of Africa as "elegant and dignified." He achieved this by historicizing the African continent alongside the great European civilizations of Greece and Rome, two popular Carnival themes.[26] As a matter of fact, in 1957 Harold Saldenha's mas band, *The Glory That was Greece,* was favored to win the Band-of-the-Year title. Some Carnival aficionados interpreted Bailey's triumph over Saldenah as Africa's triumph over Europe (colonialism). Bailey's very bold step of re-presenting Africa, albeit as a historical mas, publicly validated the continent and made it worthy for blacks to reclaim it as the ancestral homeland.[27]

Similarly, Williams sought to reevaluate and reposition the island's African descendants and their cultural practices. For example, in his foreword to Errol Hill's play *Ping Pong* (Williams in Hill 1955:6), he stated,

> These [ordinary people] are the creators of our Caribbean music, the characters of our Caribbean drama, the voters of our Caribbean democracy. It is people like these from whom the Caribbean cultural movement derives its principal inspiration.

In this statement, Williams acknowledged the political potential of the black community, who, incidentally, would later become his constituents. Having received full suffrage in 1946, "the voters of our Caribbean democracy," now had a "consanguine" candidate who selected them as the chosen ones, the culture bearers of the new nation.[28] Williams' political agenda was clear. He was building the nation from the bottom up, from a black working-class constituency. However, this black–Creole nation would be fashioned and led by a fraternity of men; women would be its loyal supporters (Reddock 1994).

This mode of (en)gendering the new nation is very typical of nationalist movements (Enloe 1990; McClintock 1995; Reddock 1996; McClintock et al. 1997). As Cynthia Enloe (1990:44) explains, "nationalism typically has sprung from masculinized memory, masculinized humiliation and masculinized hope." In other words, men's need to regain what, presumably, was lost during previous political regimes—their manhood/masculinity, their pride, and their reputation—is a primary impetus of nationalist movements. Therefore, nationhood has to be imag[in]ed through the male. Eric Williams's immediate foray into the political arena on the heels of his termination from the Caribbean Commission in 1955, seems to illustrate this idea. Frustrated and angry at the commission's policies regarding the region, Williams may have felt insulted and humiliated by the body's action. Reportedly, they offered him a job "requiring [him] to work in a subordinate capacity to one of the very men who sat down in secret session in Puerto Rico and decided unanimously not to renew [his] contract with the Commission" (Cudjoe 1993:164). In a subsequent address, regarding his tenure at the Commission, he claimed a need "to clear my name and reputation from any imputations of inefficiency or failure" (Cudjoe 1993: 160). Applying Enloe's theory, it could be said that Williams's entrance into local politics was, in part, a strategy to reclaim what he viewed as having lost, his "reputation," a signifier of his manhood. Paul Gilroy's discussion of the imagining of racial communities through black masculinity also resonates here. As he notes (Gilroy 1992:194), "the integrity of the race [nation] is . . . interchangeable with the integrity of black masculinity, which [had to] be regenerated at all costs." With a paucity of relevant popular visual images, Carnival became the source par excellence that would provide iconic representations of the black male. Recast in Crowley's traditional mas model, maleness or masculinity was defined as black militancy (Sailor, Indian, Midnight Robber), elegance (Historical bands), and wit (Pierrot Grenade).[29] In this very public and politicized space, black males/men and nationhood became inextricably linked. However, the 1950s imag[in]ing of Carnival and traditional mas has serious implications for the significance of race and ethnicity, class and gender in the codification and authentication of mas. For the remainder of this chapter, I will address briefly what I consider to be three major implications of the costume and performance aesthetics of traditional mas on gender relations in contemporary Carnival. This discussion will illustrate the inadequacy of the traditional mas paradigm to valorize, interpret, and "make sense" of the contemporary mas.

WOMAN/FEMALE AS INAUTHENTIC

In the late 1980s Carnival, the unprecedented dominance of female maskers and their preferred costume and performance styles resulted in a gendered framing of the festival. According to Desa Philippi (1987:41), "gender operates as a system of signs, the sign woman [or man] is only meaningful within the system of signification in which it is produced." Thus the significance of Woman is dependent on the role(s) that society sets for her. In Trinidad and Tobago, as it is in most parts of the world, a pervasive image of Woman projects her as the moral and ethical arm of society. She tends to symbolize the virtuous and also the goodness in society. However, as Philippi (1987:41) goes on to explain, "Woman [also] occupies a dual position, negatively inscribed in that the phallic function rests on exception (absence) and at the same time as the category of absolute otherness that acts as the guarantee in the logic of the sign." In other words, with man posited as the "norm," Woman, as sign, is representative of the abnormal, deviant, and nonstandard. However, Woman, as other, is necessary to the concept of man. In Carnival, a self-reflexive event, these ideas of gender obtain. They are underscored in the contemporary festival, resulting in analysis based on sex and gender and not on aesthetics and style.

Local journalism proves this point. Since the 1980s, newspaper reports on the event have been fixated on the female image. Such headlines as "Carnival Is Woman" or "Reign of Carnival Women" have become popular fare. Principally, they acknowledge the dominance of female maskers in modifying the festival. The headlines also underscore what Sue Best (1995:185) describes as "the 'metaphoric' transfer of the attributes of woman to space." In other words, stereotypical "female characteristics"—shapely, sensual, coquette—are employed either to describe the festival or to signify its inherent quality. In conjunction with the headlines, newspaper reports that describe the contemporary Carnival as women "celebrating their femaleness in coquettish, sensual fabrics and designs" (*Trinidad Guardian Carnival Magazine* 1992:52) or, their disguises as "beautiful and shapely Arawaks and Caribs" (*Trinidad Guardian Carnival Magazine* 1992:1) affirm the festival's gender focus. They also insinuate "woman" as an anomaly. Throughout the recorded history of the festival, "Carnival is Man/Male" has not been a concept that requires vocalization because, in large part, maleness/masculinity, as exemplified in the traditional characters, tends to represent or signify the norm or the canon. Hence, there is rarely a need to articulate the obvious. However, deviance and difference require articulation and visualization to alert us to their exception from the norm.

The public display of women's bodies and their performances, specifically *wining,* now is disturbing to many citizens. Letters to newspaper editors reveal the populace's evaluation of women's mas. For example,

> This year's celebration, particularly Carnival Tuesday's presentation, has been noted as the most vulgar and immoral display ever witnessed on the Savannah stage. Women, particularly, no sooner spotted cameramen than they began their lewd dance, which brought the bile up in most men's stomachs.[30]

A newspaper editorial (*Trinidad Express,* February 22, 1988) shared a similar assessment.

> In 1988, the spectacle had very little to do with the parade of costumed bands but with the disgusting behavior of hundreds of women who made an obscene spectacle of themselves. . . . In skimpy outfits which apparently some of them still found to be too cumbersome, they gyrated with and against one another and occasionally with men.

While women's "lewd dance" is defined as "vulgar and immoral display" and "obscene spectacle," similar performances by male maskers are not singled out.[31] This biased evaluation and reporting of women's Carnival performance stems from a tacitly sexist framing of women's mas in their biological and social roles as mothers and wives, respectively. As one resident explained, "Women are the cradle of civilisation . . . they remain the bedrock of family life" (*Trinidad Express,* February 22, 1988). Thus, their public behavior should be in keeping with their socially prescribed symbolic roles. "The scandalous and lewd cavorting of . . . women, many of whom took the pains to simulate the sex act in full view of their audience" (*Trinidad Guardian,* April 3, 1988) was unacceptable. Curiously, this author's isolation of women "simulating the sex act" absented and absolved men of any egregious participation. If men were not participants, then women were the sole performers of the "act." Was the author's criticism aimed at the homoerotic nature of the women's performance? Maybe. Her articulated concern, however, was on the effect of the women's performance on young impressionable children. "Let us not forget that many of the viewers are small children?" (*Trinidad Guardian,* April 3, 1988). Another letter also underscored this concern: "I think it is downright shameful and even frightful to see how the *mothers* and *mothers-to-be* of our nation 'wine' and expose their bodies to all and sundry. What signals are we sending to the next generation?" [emphasis added] (*Trinidad Guardian,* February 12, 1988). Traditional mas is never framed in a discourse on paternity. This public and ontological assessment of female maskers clearly illustrates women's Carnival behavior is too often "read" or interpreted primarily in relationship to their biological role as mothers.

THE AESTHETICS OF MOTHERHOOD

Motherhood epitomizes the good and virtuous woman. As feminist writer Elaine Savory Fido (1992:283) explains, in the Caribbean "motherhood is still viewed as a most important role for women by both men and women." Janice Lee Liddell (1990:321), writing on the representations of mothers in Caribbean literature, underscores Fido's observations: "The image of mother—giver and nurturer of life: teacher and instiller of values and mores—has indeed become the most persistent of Caribbean archetypes." Liddell (1990:322) also notes that the concept of motherhood is often paradoxical: mothers are strong "pillar[s] of fortitude" while being "self-sacrificing, self-effacing wom[e]n-parent[s]." Lord Pretender, in his calypso *Mother Love* (1937), identifies the characteristics of a good mother.

> The zenith of a woman's ambition in life
> Should be to be a loving mother and a pleasing wife
> For thus they are by nature intended
> Not as overlords or slaves but to man subjected
> To join with him in love and connubial unity
> In generating humanity. (Rohlehr 1990:225)

In this calypso, Pretender presents motherhood, within the sanctity of marriage where women are subordinate to their husbands, as women's natural role. Throughout local history, the upper classes, both white and colored, have frequently used the single-mother status as a sign of the inferiority and immorality of working-class women, making poverty and immorality interchangeable conditions. However, the poor mother could be "saved" or "redeemed," *if* she were self-sacrificing. The "self-sacrificing" characteristic is spelled out in the Mighty Caresser's "A Warning to Men, Women and Children about their Parents" (1937):

> A good Mother always does things constructive
> *To help her children is her objective*
> No matter *how poor* she happens to be
> Her duty she'll perform assiduously
> Without the shadow of a single doubt
> *They'll feed you, clothe you and remain without*
> Send you to school to be educated
> So that in days to come you'll be respected.
> [emphasis added] (Rohlehr 1990:225)

Literary critic Gordon Rohlehr (1990:224–226) presents motherhood as "part of an ideology of control":

> Veneration of woman's role as wife, mother and helpmate was part of an ideology of control which was designed to deny women the possibility of successful movement beyond the home and family . . . and to deny them the sexual or social freedom which the men themselves enjoyed and cherished.

In other words, motherhood as ideology could present a confining and limiting role for women. It reaffirms the old adage that a woman's place is in the home and also sanctions the containment of women's sexual expression. Some contemporary writers of women's history have reinterpreted motherhood as a metaphor for women's selfhood or their rebirth. In "On Becoming One's Mother," poet Lorna Goodison suggests that "in some essential sense one has to become one's own mother, that is one has to create or produce oneself" (Baugh 1997: 212). In sum, motherhood is a polyvalent image and concept. It is the raison d'etre of women's lives; it can bring a modicum of respect to poor mothers; it limits women's social and sexual movement, and it can be a trope for women's selfhood and self-representation. In Carnival, however, it is motherhood as ideal (respectability) and ideology (confinement and control) that has become the unspoken aesthetic in the evaluation of women's mas.

Motherhood, thus, becomes the primary hermeneutic frame for women's Carnival costume and performance, which are judged *not* for their aesthetic value but, instead, for their adherence to societal standards of good, respectable, public dress and conduct for mothers. In contrast, traditional characters are never judged for their adherence to good, public behavior standards for fathers. Because of this prejudicial assessment, women's mas cannot be appraised solely in terms of transformation or inversion, the anthropological and sociological hallmarks of festival theory. Neither can it be evaluated fully nor be valorized through the aesthetic lens of traditional mas, which is heavily invested in fully-clothed body and stylized oral and choreographic performances. In reality, women's mas requires a new paradigm, one that offers gender as a principal unit of analysis.

"EMASCULATION" OF MEN

As self-reflexive, women's mas style resonates with their changing status in the larger society, as seen in their seemingly nonreliance on men. Journalist Terry Joseph (*Trinidad Express,* February 2, 1988) intimates this as a cause and effect of women's mas:

> There is the aspect of an albeit licentious form of liberation among women, which sees hordes of females feeling enough of a sense of security to venture

> into the mas band on carnival days *without any promise of male protection.* In fact, so secure are they that they seem to spend much of the time *taunting males who failed to perform.* [emphasis added]

Joseph's observation is echoed in social scientist Ramesh Deosaran's evaluation of gender affairs in the larger society (*Trinidad Guardian,* February 14, 1993):

> In Trinidad, we are being faced with a crisis of masculinity . . . While our young girls are pumping iron, studying harder and pushing forward, we now have young men ambivalent about their very roles in society and worse yet, confused about their sexuality. Even many of our women are finding it difficult to find satisfaction with the attitudes and performance of our young males. In fact, the very ideal of sexual equality is being threatened.

In their remarks, Joseph and Deosaran posit the idea that women's public behavior, including their Carnival performance, is reflective or illustrative of a larger societal problem, the "emasculation" of men. According to these authors, women's sense of liberation and security (Joseph) and their academic achievement (Deosaran) bear a direct correlation to men's inadequacy, both financial and sexual. For Joseph, women's feeling of liberation and security allow them to publicly taunt men "who failed to perform." Sexual impotency is also implied here. For Deosaran, women's academic and professional achievements result in their dissatisfaction "with the attitudes and performance of our young men." This perceived "emasculation" of men may explain, in large part, why many believe there is a need to publicly counteract the increasing "feminization" of the national festival with strong and assertive images of masculinity.

However, the group of traditional characters selected as a counternarrative to the "female" Carnival is problematic. Among the now sacralized traditional characters are the boastful Midnight Robber, the "savage" and violent Indian, and the elegantly dressed but equally violent Pierrot and Stickfighter. Presumably, these characters evoke a time when men were men or, as journalist David Chase (*Trinidad Express,* January 24, 1997) wrote in 1997, "when Carnival was Carnival." Judging from the choice of traditional characters, when Carnival was "real" or "authentic," masculinity was located in ethnicity (black men), physical violence (Indian, Pierrot, Stickfighter), self-aggrandizement (Midnight Robber), and male reputation (Stickfighter, Pierrot, and Midnight Robber). In this model, nonblack and nonviolent males are not "real" men. In a society that is currently struggling to come to grips with the alarming increase of domestic violence and sexual assault against women, at Carnival and throughout the year, the indirect and unbalanced celebration of male violence and aggressive behavior is unsettling, even in play.[32] The elevation or sacralization of violence and aggression sends a subliminal message that, under certain circumstances (i.e.,

Carnival), aggressive behavior is acceptable. While many residents may feel the need or urgency for a more balanced representation of gender in mas, there is also an obligation to select a more diverse array of traditional characters.[33] This may be difficult in light of the extant dependency on Crowley's cast of "traditional masques."

In their articles, Pearse and Crowley tacitly molded our perception and understanding of the origins of the modern Carnival and the costume and performative traditions of its principal characters. Applying Herskovits's theory of acculturation and a West African model of masquerade, they constructed a particular image of Carnival in which black men were the preeminent performers. In costuming, there was a marked aesthetic preference for syncretism and voluminous dress. The hallmarks of performance were a combination of aggression (Stickfighter, Pierrot), stylized movements (Dragon, Bats), verbal artistry (Pierrot Grenade, Midnight Robber), and theatrical reenactments (Historical Bands). The combined styles of these categories—men, fully covered bodies, aggression, verbal artistry, stylized movements, reenactments, and inversion—now constitute the hallmarks of canonical or authentic mas. This particular construction of the authentic in mas is heavily indebted to the 1950s political climate, which required efficacious images of blacks that paralleled the imaginings of a new nation.

More recent scholarship has begun to challenge the focus on the male maskers (Miller 1991; Franco 1998; Davies 1998). Molly Ahye (1991), in her analysis of the polymorphic nature of Carnival, proffered gender as an effective analytical tool. She noted that women experienced Carnival differently from men, and vice versa. For example, men play mas "with a strong commitment to some cause or other . . . some use it to socialize . . . [or] to stalk, snare and consume their prey" (Ahye 1991:403–404). By contrast, Carnival allows women who "are plagued by the stress of life, stymied by tradition . . . [to] reach the grand climax . . . to explode with galvanic energy" (Ahye 1991:407). Despite the very sexual and reductionist connotations, Ahye veers from the well-worn, and often inaccurate, authentic–inauthentic paradigm. Her approach allows analysis of distinct women and men's mas, gender construction in mas, sexuality, and the complementarity of male and female styles of masking. While I agree with Ahye's call for a gendered lens of analysis, one must be careful not to flip the coin from a male-centered to a female-centered mas paradigm. Neither addresses the complexity or polyvalence of the festival.

In sum, the nationalist climate of the 1950s greatly affected the particular patterning of the traditional or authentic in Carnival. However, it did not facilitate the type of analysis that would have revealed a distinct women's style that was markedly different from men's. The image or representation of women had to be symbolic or subsumed into a master narrative. Crowley and Pearse were men of their time and their convictions. The *CQ* special issue is a testimony to their training, vision, and political consciousness. But times have changed and at the dawn of the twenty-first century, their post-World War II imag[in]ing of mas is inadequate as the sole or primary model to evaluate or contextualize women's mas. We need a new paradigm to evaluate the contemporary mas; one that would allow for a more panoramic and democratic view of the festival, one that would value the contributions of *all* participants, irrespective of race, class or gender.

NOTES

1. The twin-island state is Trinidad and Tobago. In this chapter, when I use the term *Trinidad Carnival*, I am referring specifically to Port of Spain, the main Carnival venue. Therefore, Trinidad Carnival, here, is actually Port of Spain Carnival.

2. Wining refers to gyrating pelvic movements.

3. The aesthetic of contemporary mas is realized in the skimpy and sexy costuming of such bands as Barbarossa, Legends, and Harts, the Younger Generation. When I mention the contemporary women's mas, I am referring specifically to the skimpy and sexily dressed female maskers.

4. *Mas* is an abbreviation for masquerade. It is the popular term used in Trinidad and Tobago to describe the costumed performers who parade on Carnival Monday and Tuesday.

5. *Jab Jab* is a creolized version of the French *diable* or devil.

6. This quotation was taken from an interview I conducted with Crowley in 1984.

7. This article, "Traditional Masques of Trinidad Carnival," may have been initially conceived by Andrew Pearse. In his unpublished notes and papers, housed at the University of the West Indies, St. Augustine, I found a very detailed outline of this article. It is possible that Pearse created the outline and Crowley completed the analysis.

8. Jamette is a creolization of the French *diametre*. The term describes those at the periphery of society. In nineteenth-century Trinidad, the jamette class defined working-class blacks who lived in urban areas and, reportedly, indulged in criminal or dubious activities.

9. The French migrated to Spanish Trinidad in the late eighteenth century. Many were royalists fleeing the French Revolution or the economic downturn in the French colonies. They quickly created a very distinct French society. In 1797, the island was capitulated to the English.

10. The term *Fetes champetres* translates as country or open-air party or celebration.

11. The "coloured middle class," in this context, are free men and women of mixed European and African ancestry, generally with fair or light complexion. By 1810, they were the second-largest ethnic and cultural group, after the slaves. They valued European culture but were also race conscious. Historian Bridget Brereton in *Race Relations*

in Colonial Trinidad explained that the colored middle class "stressed racial consciousness . . . to 'disprove' the theory of the innate mental infirmity of the African race" (1979:6). In a somewhat twisted logic, the colored middle class believed that by acquiring European values and cultural practices they were negating the Eurocentric perception of African inferiority.

12. After the capitulation of the island to the British in 1797, the free coloreds lost many of the privileges that they had previously enjoyed under Spanish law. The British under Governor Picton introduced barbarous legislation as a way to keep the coloreds in a subordinate place. One example was the right to flog a colored man or woman, free or enslaved, for any crime she or he may have committed. They were required to pay $16 for a permit to host musical events in the privacy of their homes. In 1824, a prominent colored man, Jean Baptiste Philip, presented a scathing report to Secretary of State Balthurst in London. Titled *The Free Mulatto Speaks,* the report presented the abuses that the free colored community in Trinidad suffered under British governance. The British Parliament, on the basis of Baptiste's report, finally ordered the repeal of the new discriminatory legislation. After 1826, free coloreds were no longer required to obtain a permit to host musical events in their homes.

13. The Emancipation Proclamation was effective on August 1, 1834. However, planters complained about their impending losses if the slaves abandoned the plantations. A six-year apprenticeship period was permitted. In 1838, slavery was abolished in the Anglophone Caribbean.

14. Canboulay is a creolized form of *cannes brulees* or burnt cane. After emancipation, freed blacks opened Carnival, midnight on Carnival Sunday, with the Canboulay performance, a reenactment of estate procedures to quell fires.

15. The Pissenlit or bedwetter wore a transparent nightgown and carried a "menstrual cloth." It was actually a white cloth dyed or painted red.

16. In an attempt to remove the fighting and violence from the nineteenth-century Carnival, local authorities tried to outlaw the carrying of sticks during the festival. In 1880, under the leadership of Captain Baker, the police were successful in getting the maskers to parade without their sticks. However, in 1881, the maskers refused to abide by the proclamation, which prohibited the carrying of sticks in the streets during Carnival. A confrontation ensued between the maskers and the police, resulting in casualties on both sides. Eventually, groups or bands of stickfighters were banned from the street Carnival.

17. The military characters were based on personnel on board ship. Hence, the Stoker danced incorporated elements of his occupation of stoking the fire.

18. This type of costume was popularly known as cloth mas. This term made reference to the large quantity of cloth used to fabricate the costume.

19. Sumari was performed by East Indian males.

20. At one point, boys and girls danced the Maypole. Now, mostly girls participate in the dance.

21. In the early 1950s, Andrew Pearse was a visiting professor at Northwestern University, where he met and worked with Melville Herskovits. At this time, Daniel Crowley was a graduate student of African art under the tutelage of Bascom and Herskovits.

22. The Sande or Bundu society, among such groups as the Mende, Temne, and Vai, is the only female society in which women wear and dance with wooden masks.

23. As a student of African art under the tutelage of William Bascom, Crowley was very familiar with West African masking practices.

24. Williams is drawing on W. E. B. du Bois's concept of the Talented Tenth. Du Bois believed that the duty of the 10 percent of African-Americans who constituted the intellectual elite was to educate and lead the less fortunate masses. See his *Dusk at Dawn* (New York: Shocken Books, 1940).

25. This Carnival portrayal was judged in the Indian (Native American) or Warrior categories. *Heroes of the Dark Continent* depicted Africa as wild and uncivilized.

26. By using the structure and costume aesthetic of the historical mas genre, Bailey cleverly re-presented Africa as having a history that was worthy of portrayal. The sumptuous quality of many of the costumes also placed the band, and Africa, in the pretty mas category.

27. The concept of homeland was important to Eric Williams. Prior to the 1950s, Africa was not valued as an acceptable homeland. By 1962, the year of independence, Williams would put forth Trinidad and Tobago, the newly independent nation, as the new motherland. In a famous speech, he declared, "There'll be no mother Europe, mother India, or mother Africa, only mother Trinidad and Tobago."

28. Williams's particular imagining of the new nation had its parallel in the visual arts. Black artists began to look to Trinidad's landscape, its people, and their folk practices for inspiration and subject matter. For example, such artists as Boscoe Holder and Dermot Louison painted the local landscapes as serene and timeless. Noel Vaucrosson's *Bele* (1957) depicted the popular drum dance that eventually became one of the national dances. Alfred Codallo's *Kalinda* (1957) and *Wake* (1957) also made reference to the cultural practices of the black folk. Dancer and choreographer Beryl McBurnie would include such folk dances as Bele and Bongo in her company's dance repertoire. The cultural and political visualizations of the new nation were intertwined and, also, heavily invested in the black folk and their practices.

29. Black militancy was a mixed bag. While the Military and Indian mas may have symbolized some degree of subjectivity and agency, these portrayals were popular among the nascent steelbands. With the exception of 1954, fighting among steelbands occurred every year of the 1950s.

30. *Trinidad Guardian*, February 22, 1988. In 1988, in the first live television broadcast of Carnival, many women maskers used the media to perform exaggerated versions of wining.

31. Some newspaper articles inadvertently included men when they mentioned the behavior of adults. However, none of them singled out men for their Carnival behavior. Only women were, and are, repeatedly singled out for their "obscene" behavior.

32. I use the word *indirect* because I know that the supporters of the traditional mas characters will say that they are not supporting violence and aggressive behavior. The point that they are missing, however, is that a character's costume and his performance are inextricably linked, and we can't have one without the other. For example, the Midnight Robber is not a Midnight Robber until he gives his boastful speeches. A Midnight Robber who does not recite boastful speeches is generally dismissed; he is an imposter. So when we lavish praise on a Robber or Stickfighter, we are also praising his unique performance, be it boasting or fighting.

33. While many lament the absence of men in contemporary mas, this does not present an accurate picture. There are many men who play mas, and there is also a large

contingent of men who are the musicians providing music for Carnival bands. Men also provide security for many of the bands with large numbers of women dressed in sexy costumes. Men are also involved in the behind-the-scenes organization. Therefore, men are very active in mas, both in front and behind the scene. They are just not the numerical majority.

2. The Masquerader-Anthropologist: The Poetics and Politics of Studying Carnival

Patricia A. De Freitas

THROUGH THE EYES OF A DEVIL

The morning was cool as I emerged from the darkened house and walked along Western Main Road for a pre-arranged meeting with friends. It was *jouvay* morning in Trinidad, and I was on my way to join a devil masquerade band. Popularly explained as a derivative of the French *jour ouvert* (daybreak), the patois *j'ouvert* (pronounced *jouvay*) is the ritual beginning of the two-day Carnival of the streets. Excitement, carried through the air on a cacophony of rhythms, seemed to come from everywhere—the hills in the north, residential Woodbrook to the south, unsleeping St. James in the west and Port of Spain's core to the east. I felt situated in a "space" larger than my eye or ear could contain or discipline. Time, too, stretched beyond the present into the past, as the rhythms pulsating in the shadows of the night evoked memories of pure delight when, as a child, I was awakened by the sound of music in the street, a signal that Carnival had begun. The music was gentler, in those times, the sound of unamplified steel or string, but it brought the same excitement that propelled me out of bed and onto the street. The magic, meaning and mystery of Carnival went unquestioned, then, as I, "the native," was annually inserted into a world inhabited largely by musicians, calypsonians and masqueraders who brought delight, and sometimes terror, to adults and children alike. Now, I walked the streets as an anthropologist, an observing jouvay participant, seeking cultural understanding. I felt like the quintessential masquerader, negotiating two identities—*native* and *non-native, self* and *other*—viscerally engaged, yet hyperalert to the sights, sounds, and smells that filled the early morning air.

The Main Road was bustling with people and traffic going in both directions. Some people walked purposefully and briskly; others simply ambled along waiting to join a Carnival band on its way to downtown Port of Spain. Groups sat "liming"[1] on street corner curbs and walls, while there were the few, either sleep deprived or drunken casualties of a long night of feting, who drifted from side to side, seemingly oblivious to the spirit of excited anticipation that saturated the air around them. I looked at my watch—it was 1:00 AM.

Temporarily constructed sidewalk bars, each blaring music from huge speakers, had their fair share of customers. Orange, corn, peanut, and sweet drink vendors also enjoyed a brisk trade. Play and trade, pleasure and work, festive space and marketplace: here was the co-mingling of categories usually kept analytically separate within our academic traditions (cf. Stallybrass and White 1986:27–30). More often than not, Carnival has been represented, both by local and foreign commentators, as the site of *communitas,* a playful domain partitioned off from the rational and economic "real" world. The influential theoretician of Carnival, Bakhtin, himself conceptualized the fair and market as festive space outside the "serious" world of trade and commerce. As a site of laughter, Carnival was represented as inverting and suspending the hierarchical world of officialdom. Assuming the economic–festive separation inherent in capitalist rationality, Mikhail Bakhtin simplified the paradoxical enmeshments between the two spheres (Bakhtin, 1968:255). At the Roxy Roundabout, however, itself an intersection of roads from St. James, Woodbrook, St. Clair, and downtown Port of Spain, I noted a Carnival space both festive and commercial, where work intersected with pleasure, and poorly dressed boys, with sacks on their backs, competed for the discarded and redeemable beer bottles of revelers.

Woodbrook was pulsating with sounds and movement as I joined the group of friends with whom I had arranged to *play mas*[2] It was 1:30 AM as we drew near Adam Smith Square, the gathering place of our jouvay band. Bodies glistened brown, black, and bronze under streetlights, shadowy figures smelling of freshly applied paint and cocoa. We took our place in line to complete our initiation into the tribe of cocoa devils. Buckets of dark, thick liquid stood semifull on the grass before us for our anointing. I shuddered at the thought of the messy, cold morning bath. Others obviously had the same misgivings. A female devil ahead of me requested the self-appointed "priests" to apply a few streaks on her face and hands. Another daubed baby oil on her skin before her ablutions. While some chose to be partially and selectively covered, most went for the total transformation that the "high priests" were only too happy to oblige. "Wey you want it?" my anointer asked as I arrived at the head of the line. In a spontaneous burst of daring and courage, I said, "All Over!" "Da's de spirit, man," he said approvingly as he cupped the liquid in his hand and poured it all over me. I braced as I felt the cold liquid on my face; it ran down my back and covered my clothes. Another man smeared my hands, legs, and feet. My transformation was now complete. I began to understand the words of Ken, a veteran Dragon masquerader whom I had interviewed a few weeks earlier, "Every dragon man does smile behind he mas."

Behind the devil mas and mas(s) of devils was the smiling "native," transported through the sensations of sight, pulsating sound, smell, and touch into a world both familiar and pleasurable. The visceral memory of past Carnivals, plus my physical insertion into that mass of bodies dancing to pounding brass, evoked a sense of a collective Self, a "peoplehood" (Fox 1990:3), of which I felt a part. It was an experience of "re-membering," connecting me both to "the pleasure of memory that is physically recalled" (Gotfrit 1991:176) and to a community, felt and not simply "imagined" (Anderson 1983). Sensual pleasures are not easily represented in the static, rationalist language of academic discourse. Yet it is precisely through these intangibles, in the well-being and belonging evoked, that Carnival becomes a compelling vehicle and metaphor for many Trinidadians in the construction of a collective Self.

Paradoxically, playing devil mas was a new experience for me. As "native," I had participated in Carnival in several different ways, but never had I experienced the world of jouvay devils from the inside. As a child in St. James, I had feared these fierce-looking creatures: bareback men smeared with molasses, grease, or "blue," who emerged every Carnival with long nails, horns, forks, red tongues, and wiry little tails, beating oil tins and blowing whistles to the refrain, "pay the devil, *jab jab*."[3] Over the years, the Carnival devils grew fewer and less fierce. Transformed in behavior and rarely seen patrolling the city in small troupes,[4] "tamed" devils are now found in hordes on jouvay morning, "dirty" creatures who occasionally "attack" through hugs and rubs, leaving their victims covered in a variety of substances—mud, cocoa, paint, grease. For this reason, I had avoided the jouvay devil bands in adulthood, viewing them with some distaste. But on that cool morning, anonymous, playful, and unconcerned with my physical appearance, I got some inkling of their attraction.

This, then, was a plunge into the Other of Carnival for me, a native discovering another dimension of self in an experience of the unfamiliar. Further, this cocoa devil was more than a smiling native: she was also a reflexive jab jab, an "other," if you will, desperately trying to "discipline" the experience within a discourse on identity that assumed the Self–Other oppositional categories. To what extent was this Trinidad's rite of reversal, an inversion of the norm? Or was this in fact a performance of Self, the expression "writ large" of Trinidadian identity, the natives' perception of a collective Self that lives behind the mask of everydayness? Paradoxically, an "insider" and "outsider," I set off on a jouvay pilgrimage through the streets of Port of Spain.

THE QUEST

My search that jouvay morning was for understanding through observant participation. As a "native" whose adolescence paralleled Trinidad's movement to political independence, I was attracted to anthropology because of its claim to take "the native's point of view" seriously. I saw anthropology's methodological and analytical tools as useful allies both in dismantling its own "etic" representations of Trinidadian reality and in uncovering cultural forms that shaped and defined Trinidad's peculiar response to the colonial experience. I had, therefore, joined the ranks of an increasing number of anthropologists, who were interrogating the dichotomous constructs of native/foreign, Western–non-Western to critically examine the positionality of the researcher (see Elder 1966; Srinivas 1967; Nakhleh 1979; Fahim 1982; Ohnuki-Tierney 1984; Jackson 1987; Altorki and Fawzi El Sohl 1988; Narayan 1989, 1993; Stewart 1989; Abu-Lughod 1991; Limon 1991; Kondo 1996).

Carnival, with its songs, music, and masquerade, seemed the most "natural" point of entry into "local" culture for two reasons. First, Carnival is a salient symbol, albeit highly contested, of Trinidad's cultural identity in nationalist discourse, with many Trinidadians, especially from urban areas, cultivating a self that is expressive of the carnival ethos. Secondly, Carnival had personal significance for me as a native of St. James. When I was a child, it was a time of mystery, magic, joy, and poetry when the appearance of masqueraders and the sound of steel from Cross Fire, Tripoli and North Stars steelbands provided the opportunity to dance on the streets. While it was one of many seasonal celebrations that punctuated my young life, Carnival increasingly became the privileged site where my sense of national identity was shaped and constituted.

The purpose of this chapter is not to report on "what" I found at the end of my study. That has already been done elsewhere (de Freitas 1994, 1999). Instead, I want to grapple with the "who" and the "how" of the quest. This is especially important in light of the recent development of World Carnival conferences in the United States and Trinidad, and the increasing number of studies, by both local and foreign researchers, that attempt to understand the Carnival phenomenon and its relationship to both local and diasporic communities (Cohen 1982; Alonso 1990; Liverpool 1993; Crowley 1996; Burton 1997; van Koningsbruggen 1997; Green 1998; Riggio 1998). A focus on us, the "students" of Carnival, allows us to recognize that we, too, are part of the Carnival performance. Stuart Hall, reflecting on the relationship between identity and representation, suggests "perhaps, instead of thinking of identity as an already accomplished fact, which the new cultural practices then represent, we should think, instead, of "identity" as a "production," which is never complete, always in process, and always constituted within, not outside, representation" (1990:222). Just as Trinidadian identity is, in part, constituted within the performance of Carnival, so, too, scholarly and textual representations of Carnival bend back to shape and constitute the event itself.

As such, then, for "natives," the representation of Carnival is highly politicized. At issue is the question of power and the right to represent local realities. It is part of the much larger attempt to detach from the colonizing grip and gaze, which all too frequently misrepresented and denied validity to local cultural practices. Derek Walcott, for example, in his 1992 Nobel lecture, framed the recognition of his own work against the backdrop of the colonizing gaze and grip:

> Here, on the raft of this dais, there is the sound of the applauding surf: our landscape, our history recognized, "at last . . . The Antillean archipelago was there to be written about, not to write itself, by Trollope, by Patrick Leigh-Fermor, in the very tone in which I almost wrote about the village spectacle at Felicity, as a compassionate and beguiled outsider, distancing myself from Felicity village even while I was enjoying it. (Walcott 1992:10)

Additionally, the representation of Carnival is not simply about who has the right to study or represent Carnival. It is also about who best *can* really understand and represent Carnival, not simply its social functions, but its rational and nonrational meanings for its participants and nonparticipants alike. The contest over representation is both about "politics" and "poetics," about who has the authority, both politically and epistemologically, to study and represent Carnival. Kevin Yelvington raises this precise issue in relation to studies of ethnic relations in Trinidad. For him, the jury is still out as to who, native or foreigner, is best positioned to give a "more accurate, more sensitive, and more bias-free" account of Trinidad's social reality (1993:16–17). These are the questions I grapple with in the context of an anthropological discourse and practice that framed my study of Trinidad's Carnival.

BOTH "NATIVE" AND "ANTHROPOLOGIST": TRANSGRESSING THE BOUNDARIES

Anthropology, at least in the tradition influenced by Malinowski, stresses the importance of the "native's point of view" and "native voices" in understanding cultural realities. To understand the meaning and function of cultural practices, an anthropologist is required to enter into the reality of the cultural Other through the practice of participant observation. The ability to both "stand outside" through observation and "enter into" through participation are considered essential qualities of a good anthropologist. In this discourse, "anthropologist" and "native" have traditionally been constructed as oppositional identities, the first as "the researcher," the other as "the researched."

The "normal" historical task of the anthropologist, then, has been to journey from "the familiar" to "the unfamiliar," from "home" to "abroad," from "outside" to "inside," and then back again in order to interpret–represent for both "foreigner" and "native" the experience of cultural difference. The role of the "native" has been the inverse to that of the anthropologist. The native provides access to "insider" information and performs the role of consumer and/or critic of the knowledge produced. These identities and roles have also been geographically anchored. More often than not, the "anthropologist" is positioned at the "core" and the "native" on the "periphery" of the so-called civilized/developed world. It is not simply a position of difference, but a position and relationship of power between the researcher and researched. The displacing or blurring of these identities was seen as subversive to the identity of the discipline itself. In his searing critique of anthropological practice, Bernard McGrane drew attention to the dilemma posed for the anthropologist doing "participant observation":

> Anthropology's field ethnologist exercises his utmost effort to become a native and herein reveals the paradox at the basis of anthropology: if he succeeds he fails and disappears. As [Carlos] Castaneda's works make manifest, if he becomes a native, if he submits to that absolute laceration that alone gives him access to the "other world" he can no longer be an anthropologist, he can no longer do anthropology, for the tiny pivotal reason that then "anthropology" does not exist. It ceases to be and ceases to be conceivable. (McGrane 1989:126)

I, like a growing number of anthropologists, chose to transgress the boundaries that kept the categories of "anthropologist" and "native" distinctly separate. Dissatisfied with what I considered to be the (non)- and (mis)representations of Caribbean cultural realities, I sought an emancipatory Self-understanding from within. Doing ethnography became my way of exploring Self-identity and community, an impulse and practice that has much in common with so-called "minority" scholars, who seek to carve a discursive space within academic disciplines in order to expose their assumptions and silences. My anthropological journey, therefore, was the inverse of the norm. My trip to the field, as a "native" crossing borders, was not the usual movement to the Other, but a journey "home." The bogey-man, lack-of-objectivity, leveled against "natives" studying their own cultures, was (and is) a non-question for me. The presumed scientific ideal of "objectivity" or "bias-free position," which claims the possibility of a neutral and privileged "outside" place from which we can see "truth" more clearly was clearly untenable. Every view is a view from somewhere, and the "outsider" view is itself positioned within a much larger complex of historical, political, and economic enmeshments (Abu-Lughod 1991:141). Instead, I reframed the issue within the concept of reflexivity,[5] claiming for the "native" the possibility of reflexive analysis within her home culture. Denying this possibility to "natives" assumes monolithic, constraining cultures in which we are all hopelessly entangled.

I was not long in the field before I began to experience a rupturing of the distinct categories constructed for "native" and "anthropologist." I was neither the self of the undifferentiated "native," nor the other of a "non-native" anthropologist. Abu-Lughod (1991:137) uses the term coined by Kirin Narayan, "halfie," to describe this anomaly, but it does not quite capture the complexity of leakage between and within categories. The "native" anthropologist is "not One, not two either" (Minh-ha 1989:94). I was caught at intersections of color, ethnic, and gender differences within the "native" category, and entanglements (ascribed and felt) between the categories of "insider" and "outsider."

From the Trinidadian perspective, the category of Otherness, conceived as radical difference, distance, or unfamiliarity is particularly troublesome since we are widely exposed to the technically advanced societies of late capitalism through commodities and media representations. Occupying fundamentally different positions in the global order of things, the European or American anthropologist and the "native" experience each other's cultures differently. The cultural commodities flowing from the "periphery" to the "core" of Western–Northern cities can hardly be compared to the flood going the other way. This in no way suggests that "peripheral" peoples are simply passive consumers of global capitalist products, but this unequal flow of information and goods does shape one's experience of the Other. Before journeying north, I "knew" the United States and Canada in ways few northerners "knew" Port of Spain before journeying south. The Northern Other is generally familiar to "natives," while our Otherness is largely experienced as strange and exotic.

As a "native" anthropologist, I identified easily with the local milieu. In my fieldnotes, there are few "humbling-funny" stories of cultural miscues, faux pas of etiquette or culture shock. I looked, spoke, and acted "native" and was perceived as such. When questions about my "origins" were posed, they were always framed within the Trinidadian geographical or familial context. Carnival, culture, and identity are topics widely debated on the island, and my interest in them was a confirmation of my Trinidadian-ness. I was included as a native in the "view from the beach," as locals observed the new "discoverers" who stepped ashore from modern-day Santa Marias, Pintas, and Ninas in search of "sun, fun, and rum." Networks of family, friends, and acquaintances provided a basic infrastructure of support, interest, and critique of my work, and strangers often confided "insider" information to me:

> I don't tell everybody this, you know, but you are one of us and I know you will not misquote what I tell you. That's why I 'fraid those foreign people hanging around with their cameras and ting. They say they not making no money on it, but that ent really the problem as far as I am concerned. It's how they going to present the ting that could bring plenty trouble." (Sonny)

> I am going to talk to you as a Trinidadian because I think you will understand. It really have *jumbie*[6] in mas, you know. People from America will laugh at me, so I usually say nothing—but I experience *jumbie* here in this mas camp[7] at least on two occasions." (Roderick)

Many people with whom I spoke were concerned about being quoted inappropriately. It was precisely because I was "native" that they presumed I would know that Trinidad "is a small place" and that their words, if published, could be traced and "could bring plenty trouble."

Ironically, on one occasion, I found myself in the role of "native informant" to an anthropologist from the United States. I was referred to my foreign counterpart by a librarian and introduced as "a local expert" on Trinidadian culture. An interview was scheduled to which he brought very tightly focused questions, which restricted any possibility of interrogating so-called Otherness on its own terms. His data search resisted my attempts to insert the "ands," "ifs" and "buts"—and "the poetry"—necessary for understanding and theorizing. The interview left me frustrated and annoyed.

More than existential discomfort, this experience raised issues for me about the production of anthropological knowledge. The problems had less to do with the attitude and manner of the researcher, which was impeccable, but more with the structural model out of which he operated. Traditionally, anthropological knowledge and Trinidadian cocoa production share much in common. Both are gathered in the field, processed and refined in the "mother" country, and sent back for consumption by the local population. Frequently, the "native's" ethnographic presence goes together with his or her theoretical absence (Fabian 1990:771), reinforcing the notion that reflexivity is not the prerogative of the native. For a local anthropologist, this model of knowledge production is epistemologically, politically, and ethically unacceptable.

My early fieldwork experiences "played mas" with my anthropologist and native-informant categories, alerting me to colonial practices which reduced "informants" to sources of raw "insider" data. As McGrane puts it:

> Anthropology's participant observer, the field ethnologist, appears on a concrete level to be engaged in intercourse with the "natives," with the non-European Other. Analytically, the intercourse or dialogue is a fantasy, a mask, covering over and hiding his analytic monologue or masturbation. Analytically, to continue the erotic metaphor, he [*sic*] never loses control. (1989:125)

I, therefore, tried to engage in "structured conversations" rather than "interviews," and became increasingly comfortable with the "negotiation of reality" that ensued during discussions. As a fellow native, people assumed that I had an opinion and they wanted to hear it. As an anthropologist, they interviewed me on the nature of my study, its purpose, its benefits. On four occasions, "interviewees" requested that I record and give them a copy of our conversation, not for "copyright" purposes, but to mull over new insights that our sessions together may have produced:

> We have to be nourished, we have to have these conversations. At first, I told you I didn't know what I was going to say, but now I am talking more than ever. You see the point? All because we have established a platform, a position from which I can pick up, and therefore, I utter by way of invitation. If you were ridiculous, if you were not open, I couldn't. If you were purely intellectual, you just that. But we're involved in the matter of the spirit, the human spirit lends to the human spirit. You see the point I am making? (Roy, a poet)

As a Trinidadian, I was acutely aware that informants were disinclined to be used as raw data banks for the mining of theories elsewhere. Many were themselves engaged in reflexive theoretical discourse, and included me, as co-native, in that search for Self-definition and valuation. This ethical proximity not only undercut the comfortable notion of the subject–object, researcher–researched in academic knowledge production, but demanded that I take local interpretations seriously within my own anthropological representations.

The category of "native," however was not unproblematic. Who and what constitutes the "real Trini" is a hotly contested subject, and includes the question of who, within the category of "native," has the right or authority to best constitute and represent Trinidad's culture. Within the Trinidadian context, I was not simply an undifferentiated "native." As a student of Carnival, I felt and was perceived as "Other" in a variety of contexts, my difference marked by gender, color, urbanity, class, ethnicity, and life lived abroad. My incursion into anthropology had been fueled by my desire to explore the cultural traditions and practices that had been erased from hegemonic discourses and practices. I, therefore, consciously journeyed across borders into the "unfamiliar" male world of stickfighting and rum shops, went to the rural districts of Guayaguayare, Mafeking, and Paramin, and hung out with the "Bats," "Wild Indians," "Dragons" and Jab Jabs (devils) of Carnival. My "blackness" in North America became unmarked in Port of Spain, "red" in Guayaguayare and Arima, "brown" in Barataria, and "white" in Mayaro, where much to my amusement I was asked by a fisherman, "white lady, you want to buy a fish?" An "insider" in Port of Spain, I felt myself to be an "outsider" in Mayaro and Guayaguayare, yet I was considered an "insider" by each village in relation to the other. Within Port of Spain itself, I felt an "insider" in the St. James area, an "outsider" in the Burro's Den Rum Shop in Belmont. And overall, I was "outsider" by virtue of my association with a Canadian university and my interest in, and persistent questioning of, phenomena that most Trinidadians consider ordinary. For most, these various and context-dependent identities created no significant barriers to our "structured conversations," but for the Mayaro man, who refused an interview because I was "a *woman* from outside the village," it did matter. For me, the categories of "anthropologist" and "native" bled into each other, and I and others (re)acted accordingly. I found difference in the familiar (Stewart 1989:14), and commonality in the so-called unfamiliar. There was no seamless native Self of which I was unproblematically a part, nor was I the stranger anthropologist in a land of distinctive Others.

IMPLICATIONS FOR ANTHROPOLOGICAL ETHNOGRAPHY

My experience as a "native" doing ethnography "at home" raised several questions, which I continue to grapple with as a practitioner of anthropological ethnography. These questions involve the "who" and "why" of doing research. Historically, most anthropologists traveled from so-called First World "cores" to Third World "peripheries" to study cultures or institutions considered different from their own. By definition, then, "anthropologist" was almost always "the foreigner," who brought the outsider's Eye/I to local realities and saw patterns and meanings not immediately evident to "natives." However, the anthropologist was not just any outsider; for example, she or he was not someone from a similarly positioned "developing" island or region. Typically, she or he was "the foreigner," whose home location was in the so-called First World.

Anthropologist–native views, then, so central to the anthropological project, were embedded in a larger set of asymmetrical relations and locations. Further, their personas were located in social and psychic orientations toward the subjects or field of study. The anthropologist was typically "the outsider" and the native, "the insider." Paradoxically, it was the subjects of research, "the natives," who brought the "outsiders'" Eye to the culture of anthropology itself, to unmask the power asymmetries, motives, ideological assumptions, and effects of representation on "native" cultures and subjectivities. It was this recognition that led me and other "natives" to claim the right to study our "home" cultures.

My journey to the field was a journey "home" then. I identified, and was identified, as "native," and had consciously claimed the "insider" position as the privileged location from which to do anthropological ethnography. I was claiming my right as "native" to Self-representation within an asymmetrical global order in which the "native's voice" is either muted or mediated through the narratives of the anthropologist Other. In the case of the Caribbean, a region frequently "written about" by outsiders, but not "writing itself," I saw myself as an engaged participant in a common struggle for the right, as Trinidadians, to narrate ourselves both in performance and text. Among others, a self-conscious goal was to capture the cultural nuances and local meanings—the poetry of Carnival—for the purpose of evoking "recognition" in native readers. This stance as anthropologist is an intensely "political" act, as it privileges the "native" both as narrator and audience and re-centers the anthropological project from the "core" to the so-called "peripheries."

The anthropological task, however, is multiple. As Talal Asad remarked almost two decades ago: "But anthropologists don't only do field work: they analyze ethnographic material, make cross-cultural comparisons (based on other people's reports), and even, on occasion, criticize the work of other anthropologists" (Asad 1982:285). In fact, it could be argued that anthropology's ultimate goal is to promote an appreciation and understanding of the human endeavor as it is manifested through time and space. This requires the ability to stand both "inside" a culture, as well as "outside" in order to see the patterns, connections, and differences that exist within and between human societies and configurations. As a "native" doing an anthropological ethnography of Carnival, I was also conscious of this task. The challenge was that of evoking recognition, as well as providing new perspectives on the event.

Within the culture of anthropology, the view from "inside" provides the profound meanings, visceral experiences and nuances of "native" cultural practitioners. The view from "outside," on the other hand, is critical in unmasking the so-called "natural" order of things and the web of unquestioned assumptions and patterns that underpin social life. These views, however, were traditionally located in space and persons; for example, homologies were created between insider–native–peripheral cultures and outsider–anthropologist–core cultures. Until the objections of "natives" within the last few decades, it was assumed that the anthropologist–outsider position was the privileged site of producing epistemologically sound anthropological knowledge. Counterclaims for the native–insider position are now part of anthropological discursive practice. Kevin Yelvington claims that the jury is still out on whether the foreign or native scholar is better positioned to produce scholarly work that is "more accurate, more sensitive, and more bias-free," (1993:17). His solution is to include multiple voices, both native and foreign, in his volume, *Trinidad Ethnicity,* perhaps to let us, the jury, decide whose work better captures Trinidad's cultural reality. While very commendable, this approach leaves the binarisms and homologies so endemic to anthropological discourse untouched. Further, his introduction of the "jury" concept suggests that there is a better position per se, located in one of two homologies, from which to "capture," explain, and interpret the meaning of Carnival.

Given the political and epistemological questions that emerged from doing fieldwork "at home," I want to argue for an anthropological praxis that is more responsive to the historical context in which knowledge is produced and consumed. I wish to underline three points in this regard. One has to do with the taken-for-granted homologies that exist in anthropological discourse. These need to be unhinged in order to attach the notions of "insider" and "outsider" to perspectives, rather than to roles and geographical locations. Both views are required to do the anthropological task. It is through the experience of Otherness that we gain a more profound understanding of the Self. Similarly, it is through the Self—and not in spite of it!—that we understand the Other. "Natives" can, and often do, bring "outsider" perspectives to their own and other multidimensional societies. Conversely, "anthropologists" are themselves "insiders" of their own native cultures, and as such, are as entangled in cultural and political webs as are the so-called "natives" of anthropological discourse. All scholars who engage in anthropological work are in fact "natives" of some cultural space and time, but what makes them "anthropologists" is the ability to be reflexive, that is, the ability to stand "inside" and "outside" their native cultures and bend back on them in order to understand, appreciate, and critique them. It is also as "natives" that they move into Other places and times as anthropologists. In this movement, they must simultaneously draw on and stand outside their "nativeness" in order to understand, interpret, and make comparisons.

Thus far, my argument for detaching the native from "insider" and anthropologist from "outsider" would suggest that the subject position, native versus foreign, is not of great significance, and that what really matters is the ability to be reflexive. In principle, yes. But the issue is not simply one of epistemology. It has a political dimension, given the linkage, in theory and practice, between anthropologist–hegemonic cultures and native–subordinated cultures. Most anthropological studies have been produced by Western European and North American scholars on communities and institutions in the so-called Third World. Studies by "Third World" anthropologists about "the West" are few (Asad 1982:286–287). This asymmetry is indicative of a world (dis)order, which not simply divides the world into "outsiders" and "insiders," but also into the hierarchical categories of "above" and "below," "cores" and peripheries." For the typical anthropologist, then, the view is not simply one from "outside"; it is also from "above." Conversely, the native's view is popularly understood to be the one from "below." This must be factored in to any consideration of the merits or demerits of an anthropologist's position with regard to the subjects studied. It is a question not only of what anthropologists can see, but also of what they are allowed to see, given the subjects' perception of her or his position in relation to theirs. The view from "above" is limited in ways that the view from "below" is not. Because of the penetration of dominant cultures globally, subordinated peoples are known to develop a "double consciousness" that allows them the possibility of navigating the worlds of "above" and "below." Until anthropologists work to dismantle the homologies that underpin anthropological theory and practice, they will constantly have to justify their right and ability to produce "local" knowledge, especially when produced from the subject position of "outside-above."

My second point relates to the purpose of anthropological knowledge. In developing criteria about who is better positioned to study cultural phenomena, we must consider not only the subject position of researchers, but also the purpose of their work. The anthropological quest, at its best, is to document, interpret and explain the human journey in order to help us better understand ourselves as human beings. For some, understanding is the ultimate destiny; for others, understanding is sought for social purposes. To mine this knowledge, the anthropologist is required to experience cultures from the "inside-out" and/or the "outside-in." Several activities, already mentioned, allow her or him to do so (Asad 1982:285). In the Caribbean, where anthropological knowledge has largely been produced from the "outside-in," and from "above-down," ethnographies written from the "inside-out" are necessary and needed. Ethnographies, by and about Trinidadians, that evoke both recognition and understanding, can have the effect of empowering other Trinidadians. The debate over who can best represent local reality must engage not only the epistemological questions, but also the audience and social purpose for which the work is intended. Perhaps this is the main contribution of the "local" anthropologist in this historical moment of colonial legacies and global asymmetries. But the anthropological task is larger and multiple. The anthropologist must leave "home" culturally and/or intellectually in order to engage the perspectives of others, including "foreign" anthropologists. The "foreign" anthropologist does have a view, but it is not the only—and far less!—the privileged view. It is through an ongoing process of engagement, dialogue, comparison, and even argument that knowledge will be produced and reconstructed, tested by its ability to evoke recognition, promote understanding, interrogate power, and suggest new possibilities for human living.

My last point specifically addresses the study of Carnival by native Trinidadian anthropologists. Given Trinidad's colonial legacy, I wish to underline the importance of their work as a way of articulating the local experience from the "inside-out." However, it must be emphasized that the category of "native" is not seamless. Within Trinidadian society, not every "native" is presumed to have a privileged view of Carnival. Gender, class, color, and ethnicity are often salient categories in determining the validity and authority of an "insider's" knowledge. The authority and right to represent Carnival is part of the much broader debate about the "ownership" of the festival. The "native" researcher's position, then, albeit an "insider's" view, is itself part of the politics of Carnival. Just as Carnival remains a dynamic cultural performance because it registers, fuels, and negotiates contests in Trinidadian society, so, too, must studies register this dynamism and critically engage with any "script" that attempts to fossilize and capture, from one seamless "native" position, why and how Trinidadians play their yearly mas.

NOTES

1. The rough equivalent of "hanging out" for Americans. The local word connotes taking pleasure in so-called nonproductive activity. Trinidadians describe themselves as great *limers,* and Carnival as the greatest *lime* of all.

2. *Mas* is derived from the word *masquerade* and is used to denote the masquerade, masquerader, or Carnival itself. As used by Trinidadians, *mas* communicates dynamism and action. A person becomes a mas in moving and performing. Revelers *play mas* on Carnival days.

3. *Jab*—a patois word from the French *diable* (devil).

4. A few small troupes of devil masqueraders from Paramin Village in the Northern Range of hills have recently been appearing in the Port of Spain Carnival spectacle, encouraged to do so by the National Carnival Commission in its attempt to preserve the "long-time" masquerades.

5. I use *reflexivity* in the general sense employed by interpretive anthropologists: the ability to bend back on one's reality in order to represent, analyze, critique, and shape it. It is not used in the specific way proposed by Watson (1991:79–81), namely, the constituting of reality through our ethnographic accounts. My usage, however, does not exclude Watson's specific meaning.

6. *Jumbie* is a local word for spirit or ghost. Jumbies can sometimes cause harm and are generally feared.

7. A mas camp refers to the location where Carnival costumes are made and displayed, and where registrations are taken from those who wish to participate in a masquerade band.

3. Authenticity, Commerce, and Nostalgia in the Trinidad Carnival

Garth L. Green

> Stamped on that image is the old colonial grimace of the laughing nigger, steelbandsman, carnivalmasker, calypsonian and limbo dancer . . . trapped in the State's concept of the folk form . . . the symbol of a carefree, accommodating culture, an adjunct to tourism.
>
> —DEREK WALCOTT 1970:7

> Middle class intellectuals . . . occup[y] an absurd and comic position both champions of a fast-disappearing "traditional" [culture] *and* unchallenged masters of the modern media . . .
>
> —PRICE AND PRICE 1997:16

Trinidadians, tourists, and international investors learn about the Trinidadian Carnival and its history through a great number of sources: newspaper and magazine articles, television shows, and interviews with prominent Carnival designers and masqueraders. These numerous sites of public discourse contribute to the formation of images of the Carnival that inform these diverse audiences about the history of the Carnival as well as that of Trinidad and Tobago and its people. It is, in part, through such sources of information and education that the people of Trinidad learn to interpret their experience of the Carnival of the present. The past Carnival serves as a point of reference and as a model. Many of these historical representations are created in a mood of loss and longing in which the current Carnival is implicitly portrayed as a degraded iteration of the Carnival of the past. This nostalgic mood drains the current Carnival of significance by placing authenticity, immediacy, and presence in the Carnival of the past.

During the period of my fieldwork from fall 1992 to spring 1994, I found that the narrative dominating discussion of the Carnival in Trinidad possessed traits similar to those of the more general nostalgia narrative summarized by John Frow as a decline from "use value to commodity, from immanence to instrumentality . . . from the world as being to the world as simulacrum" (1991:

142). This narrative described a fear that the Carnival has been commandeered by commercial interests, dominated by economic and touristic imperatives, and divorced from the spirit of Trinidadians. The story of the current Carnival compares it with the Carnival of the colonial era, which satirized, mocked, and criticized the colonizers and the colonial regime. The narrative portrays the pre-independence Carnival as the prime example of the creativity, wit, and resourcefulness of a unique Trinidadian people; a people that deserved to govern themselves.[1]

At the same time, I encountered another narrative about the Carnival that expressed a desire to intensify the "decline" from use-value to commodity. By this I mean that many officials interested in economic development and participants in the Carnival sought to expand the economic potential of the Carnival—to make it more a profitable and viable enterprise. Rather than this being seen as a "bad thing," that is to say, a process undermining the authenticity of the Carnival as an expression of the genius of the people, it has become highly desired (Nurse 1996). Artisans, entrepreneurs, and political leaders wish to make the Carnival a more attractive tourist event. In the early 1990s, the rhetoric of economic development merged with that of cultural nationalism in promoting the Carnival as the basis for cultural tourism. Despite what may have been a happy convergence of cultural pride and competitive advantage, a paradox emerged. The paradox of the nationalist entrepreneur or entrepreneur of nationalism is that in order to intensify the commodification of the Carnival, it must be presented as though it is actually "authentic" or "'noncommodified." Tension arises between a desire to maintain a putative authenticity and a desire to locate that authenticity in the past.

In this chapter, I consider the political implications of different forms of nostalgia that social actors deploy to inform and guide their representations of the history of the Trinidad Carnival. Calypsonians, political leaders, and culture brokers wield the concept of "tradition" as a weapon in discussions and performances about the history of the Carnival in Trinidad and Tobago and its place within a national cultural assemblage. Those in positions of cultural leadership attempt to control the depiction and interpretation of the Carnival's history.

Ethnographically I focus on two case studies: first, I examine a special Carnival show and competition devoted to "traditional" Carnival characters, the Viey la Cou. Second, I consider a tableau of carved figures depicting a famous 1959 Carnival band created by a man who participated in that band. Each example emerges from a precise social location, articulates a vision of Carnival, and, invokes the past to comment on the present. Both cases are part of the greater effort to educate the public about Carnival. The first is the product of a group of patrons of the arts who very self-consciously wish to educate young

Trinidadians and visitors about the types of masquerades and performances that were popular from the early 1900s until independence in 1962. The second arose out of an individual's need to heal himself through creative expression; only by chance did it later come to serve as an instrument of public education.

I argue that forms of nostalgia and the representations of the past that they engender are influenced by current political and economic agendas. People in positions of cultural authority, such as those who work for the government or the tourism industry, wish to articulate a past that can both instill a sense of national pride and serve as the basis of a viable cultural tourism industry. The Carnival history depicted by such cultural brokers highlights those aspects of Carnival that emerged during the period of opposition to colonial rule. I contend that a particular form of nostalgia, a hegemonic nostalgia (K. Stewart 1988) inspires the development of various Carnival shows and performances that create a system of valorization in which the Carnival characters, costumes, and performative styles as well as a system of costume production purportedly characteristic of the past are deemed better than those of the present. I conclude that such nostalgic impositions of standards of evaluation implicitly denigrate and ignore the ways in which the majority of Trinidadians currently celebrate the Carnival. The inability of cultural brokers and educators to understand how the current Carnival speaks to important concerns of Trinidadians indicates the cultural gap between those who administer and manage the Carnival and those who actively participate in it.

One strong motivation for promoting the vision of Carnival favored by those in positions of cultural authority and influence is to instill a sense of cultural pride in the young people of Trinidad; this is an understandable goal given the denigration of Trinidadian cultural practices during colonial rule.[2] However, public education is not the only goal of these projects. The traditional Carnival characters actively promoted are part of an attempt by the National Carnival Commission, the administrative body that oversees the Carnival, to create a codified folk art that is comparable to other national cultural forms around the world. This effort is linked to broader efforts to develop the cultural tourism industry in Trinidad.

NOSTALGIA

Nostalgia is a valuable concept for analyzing the politics of memory and for thinking through how people deploy representations of the past to articulate different ideas about cultural value, contributions to national culture, and identity. Several theorists (S. Stewart 1984; Turner 1987; K. Stewart 1988, 1996; Jameson 1989; Frow 1991) have offered valuable ways of differentiating among forms of nostalgia and have provided models of analysis. One common factor is the analysis of the social, historic, political, and economic conditions out of which nostalgic attitudes emerge and in which they are deployed in concrete social struggles. Here it is useful to distinguish between nostalgic rhetoric and what I call nostalgic enactments. Nostalgic enactments are specific events that emerge out of representations of the past. They reveal a politics of historical reminiscence and representation that influences how the people who participate in them or view them come to understand their histories. These nostalgic activities are ways of doing and being that concretize identity and identification. It is in the charged representational and experiential space of art galleries, cultural shows, and even souvenir shops that we find a fluid movement between individual memories and representations and collective memories and representations. Through this dialectical process, people attain and demonstrate understanding of their national identity through particular activities and representations of those activities.

All nostalgia is necessarily selective, as is memory in general, but nostalgia suggests a certain longing and desire for what was past, lost, and can never be again. Nostalgia is about attempting to re-create what cannot be regained. There are two key moments in nostalgic enactments. The first involves rhetoric and concerns marking specific aspects of the past as valuable, as possessing greater authenticity, and as indicating how the present lacks some essential component of vitality. The second process involves attempts to re-create that past period or condition in some kind of insulated environment. We may then distinguish nostalgia from other forms of memory by exploring just how a yearning for what was past but cannot be regained is constructed through nostalgic rhetoric and nostalgic re-creations.

Bryan Turner (1984: 150–151) examines the development of the concept of nostalgia in Western art, philosophy, and social theory and identifies four elements of the nostalgic modeling of the past and its relationship to the present:

1. A sense of historical decline from a mythologized 'golden age' with which contemporary social life is compared and found wanting.
2. A sense of the absence or loss of personal wholeness and moral certainty in which religious and moral values have been undermined by the development of capitalist relations, urbanization, and secularization.
3. A sense of the loss of individual freedom and autonomy because genuine social relationships have disappeared with the bureaucratization of everyday life and the subordination of the individual to instrumental reason.
4. A sense of the loss of simplicity, personal authenticity, and emotional spontaneity.

The nostalgic mode of thought describes a decline, an absence, and a loss of freedom, authenticity, and genuineness. At the base of all of these elements is a sense that life in the past was more grounded, direct, and fundamentally human. The nostalgic critique of the present condemns the increasing alienation of the self, growing social isolation, the deterioration of community, and the replacement of social relationships with individualistic consumerism. All of these elements are present in the forms of nostalgic thinking and modeling that I found in Trinidad.[3]

VIEY LA COU

Viey la Cou, loosely translated as "the Old Yard," is a traditional Carnival character show and competition that emerged out of a desire to preserve what its organizers believed was the Carnival of the past. It occurs on the Saturday before Carnival in the parking lot of Queen's Hall, a performance venue at which numerous kinds of entertainments, including concerts, plays, and Christmas pageants, are held. The Queen's Hall Board, an administrative body made up of prominent members of the cultural community as well as business leaders interested in the arts, established the show in 1988. The show features what have come to be known as traditional Carnival characters, among them Dragon, Midnight Robber, Devil, Imp, Minstrel, Moko Jumbie, Clown, Bat, Borroquit, Dame Lorraine, Fancy Indian, Jab Molassie, Jab-Jab, and Pierrot Grenade.[4] The participants in this exhibition compete for prizes in their respective categories under the auspices of the National Carnival Commission (NCC),[5] which has incorporated the show into its annual calendar of events. In addition to the competition, local artists and merchants set up booths displaying small watercolors of island scenes, tee-shirts with colorful original designs, locally crafted jewelry, and concession stands featuring local foods. The presentation of Carnival characters becomes an opportunity for audience members to enjoy not just a demonstration of Trinidadian folk life, but also current forms of cultural and entrepreneurial creativity.

In the blazing tropical sun, tourists, children, and members of the local middle class sit in hastily constructed stands and admire the costumes and performative styles that once dominated the streets of Port of Spain on Carnival Monday and Tuesday. Giant loudspeakers tower over the heads of spectators and performers, broadcasting the complex harangues of the Robbers, the "robber talk," and other oral performances associated with the masquerades being judged (Wuest 1990; Honore 1998).[6] Unfortunately, due to technical problems with sound equipment and the audience's lack of familiarity with the meaning

Fancy Indians playing their mas for the judges and spectators in the parking lot of Queen's Hall at Viey La Cou, 1993. Photograph by Garth Green.

of the performances, it is often difficult to understand what the performers are saying. Many tourists I spoke with were a bit dumbfounded as to what was going on. Inside Queen's Hall, calypsonians attempt to re-create the extemporaneous clashes of wit characteristic of pre-independence calypso performances, known as *extempo kaiso*.[7] Other forms of performance associated with the Carnival of the past are staged as well.

This competition–display has become an increasingly popular event on the Carnival calendar, not only for locals looking for an educational experience for their children but also for tourists seeking a sanctioned and approved cultural show. What is striking, at least to many Trinidadians, is that the characters are rarely played any longer in the Carnival that goes on outside of the secured gates of the parking lot. The current parade of Old-Time Carnival characters occurs in the middle of the afternoon a few days before Carnival Monday. The Viey la Cou showcase environment creates a bubble of safety in which the characters are called upon to perform outside their traditional context, which was traditionally early in the morning. By being taken out of the context of active and current Carnival performances and given this special time and place of performance, the "Old-Time Carnival" characters are highlighted as *historical* rather than as contemporary.[8] The degree to which these performative forms are distant to the Carnival as known by the majority of Trinidadians is indicated by the explanations about the content and meaning of the performances provided in a handout distributed to the spectators.

The event has the air of a middle-school pageant. Many children now play these Old-Time characters as part of state efforts to educate them about the history of the Carnival (and by extension, of Trinidad and Tobago), through the junior Carnival program in the schools (Harvey 1984; Liverpool 1990). Large numbers of children in similar Old-Time Carnival costumes tag along with many of the performers. With a great sense of moral satisfaction, commentators applaud the presence of children as evidence of the continuation of tradition. A pamphlet (Springer and Rogers 1993:2) distributed to the paying audience explicitly spells out the educational and moral project of the Viey la Cou:

> Viey La Cou is a continuing attempt by the Board of Management of Queen's Hall to bring back the disappeared and the disappearing characterisations from the oral and choreographic traditions of the Old Time Carnival street theatre, into the people's consciousness, particularly the young and impresionable [*sic*], so that this form of masquerade, its music, its song and its dance, do not become entirely and irrevocably lost to us. The endangered species of the Old Time Carnival must be saved for future generations. To this end, the Board has also sought to involve students from a number of schools in the area. Their teachers see the value of the project and over the years the children have presented many and varied Old Time Carnival characters portrayals.

The natural history language of the pamphlet, its likening of the Old-Time Carnival characters to "endangered species," indicates the sense of urgency and impending loss that marks the efforts of the middle-class cultural supporters of the Queen's Board.

But just what species are considered endangered and who has characterized them as such? While these traditional characters clearly mark continuations with the past, they are not the only characters that were played. One never hears calls for resurrecting Pissenlit,[9] Bajan Cook, Policeman and Thief, Yard Sweeper, Cow, or Bear. These masquerades are not of the same type as those performed in the competitions. The principles guiding the choices reveals a politics underlying the choice and marking of certain aspects of a collection of practices.[10] The forms highlighted are those that were once significant in the past as part of significant political and cultural struggles. The return to these characters in the present suggests a social archaeology in which characters that demonstrate a certain kind of wit or creativity that is no longer threatening to a middle-class sensibility are appropriate for tourists. There is little to differentiate the principles of inclusion and exclusion here from those exercised by middle-class Carnival reformers in the late 1800s and early 1900s.[11] These characters live only because they have been swiped and laundered by well-meaning middle-class folklorists to be deployed in educational settings, as if they still represent the cultural and political struggles of grassroots people.

Infusing the Viey la Cou is what Kathleen Stewart (1988:227) calls a hegemonic, as opposed to a resistant, nostalgia. Hegemonic nostalgias are those of the middle class or of mass culture, while resistant nostalgias emerge out of the working class and a desire for "local, nameable" places. She argues that all nostalgias posit a lost past. They create, out of unnamed and undifferentiated space and time, particular times and places in which subjects can form meanings that have reference to particular social contexts. The differences among nostalgias lie in the social position of the "nostalgic" person generating it, and, it would seem, in that person's power to impose or disseminate his or her vision of the past. Stewart suggests that nostalgia is a narrative practice that makes sense of the present by positing the existence of a past, no-longer extant, "other" world in which meanings are grounded ideally.

The Carnival of the past is also considered more virtuous than the current more hedonistic one because it was allegedly less dominated by commercial elements or by vulgarity. This vision of the Carnival of the past also locates authenticity in particular places and practices such as stickfighting in Arima; Devil mas from downtown Port of Spain; Indian mas from San Fernando; or Blue Devil from the mountain area of Paramin (Bellour and Kinser 1998, Harris 1998; Walsh 1998). Authenticity is displaced both temporally and spatially. The "real" Carnival—the implied meaning suggests a Carnival that is deeply tied to place and community and is free from the taints of the tourism market—may be found in places far from the centers of economic and political power in Trinidad, such as suburban Port of Spain. Suburban Port of Spain is also the location of the middle classes who populate the large Carnival bands that are seen by the Carnival intelligentsia as undermining its historical significance by turning it into nothing more than a party in flimsy costume.

Different classes recreate the Carnival according to their vision and desires for the future. The Carnival may be open to this kind of development as it does not rely so heavily on the mediating role of the artist to articulate that vision.[12] However, not all representations and re-creations are equal, not all have the same social force or persuasive power. The Viey la Cou show is one activity in the complex reconstruction of the Carnival by the newly emergent middle class that prides itself on its media savvy, marketing prowess, and ability to mediate between Trinidadians and the global economy.

Fredric Jameson relates formal innovations in cultural forms to "the new and emergent sense of history of the triumphant middle-classes as that class [seeks] to project its own vision of its past and its future, and to articulate its social and collective project in a temporal narrative distinct in form from those of earlier 'subjects' of history" (1980:522). He points us toward an examination of how some Trinidadians tell themselves their history and how they experience it. It may be possible to see the Carnival as an ongoing creative project in this way, one that relates the development of a cultural form to an emergent, triumphant class vision of its past and future.

A hegemonic nostalgia establishes "codes of distinction and good taste" that "purify" and "reify" the social world (K. Stewart 1988). This mode of nostalgia emphasizes the power of a critical and discerning self to make creative choices about quality and aesthetics, the individual self that "acts on life" and can fashion an imagined social world through the exercise of good taste, imagination, and choice. In hegemonic nostalgia, the individual's ability to distinguish among those elements of the past that are worthy of being remembered is paramount. Clearly the people on the board of Queen's Hall would consider themselves the most discerning members of their class, most capable of identifying the more deserving elements of the Carnival of the past to be preserved and promoted. It is these members who mark those masquerades most worthy of being "saved" from extinction. Their aesthetic choices valorize certain masquerades over others, and they choose which "good" or "authentic" objects of the past are to be displayed in the home, presented in the museum exhibit, or hoarded in a private collection.

Heritage often serves as an anchor that provides stability and secures identity in times of great social unease and confusion. The vision of the past to which cultural preservationists cling compels them to bring out the Old-Time masquerades for show. And yet, the clarity and confidence with which the Queen's Hall board asserts which masquerade forms shall be preserved and which forgotten, which shall finally receive their place in the sun, only underscores just how those forms are dying out. One of Trinidad and Tobago's foremost masquerade designers, Peter Minshall, believes that these forms faded from view not because of any social insecurity on the part of rising generations seeking to forget the past as a shameful memory of colonial domination and poverty, nor from a lack of adequate education of the youth, nor because of the influence of the North American media and artistic and musical forms. The old forms of masquerade have lessened in importance, Minshall asserts, because they are no longer relevant to the everyday social life of the majority of the population.[13]

Many scholars of Carnival with whom I spoke believe that Carnival is about innovation, novelty, and the new. They suggest that the Carnival is always changing and developing as an expressive form. It is to be expected, and preferably to be encouraged, that new forms of masquerade and celebration emerge to express the aspirations, fantasies, and perhaps anger of the current generation of masqueraders. Ambiguity and improvisation mark the Carnival and underscore how its aesthetic and practice capitalizes on the unforeseen and highlights the power to transform given materials, both in the sense of ideas and of objects, into one's own scenario (Greenblatt 1980:227–228). Unfortunately, the desire to recognize the significance of past cultural struggles leads to the museumifying tendency of national folklorists and the commodifying tendency of tourism entrepreneurs.

In Trinidad and Tobago, the borrowing, hiding, reusing, and redirecting of cultural material is celebrated as a sign of creativity in the face of political oppression and material poverty (Segal 1993, 1995). At the same time, the nationalist cultural and political project calls for purging the national culture of allegedly "foreign" elements alongside a desire to purge for the sake of authenticity (Scher 1997). In this view of cultural authenticity, culture is reduced to a collection of particular kinds of things. The concept of culture that informs this impulse to purification seems almost Boasian in nature—a confusion of the thing as "culture," with culture understood as a collection or assemblage of "products" or "distinctive practices." At the same time, the processes and conditions that enable and encourage their creation are elided and the social relationships through which they are made and experienced are ignored.

While recognizing the urgency with which some cultural preservationists seek to return to older forms of masquerade, I suggest that cultural borrowing does not lead to total homogeneity or conformity with a putative hegemonic capitalist culture as imposed from the United States, nor to a loss of authenticity. The acquisition of new forms, by force, insertion, or borrowing, makes for new possibilities. In fact, it can be argued that the history of the Carnival is replete with many examples of how cultural forms from outside Trinidad have been reconfigured and given new meanings. Here, a central question arises for nostalgics and marketers alike: "When is the Carnival no longer the Carnival?" That is to say, what aspects of Carnival are considered essential? Which elements are vital to its legitimacy and historical identity and which are not?

The handing down of tradition requires symbolic interpretation and is continuously reinvented in the present because current performative styles are never completely isomorphic with those of the past. Moreover, the understanding of the performance is generated from contexts and meaning in the present. As Handler and Linnekin have stated, the idea that "one should do or preserve something that is 'traditional' is already to reinterpret and change it" (1984: 270). Once people are told what the meaning and importance of the Carnival is, they undertake their activity with an attitude that leads them more self-consciously to enact "national culture." Playing mas or going to a mas camp, panyard, calypso tent, or any other Carnival show becomes an exercise in cultural patriotism. It is as though one is trying to live out the tourist guidebook. In the Viey la Cou, the Old-Time mas players display a self-consciousness that is heightened to the greatest degree. The larger society's notions of traditional and cultural identity are incorporated into the self-image of these masqueraders as the meaning of "traditional mas" has changed to one of purity and authenticity whereas it was, in its own time when it was not "traditional," one of violence and vulgarity. The Viey la Cou exposes the tension between threatening the social order and being sanctioned by it. This tension characterizes the awkward position of the Old-Time Masquerader and even of the Carnival itself. Through its sponsorship of the Carnival, the state recognizes a destructive oppositional force and thoroughly tames it by offering prizes and praise. Trophies and prize monies have replaced the balata clubs and truncheons of late nineteenth-century Trinidad that were that era's chosen mode of restraining Carnival enthusiasts.[14]

The Viey la Cou is but one example of a larger trend I observed during my time in Trinidad. It was clear to me that an emergent Carnival intelligentsia comprising government ministers and bureaucrats, culture and heritage administrators, cultural entrepreneurs, and scholars often exhibit in their public statements and commentaries nostalgia for a "Golden Age of Carnival."[15] With special reference to the masquerading aspect of the Carnival arts, this period is marked by careful attention to craftsmanship in costume design and production, intense devotion to research, historical authenticity and accuracy, and a concentration on the adoption of a unique persona in a masquerade performance marked by cleverness, wit, and satire. Furthermore, the system of cultural production associated with the "Golden Age" resembled a mystery school, or a medieval guild, rather than the near factory-like assembly processes of today. In the "Golden Age," designers, artists, artisans, and performers made art and culture. Today, the rhetoric suggests, business people make commodities and profits.

Middle-class culture brokers, such as those who created the Viey la Cou, possess the social capital, financial resources, and bureaucratic authority to concretize their "memories" of the Carnival through the creation of shows, competitions, and exhibits. Their nostalgic practice is embedded within hierarchical social relations with serious political and economic implications, and yet in both the experience and interpretation of these representations and practices, audiences may generate counter-narratives and invoke an alternative historical consciousness. The second case study is just such an alternative imagining of the past.

Day of Glory by Leighton James as seen from the front. Note the figure with shepherd's robes and raised shepherd's crook chasing after the figure in fatigues, 1993. Photograph by Garth Green.

FLOWERS AND FRUITS

One day I went with a group of friends to the Barataria E. C. Primary School to see a tableau of Carnival figures titled *Day of Glory. Day of Glory* depicts what was perhaps one of the finest bands ever to appear in the Carnival: Cito Velasquez and Geraldo Veira's *Flowers and Fruits* from the 1959 Carnival. The story of *Flowers and Fruits* is particularly poignant, for it was never seen in its full splendor by the judges in the "Big Yard," the Queen's Park Savannah (the prime competition and judging venue), because it was nearly destroyed after being caught in the middle of one of the most violent steelband clashes ever to occur in Trinidad.[16] Clearly, the experience was the most profound kind of loss, a sense that the band was never able to enjoy what could have been its greatest moment of public recognition due to the tragedy of the steelband clash. Most of the band's flowers and fruits and many of its pans were destroyed in the confrontation. Still, the band finished in fourth place.

The creator of the tableau, Leighton James, is a retired laborer in his late fifties. He lives in Barataria, part of the densely populated East–West corridor that

Detail of Soda Vendor from *Day of Glory* by Leighton James, 1993. Photograph by Garth Green.

runs along the Churchill-Roosevelt Highway from Port of Spain in the west to Arima in the east. James worked with and still lives around the corner from Cito Velasquez, the much honored and respected wire bender whose surrealistic headpieces for fancy sailor bands and innovative designs for Kings and Queens throughout the 1950s and 1960s are legendary. In 1959, James was an eighteen year-old musician whom Velasquez asked to help bring out a section of the band.

Over the course of two and one-half years, James carved more than 180 figures out of teak and recreated not just *Flowers and Fruits* and the steelband Rhapsody, but also the entire feel of the Carnival of the late 1950s. The tableau covers about 17 x 4 feet and contains sixty fancy sailors, thirty panmen, and about ninety other characters. Other materials used in the construction of the figures and items in the tableau include papier-mâché, styrotex, plastic, fiberglass, and wood for the fruits and other objects. The flowers are made of silk and the pans are from tin cans.

Scattered throughout the tableau are characters from the traditional Carnival: a Jab-Jab cracks his whip; a robber blows his whistle before delivering his litany of deadly accomplishments; minstrels strum their banjos. Other finely detailed and crafted figures enhance the atmospheric totality of the work: a soda vendor sitting before a washtub filled with ice and soda adjusts a bloody ban-

Detail of pan and "Fruits" section from *Day of Glory* by Leighton James, 1993. Photograph by Garth Green.

dage covering a sore on her lower leg; a full-figured vendor, her head protected from the sun by a big hat, sells roasted corn; a policeman cautions an overly exuberant masquerader; a man cups his hands around a match as he lights a cigarette; another man is having his pocket picked.

There are humorous and ironic references as well. A figure dressed in a sailor costume empties his beer against a tree, yet from behind it appears as though he is relieving himself. A majorette in the band has lost her slipper. She turns and bends to put it back on before the band rushes past her. One steelband supporter pulling the pancarts is about to have his foot crushed under a wheel and grimaces as he anticipates the impending injury. A little boy points him out to his mother.

At the head of the band we see a figure dressed in flowing Arab robes, carrying a shepherd's crook, rushing headlong into the band and away from his pursuers. He is from the steelband Desperadoes that is playing *Noah's Ark.* A figure in fatigues, a soldier from San Juan All Stars' *Battle Cry,* rushes into the band. The flagman for *Flowers and Fruits* is losing his balance. This is the moment before the clash destroys the presentation and before the bottles begin to fly, before the cutlasses "swish the air," and the cleaved pans clatter into the street. This is Carnival: the feeling, the movement, the multiplicity of simultaneous events, the great number of small personal stories out of which people construct their ideas about the event.

No exhibit, painting, sculpture, or written description had ever come as close to capturing the Carnival for me as did these figures. Their dynamism sets this work apart from all others. We see a panman stumbling to coordinate his walking and playing, the struggle of a fancy sailor with his huge soursop headpiece, a woman drunkenly leaning against a friend for support, the snowball vendor holding out change for a customer and the customer poised to collect it. This work of art was unlike the somewhat dingy, ragged, and desiccated folk culture found in some of the cultural shows and distorted into either a pretty tourist spectacle or a dreary educational exercise. There was no musty odor, no shabby lifeless costumes quietly decaying in a dimly lit exhibit hall such as is found in the National Museum.

After we had viewed this extraordinary work, friends who knew the director of the National Museum and other well-placed figures attempted to convince them to purchase it for the museum. Unfortunately, however, there were no funds for such acquisitions. The museum could buy a small number of the figures—three, maybe four—but not all of them. They offered James about TT $4000 (about US $700). Alternatively, they suggested to James that he simply donate the entire ensemble of figures. James, however, did not wish to see his work broken up because it was the ensemble of figures that communicated the meaning and importance of the Carnival to him. He also felt that he deserved to be appropriately compensated and recognized for his artistic efforts.

Certainly one can appreciate James's position. Equally, one can also acknowledge the hardships facing the National Museum in its efforts to procure new works of art, given its meager budget and lack of governmental and public support. Despite the government's frequent pronouncements that the Carnival represents "the genius of the people of Trinidad," funds to support the arts are insufficient. The reluctance to provide funding for Carnival is evident in the act of parliament that created the National Carnival Commission, an act that called upon the NCC to guide the Carnival to financial self-sufficiency. One of the main difficulties facing those in charge of realizing this goal is confronting the fact that the public does not want to pay for Carnival products. The Carnival is often seen, they claim, as a kind of national property for which people should not have to pay. For example, there is a large bootleg market in calypso and steelband recordings; some performers and promoters attempt to skirt the payment of royalties.

There has been an emerging tension within the larger Carnival community regarding the relationship between Carnival as an art form and Carnival as a livelihood. On one hand, culture brokers say the Carnival arts are a kind of folk art that people spontaneously generate out of their desire to express themselves through the medium of Carnival. In fact, many Carnival performers are not professional or full-time artists or performers. Equally, there are a large number of costume designers, calypsonians, and steelband players that are able to make a living pursuing their art. Many additional artists would like to be able to pursue their art full time as well. One factor in favoring certain old forms of masquerade is that such forms are seemingly not professional, and that is what makes them so unusual and worthy of commemoration. We are confronted with the paradox of cultural tourism in which authenticity becomes the determiner of international touristic value. To pay James and other artists like him for their work is to acknowledge the commodification of "culture." Commodification reduces "authenticity" as a folk art product. Hence control over material representations is vitally important. James has never relinquished control. The figures with their silk flower and papier-mâché or plastic fruit headpieces are now stored in individual cases in his garage.

James's relationship to the history of the Carnival he depicts is in stark contrast to that of the creators of the Viey La Cou. James does not present an idealized working-class Carnival populated by masqueraders in hand-made costumes performing original dances and engaging in oral combat. He conveys the complexity of the Carnival as he knew it; its humor, its strains, its tensions, its violence, pathos, and exuberance. *Day of Glory* can be interpreted as an example of what K. Stewart (1988) calls resistant nostalgia. It has a level of specificity that "resurrects" direct lived experience from the deathly silence of the past. While James was a part of *Flowers and Fruits,* there does not seem to be a yearning on his part for a return to this time. It seems to be a commemoration, a celebration of the experience, immediate, and yet it manages to capture the spirit of Carnival that remains constant despite changes in the music, in the forms and types of masquerades and masqueraders, and in the administrative context within which the Carnival occurs.

James's tableau evokes what K. Stewart (1988) calls a resistant nostalgia that counters the distancing and decontextualizing practice of hegemonic nostalgia and the glorification of the discerning self as seen in the case of the Viey la Cou organizers discussed above. The tableau emphasizes how the meaning of the event is heavily dependent upon its context and can only be made and read in a "context" that is not just a "background" for the "facts" but its very inspiration—its enabling condition"(K. Stewart 1988:228). The creation of meaning in resistant nostalgia relies upon a reassertion of the significance of context out of the abstract and alienation of "hierarchies of distinction" that mark hegemonic nostalgia. Rather than raising, glorifying, or distinguishing the self that acts on the world, resistant nostalgia emerges out of a desire "to act in a world that surrounds" (ibid.).

Flowers and Fruits grows out of the desire to recall the history of place; the world in which James and his compatriots acted *in* rather than a world of objects acted *on* with fixed meanings, as the traditional characters are rendered in the Viey la Cou. The tableau emerges out of a longing to remember what happened, to resurrect through narrative that which is being forgotten. Stewart suggests that in being surrounded and "haunted" by images of the past, the resistant nostalgic reinscribes the landscape with meaning and moves through a world of significance. For James, the glory and pain of the band *Flowers and Fruits* is recalled in his tableau. In the work, his own experience is revalidated and reinvested with significance.

I began this essay with the question of how different representations of the Carnival of the past and by implication the social context within which it took place, are deployed politically by differently situated social actors in Trinidad and Tobago. I contrasted two examples of what I call nostalgic enactments, the Viey la Cou presentation and the individual work of art, *Day of Glory.* I argued that these two visions of the Carnival of the past—one emerging from a position of middle-class cultural guardianship explicitly seeking to inform and educate; the other emanating from a working-class individual with a desire to commemorate an event of great personal significance—suggest contrasting politics of memory. Drawing on K. Stewart, I differentiated between hegemonic and resistant nostalgias to explore the differences between these two ways of representing the Carnival of the past. However, perhaps even positing such a distinction between hegemonic and resistant forms of nostalgia is itself part of a hegemonic nostalgia that places authentic, true voices among the working class or the otherwise dispossessed and avoids confronting the problematic interrelationship among different ways of remembering and narrating the past. Such a dichotomy may be a good place to start, in that it suggests that there are different forms of nostalgia and ways of being nostalgic. However, my analyses of particular enactments of nostalgia reveal complex and contradictory motives and agendas that inform such enactments.

In their exploration of transgressive practices, White and Stallybrass (1986: 19) argue that nostalgia is a common analytical error in the analysis of Carnivals in general. They suggest that scholars may be blinded by the desire to find "genuine" opposition to hierarchies and other forms of social domination. The practices of the working classes or any other subordinate group within a society are considered to be inherently critical of existing social relations.

I question the idea that Carnivals everywhere are inherently oppositional, an idea that has grown through the application of Bakhtin's (1984) ideas about medieval and renaissance carnivals to just about anything that even remotely appears "Carnivalesque" and that includes Carnivals themselves. The Carnival in Trinidad cannot be reduced to being oppositional to, subversive of, or alternative to the established social order. Nor can it simply be characterized as supporting that social order, given the prominence of representatives of the social order, the state, and interested economic parties in its planning and promotion. Like any complex social and cultural practice, there are multiple effects and interpretations of the Carnival. Carnival may support existing relations of domination, but not as a "steam valve" that alleviates social tensions nor as a "ritual of reversal" that eventually re-establishes the social order after a sanctioned period of inversion. Rather, Carnival may support existing relations of domination by providing an opportunity for the existing forces of control to re-assert their vision of society and of the place of distinct groups within it. Viey la Cou and *Day of Glory* are both avenues through which the people of Trinidad come to learn about the history of the Carnival and the history of Trinidad. My interpretation of the Viey la Cou and the efforts at cultural preservation that motivate its organizers suggests how one vision of Trinidadian history may be imposed over another.

We should be careful to distinguish between hegemonic and resistant nostalgias in such a way as to avoid a simplistic dichotomy in which almost any reaction to oppression is raised to the level of resistance. What may have been a form of resistance in the past may no longer hold much political or symbolic power in the present. Clinging to such forms may be a form of oppression itself. The imposition of codes of performance and masquerade in the Carnival may inhibit innovation and experimentation. I suggest re-entangling these forms of nostalgia to see how they articulate and inform each other in the increasingly commodified context of the Carnival. Ideas about what the Carnival was and is are formed, in part, through performances such as the Viey la Cou, exhibitions of works of art such as *Day of Glory,* and many others. In this emerging context, notions of folk art as representative of authenticity collide with notions of art as a commodity. Contrasting ideas about cultural heritage and folk art become weapons in an ideological battle to undermine claims of cultural distinctiveness in the Carnival. Instead of artists creating contemporary works of art, Carnival masqueraders and designers become folk artists reproducing cultural heritage. Cultural heritage in the Carnival is composed of masquerade forms that were once powerful symbols of resistance, but are no longer as salient as they once were.

Nostalgic representations of the Carnival of the past by middle-class administrators and culture brokers emerge out of what seem to be competing, almost mutually exclusive, motivations. On the one hand, there is the sense that the Carnival as celebrated by most people today is not as good or authentic as the old Carnival. And yet the Carnival of today is the Carnival as made by numerous factions of the middle class over the past century. Today's Carnival is the product of constant reform efforts that have sought to eliminate working-class forms of violence, vulgarity, and exhibitory sexuality. Despite these efforts, today's Carnival is dominated by the hedonistic Carnival, the giant "lime," including its rampant commercialism, commodity exchanges in place of "craft production," and increasingly class-divided participation (which is not really new at all, but a long-standing aspect of the Carnival).

On the other hand, the desire among cultural elites grows stronger to embed the Carnival even more solidly into the web of capitalist relations and activities by making it the basis of cultural tourism, to bring in more tourists and to make more money through television presentations and video sales as well as through merchandising agreements (Green 2005). The nostalgia is for what they or their well-meaning middle-class moral protectors and predecessors have destroyed.

The hedonistic Carnival may be interpreted as a form of mass culture in that it is a lighthearted amusement, an enthusiasm of consumption, a "bread and circuses." What follows from this interpretation is the sense of alienation that Turner (1987:153) has argued marks nostalgia and is especially common among intellectuals. Here I extend the idea of intellectuals to include those "organic intellectuals" in the Gramscian sense, whose job it is to work with and create symbolic material. The intellectuals' critique of mass culture depicts it as follows:

> a loss of personal autonomy, spontaneity and naive enjoyment of the everyday world. Mass Culture vulgarizes traditional forms of cultural expression by making them available to the populace via the falsifying system of the mass media. Within the nostalgic framework of elite culture mass culture is regarded as a feature of an incorporatist ideology which pacifies the masses through the stimulation of false needs under the dominance of modern consumerism. (Turner 1987:153)

But in Trinidad, nostalgia is used to create the shows, events, and performances that are to be for mass consumption; at least that is the hope. Intellectuals further this process by conducting economic analyses of the tourism and culture industries, by generating marketing plans, and by undertaking cultural historical research to further authenticate the product in a manner that makes it more presentable to an international audience. Rather than having nostalgia be opposed to modernity, culture brokers employ nostalgia as an aspect of the cultural commodity they create and distribute. Their nostalgia imperceptibly merges with that of an international consumer, often an expatriate Trinidadian, to seal the package of Carnival goods.

NOTES

Research for this essay was conducted in Trinidad from September 1992 to April 1994 with funding from the IIE/Fulbright program, the Wenner-Gren Foundation for Anthropological Research, and the New School for Social Research.

1. Liverpool (2001) argues that the Carnival was, as his title indicates, a rite of rebellion in which the oppressed African working classes condemned their oppressors through innuendo, cleverness, and subterfuge as well as, in some cases, direct confrontation such as the Canboulay riots of the early 1880s or the censored lyrics of calypsos in the 1920s and 1930s.

2. Following World War II, the nationalist and anticolonial movement portrayed the Carnival as the centerpiece of a national culture. After limited home rule was granted in 1956, the government of Premier Eric Williams and his People's National Movement (PNM) party took administrative control of the Carnival from a variety of private groups and created the Carnival Development Commission (CDC). After the National Alliance for Reconstruction (NAR) defeated the PNM in 1986, they reorganized the CDC and created the National Carnival Commission (NCC).

3. In what may be considered an ironic twist given the subject of this essay, Turner illustrates what he means by the loss of simplicity, autonomy, and spontaneity by contrasting peasant feasts and their Rabelaisian pleasures of gluttony, vulgarity, and sensuality with the strictures and rules of modern society. In comparison with the Bakhtinian world of the carnivalesque, in the social theory of such thinkers as Freud and Marcuse modern society, and, in particular, bourgeois society, are depicted as having imposed restraints, morals, manners, and other forms of repression on the open expression of pleasure. In Trinidad, and indeed in much scholarship on carnivals in general, Carnival is portrayed as the very embodiment of spontaneity, genuineness, and personal freedom that the restraints, morals, and manners of modern society quash.

4. Space does not permit a detailed discussion of these masquerades and performances. There is a large literature on the history and development of what are now known as Old-Time Carnival masquerades: Crowley 1956; Pearse 1956; Hill 1972, 1985; Wuest, 1990; Harris 1998; Honore 1998; Walsh 1998. See Pamela Franco's essay in this volume for a discussion on how traditional Carnival characters were established in the 1950s through the collaboration of anthropologists, folklorists, and government officials.

5. The National Carnival Commission was created in 1986 to oversee the administration of the Carnival throughout Trinidad as well as to promote Carnival arts both at home and internationally. One key provision of the law establishing the National Carnival Commission is that it strive to make the Carnival financially more efficient and ultimately self-sufficient. The NCC sponsors "Old-Time Carnival" character competitions all over Trinidad during the Carnival season. The Viey la Cou is just one event, albeit probably the most publicized and well-attended.

6. Many of the Old-Time masquerades featured in the Viey la Cou have as part of their performance some form of verbal combat. For robbers, speeches would traditionally be performed when two encountered each other on the streets on Carnival day. These characters would also accost spectators and demand some kind of offering, often money. Other characters have forms of dance with which they are associated.

7. Extempo kaiso involves exchanges between calypsonians in which they alternate singing a verse that is usually an insult or "picong" of the other. They continue for a set number of rounds or until one of them exhausts his or her wit. The winner is determined either by audience applause or after the failure of a participant.

8. These characters also play on their own, in their desired way, on Carnival Monday and Tuesday, attempting to reassert their place in the current Carnival. However rather than dominate the streets as they did in their heydey, they are overwhelmed by the enormous numbers of masqueraders who participate in the huge bands of 2,000–5,000 masqueraders in what is known as "pretty mas."

9. Pissenlit, literally, "wet the bed" was popular among working-class male masqueraders in the late 1800s and involved men cross-dressing as women, wearing rags that were stained with "menstrual blood" and other bodily fluids.

10. In addition to children playing Midnight Robber, Dame Lorraine, and Blue Devil as part of Viey la Cou, the formal NCC-sponsored Children's Carnival also emphasizes "traditional" Carnival characters and the history of Carnival. The decision to highlight historical masquerade forms in the Children's Carnival, especially in the school system, possesses an intriguing meta-referential quality. It signals that the Carnival has become its own subject and may indicate the death of the living form. This is the Carnival as a simulacrum, as an imitation of itself, yet of a "self" that may never have existed. One may see it as mas playing mas, that is to say, a masquerade based on the concept and historical artifact of the masquerade.

11. An early version of this essay was presented at the International Conference on Carnival at Trinity College in Hartford, Connecticut in 1998. Several members of the audience strongly disagreed with my thesis that Carnival performances and much discussion about the Carnival was motivated by nostalgia. One member also questioned the validity of my interpretation of the fact that children were not asked to play certain controversial characters from the past. She said that it would be inappropriate for children to play such a mas. In her protest, she reinforced the point I was trying to make regarding ideas about morality and propriety guiding interpretations of the Carnival past. She argued that there were certain aspects of the Carnival of the past that were not proper, and by proper, I take her to mean, suitable for a general audience. In essence, she recapitulates the middle-class criticisms of the Carnival that have been levied against it since the late 1800s. While I appreciate the concern expressed that children be educated about Trinidadian history, I merely wish to point out that choices are made about what will be remembered and what will be forgotten.

12. In the past, the formally trained artist did not participate as often in Carnival design. In the last twenty-five years, it has become more common for people trained in theater or design to become masquerade costume designers. Peter Minshall and Wayne Berkeley are among the more prominent designers with such training.

13. Personal communication, May 18, 1998.

14. While there were numerous instances of police violence directed against masqueraders in the mid-to-late 1800s, the most notorious examples are the Canboulay

riots of 1880 and 1884, in which the chief of police sought to provoke violent confrontations with masqueraders, seen by the authorities as violent and unruly gangs of criminals.

15. Hollis Liverpool, in his incarnation as the calypsonian Chalkdust, sang "Come back to Tradition" for the 1994 Carnival, in which he excoriated calypsonians who did not employ what he considered to be the proper form and content of calypso singing, the "social commentary" form. Such songs explore issues of public interest and concern rather than the tense, humorous, or otherwise difficult relationships between men and women or celebration and partying. One person I interviewed who had served as a judge for the Calypso Monarch competitions felt that Chalkdust was part of a Carnival intelligentia that sought to impose a particular vision of what Carnival has been and should continue to be especially in its formal attributes of performance.

16. Steelbands emerged after World War II and were often (and continue to be) based in particular communities. Steelbands were often composed of people from a certain neighborhood and would usually enjoy the support of the people living in that area. Throughout the late 1940s, 1950s, and into the 1960s, the bands would occasionally come into conflict and "clashes" would occur. For many years, those who played in steelbands were viewed as dangerous people, criminals, and thugs, with whom "respectable" people would have no interaction.

4. When "Natives" Become Tourists of Themselves: Returning Transnationals and the Carnival in Trinidad and Tobago

Philip W. Scher

> Wherever Trinidadians have settled in sufficient numbers—Toronto, Harlem, Brooklyn, London, the outskirts of Caracas—they have taken Carnival with them. Yet great numbers troop back home annually from these and other places for the master celebration. For them, carnival stands as a time of renewal, of self-affirmation, which can occur in no other way. To miss carnival is to be diminished.
>
> —JOHN STEWART (1986)

> Nostalgia for a lost authenticity is a paralyzing structure of historical reflection.
>
> —JOHN FROW (1991)

Steelbands, followed by undulating columns of masqueraders dressed as sailors, made their way through the massive Port of Spain crowds, sound systems, and vendors on Carnival Tuesday in 1996 in a spirit of "longtime Carnival" or Carnival of long ago. With famous names such as All Stars, Exodus, Phase II Pan Groove, Laventille Sounds Specialists, Invaders, Tokyo, Starlift, they vied for a TT $100,000 prize to be awarded to the best steelband and masquerade on the road. This particular contest was a new feature and was instituted to bring the sounds of the steelband back into Carnival. The contest was an enormous success. In addition to the warm reception the contest's participants received from the throngs of spectators, I noticed that the steelband and sailor contest held a specific attraction for returning migrants, who participated heavily in the event itself.

In investigating the Steelband competition I saw that there were some commonalities with other competitions held during Carnival; among them were the following: (1) The role of the National Carnival Commission in the institutionalization of certain Carnival forms that were identified as endangered and that required preservation in the name both of cultural heritage and commerce and

(2) The impact of such strategies of preservation on the community of costume makers and musicians who remain dedicated to portraying and continuing such forms. Yet there is a third factor that appears here that was generally absent from other, more local competitions and noncompetitive showcases. This was the impact of preservation strategies on the emigrant population of Carnival returnees who have a nostalgic and emotional investment in seeing the masquerades of their youth maintained. In all cases of NCC-sponsored contests, organizers attempted to create tourist attractions that they hoped would both attract locals, foreign visitors, and transnational returnees who would play some part in keeping an archaic expressive form alive. Foreigners generally play very little part in such contests (although for several years I saw the odd foreigner taking part in Old-Time masquerade forms such as the Midnight Robber and Moko Jumbie). Locals tend to be attracted to showcase, competitive events such as Viey la Cou, whose characters—in their heyday—predate the lives of most participants.

Yet transnationals figured overwhelmingly in the success of the steelband and sailor event. Their enthusiasm for this event was of particular interest because the steelband as a musical form and the sailor as a costume form were *the* dominant presence in Carnival at the time when many Trinidadians were immigrating en masse to North America. In many ways, the demise of the steelband on the road coincides with this period of migration quite closely. Stephen Stuempfle comments that during the early 1960s, steelbands were near the height of their acceptance in Trinidadian society. The 1950s independence movement had included with it a swell in enthusiasm for all local, especially Afro-Trinidadian cultural forms. In the years around independence in 1962, steelbands dominated the streets and most masqueraders who took to the roadways did so behind these mobile orchestras. Yet by 1970, as Stuempfle points out, the steelband had waned considerably in its popularity (1995:170–172). Stuempfle rightfully accounts for some of this loss of popularity by pointing to the disillusionment with the independence movement in the minds of many young people. To this younger generation, the newer musical form of soca was beginning to replace the older style of calypso and pan that had dominated Trinidadian popular culture. As soca became more and more prominent, steelband certainly did not disappear. But the bands themselves were, so to speak, crowded off the streets by the louder, electronically amplified soca sound systems of the 1970s and 1980s. This cultural climate was in large measure aided by the economic phenomena in Trinidad known as the oil boom. The impact of the oil boom on Trinidad was enormous, but for this essay I want to focus on two specific factors. The first is the substantial migration out from Trinidad that began in earnest around 1965. The second is the changing demographic in the Carnival brought on by the influx of wealth into the society due to oil revenues.

REASONS FOR MIGRATION

The standard explanations for Caribbean migration to the United States apply only partially to the Trinidadian situation. Heavy capital investment in the West Indies, a rising cost of living, a booming economy in the States, the entrance of more and more American women into the workplace (thereby opening up a need for domestic labor) are merely some of the factors that have been mentioned in accounting for the waves of Caribbean migrants after 1965. In Jamaica, the discovery of bauxite meant an increase in foreign capital investment, but not an increase in employment due to the nature of bauxite mining, which requires a relatively small but skilled labor force. Capital investment may also lead to a loss of jobs through the elimination of local competition in a particular economic area: for instance, international food franchises push out smaller establishments. In other commonwealth Caribbean nations, a growing labor force and chronic job shortages produced a population in desperate need of economic options. Statistics showing the breakdown of jobs taken by immigrants throughout the heavy migration period show a high percentage working as "service industry" employees, which often meant working in the homes of American families caring for children or maintaining the household. Service positions, however, did not account for all of the jobs filled by West Indian workers. In addition to "blue-collar" employment, both skilled and unskilled, many professionals migrated to the United States bringing with them high levels of education and experience. Amounting to what scholars have termed the brain drain, the flight of professionals from the West Indies, especially Jamaica, created a dire situation in areas such as health care, upper management, and technology.

Trinidad has been one of the largest contributors to the West Indian migration outflow. However its role in this capacity must be treated slightly differently from that of the rest of the Commonwealth Caribbean. Because Trinidad already had a history of oil production and exportation, its economy took a different direction than that of its neighbors during the period in question. In 1973, in the midst of the implementation of a series of Five Year Plans orchestrated by the government of Eric Williams, the OPEC nations unilaterally began to increase the price of oil, and Trinidad suddenly saw its revenues skyrocket. During this period, the public sector increased employment dramatically and the unemployment rate in Port of Spain, which had hovered near 10 percent, dropped to just 4 percent. Yet during the same period, emigration continued and increased. For the nation as a whole, the rate of unemployment stayed relatively stable indicating that the oil boom was beneficial primarily to the capital city and to the oil-producing regions of the country. On the one hand, the rate at which emigration proceeded from Trinidad seems to have affected a smaller percentage of the population than in other Commonwealth Caribbean nations, amounting to 10 percent as opposed to 18 and 17 percent respectively for Barbados and Jamaica. Thus there was not as great a need to leave as there was in those other nations. On the other hand, there was still a significant increase in out-migration relative to the patterns established before the oil boom. There are several possible explanations for this, the most important being the transformation of U.S. immigration law that facilitated such moves in the first place. In addition, the oil boom brought with it an increase in imports, the virtual abandonment of the expansion of local production of basic goods, and an attendant rise in the cost of living. For those not in a position to benefit from the oil boom, there were still many economic reasons to emigrate.[1]

Compounding the economic motives for leaving were cultural ones. The growing dependent relationships that West Indian economies were realizing during the 1960s and 1970s also produced a stronger cultural relationship with the United States. In Trinidad, the oil boom generated a massive investment on the part of the government in terms of infrastructure. The construction of new roads, schools, telecommunications networks, electricity, and running water all facilitated a more "upscale" lifestyle for the average Trinidadian. More homes had televisions and a greater access to images of foreign lifestyles and to foreign cultural goods. Daniel Miller has noted that a preoccupation with foreign—especially American and British—culture was not new to the oil boom years, but had a history in Trinidad dating back to both British colonialism and the presence of American soldiers during World War II (1994:204–205). Yet the sudden prevalence of these images and items certainly had an unprecedented impact on the way in which Trinidadians began to think about standards of living. Speaking primarily of Indo-Trinidadians, but with a general application to all members of society Miller notices a "close association of lifestyle and place" such that North America becomes the place where, "even if one has less money, at least that money can be translated into goods which are of the requisite quality befitting the kind of person one has become" (1994:272–273).

The period of greatest migration, then, can also be seen as the period in which ties to the north become most pronounced at every level. In Trinidad, the growing intimacy in relations with North America led some members of society, especially those in the cultural elite, publishers, culture ministers, and educators, to worry about the impact such ties were having on local cultural forms. One frequently encounters a stance taken toward this phenomenon in academic literature, in the popular press of Trinidad, and in the official rhetoric of the state, marked by a growing fear of the loss of "authentic" culture (van Koningsbruggen 1997:200–202). Miller notes in these pronouncements a sense of "decline in the knowledge of traditional folklore, attached to agricultural labor, medical diagnosis and treatment, the supernatural and traditional folktales, as well as traditional foods and customs" (1994:205). The general sentiment among the educated elite is an ambivalence, at best, with regard to the nature of the country's association with things foreign. Certain influences constitute an unambiguous good, including technologies, medicines and treatments, foods, and manners. A kind of worldliness is invited, while the "loss" of local cultural forms is lamented. This ambivalence does not seem to be shared by the classes to whom these features of local authenticity properly belong (Miller 1994:206). The dynamic interplay between home and host generated by mass migration should be seen here as taking place on multiple levels. That is, the phenomenon of migration does not merely produce a population "in exile," but emerges out of global transformations that create a condition in the home society which necessitates movements of people. Yet at the same time, migration affects the home country in more ways than just politically and economically. The moves from Trinidad (as well as from other parts of the West Indies) were not always undertaken out of duress. In traveling to England, for instance, many West Indians regarded themselves as "English people" eager to dwell in the "motherland." It was fashionable to migrate. In the North American case, many who left were educated and upwardly mobile, eager to fill posts in more cosmopolitan locales (Gmelch 1992:41–61).

In any case, the attractions that drew West Indians away were part and parcel of the global processes that brought images of foreign places to people's doors, as well as unemployment to their shores. There were multiple reasons for leaving. The state's response, especially in the case of "brain drains" was to lament the loss of West Indian culture and society; countries blamed the siren song of the Western world. Yet most West Indians who left did so with the idea that they would return. Although family members were often sent for and settlement often occurred in the new country, many wanted to return and did so. If retirement to a quiet house in Tobago or to the pleasant suburbs of Port of Spain could not be effected, then temporary visits would be made. The traffic at holiday times, for instance, is enormous on British West Indies Airways, the main carrier for the region. The mobility of the Trinidadian population in America, their constant travel, creates an environment of cultural cross-pollination, of give and take. It also facilitates the creation and maintenance of a market for Trinidadian goods abroad. A significant trade in Carib beer, roti skins (a kind of Indian bread used to wrap up the curry stew known as roti), calypso CDs and other items has grown up to serve the transnational community.[2] A network of remittances from the United States helps sustain family and friends at home and is augmented by revolving credit associations known as *susus.* The neighborhoods in which Caribbean migrants have settled have been transformed physically into approximations of their Caribbean urban counterparts complete with open-air shops, music, vendors, and even a version of the "maxi taxi" system of minibuses carrying passengers along set routes through Caribbean neighborhoods. Dramatic economic transformations in Trinidad, therefore, came with cultural ones. Closer economic ties to the United States engendered closer cultural ties, especially with African American cultural forms and political ideologies. Soca, then a new musical form, is really a compound word that blends soul with calypso. The emergence of this music became the soundtrack for the Black Power movement in Trinidad, the growth of which was inspired by the new political agendas of black people in North America.

And yet the dramatic increase in the price of oil in the early 1970s also brought about enormous transformations in the demographic make-up of the Carnival. More and more women came to join masquerade bands, and the class profile of the average masquerader began to change with an increasing number of middle-class participants taking part in the annual event. By the late 1970s and the early 1980s, women were playing a much larger on the streets, and were dancing to soca. Furthermore, with the demise of the steelband on the road, the independent masquerade organizations, which was run by band leaders, came into greater prominence. The result was that steelbands were no longer commanding anywhere near the numbers of masqueraders that they had in their "prime." Many of the steelband masqueraders of the past who had dressed as sailors and joined in behind the pans in the thousands were now working and living in New York, Toronto, London, Miami, Boston, and other urban centers of North America and Britain. Yet due to the nature of this very transnational style of migration, in which continuing contact is maintained with the home country, many working- and middle-class Trinidadian men maintained an interest in the land of their birth and the cultural forms of their youth. It is these very people who responded with enthusiasm to the nostalgia-fueled steelband competition when it was introduced in 1996, some thirty years after they had left home.

STEELBAND COMPETITION AS ETHNIC TOURISM

When dealing with issues raised by the phenomenon of ethnic tourism, scholars frequently point to the level of exploitation imposed by such ventures (MacCannell 1992). The reconstruction of ethnicity for consumption by tourists is destructive and coercive, they maintain. It objectifies cultural forms and insinuates a "way of life" into a market-driven economy. Groups that turn themselves into tourist attractions become markers of the way in which dominant notions of cultural authenticity and their relation to a marketable identity have been internalized by traditionally subordinated groups (MacCannell 1992: 178–179).

But what other kinds of meanings might be generated when states create tourist destinations and attractions out of their landscapes and cultural forms for former nationals living abroad? Certainly sentimental tourism is nothing new. Places like Disney's Main Street, USA are created for nostalgic consumption by Americans who have never experienced the items preserved there that have been purportedly lost. Other examples might include tourists from Tokyo "rediscovering" pilgrimage spots in Japan (Ivy 1995). In these cases, the desire seems to be to capture a culture as if it were being recaptured, as if it should have somehow belonged in the experiences of the tourists themselves but never did. The culture and lifeway of "ancestors," or "forefathers" therefore rightfully belongs to the alienated and drained latter day "ethnics" or nationals who bear little of those ways themselves.

Yet this is not the case with many Trinidadians and Carnival. For first-generation Trinidadian Americans, who came in the mid-1960s, Carnival was a factor in their lives *even if they never had played.* Carnival is an unavoidable feature of Trinidadian life, and one has to make a conscious and concerted effort to avoid it. As John Stewart points out, "[F]or almost one-third of the year carnival accounts for a significant share of all public events in Trinidad" (1986:290). For many second-generation Trinidadian Americans, trips back "home" are regular events, and exposure to Carnival begins at an early age. In addition, the presence of, for example, the Brooklyn Carnival means that Trinidadian Americans can keep up with the festivals' events, bands, calypsos, and panorama champions, as calypso monarchs from the previous year, bandleaders, or at least steelband arrangers and performers from Trinidad are routinely invited to participate in the Brooklyn versions. For many such performers, the Carnival circuit (including festivals in London, Toronto, Miami, Boston, along with others) is a good means to earn extra money throughout the year. It is even the intent of Carnival organizers abroad and their umbrella organization—the International Caribbean Carnivals Association (ICCA)—to stagger the events in order to maximize participation by spectators, players, and Carnival artists. With all of this Carnival activity, most Trinidadians that I have spoken with are not strangers to the event.

Yet there is still an element of what Frederic Jameson has called "the desperate attempt to appropriate a missing past" (1991:19). Carnival in Trinidad is frequently referred to as the "real" event. Before many interviews that I conducted (or at some point during them), in nearly every conversation and even in polite chatter on the streets as the costumed performers skipped past, I was told that I must experience true Carnival in Trinidad. Many of the organizers and band leaders whom I spoke with maintained that the quality in Brooklyn had reached that of Trinidad; one organizer even stubbornly refused to acknowledge that there was any difference at all. Yet for the vast majority of Trinidadians who had no stake in "selling" me on Brooklyn Carnival, Trinidad was where I had to go.

Trinidad thus remains, in the words of one Carnival-goer, "the mother of all Carnivals." The festival in Trinidad, however, has another, special resonance for the Trinidadian abroad. It holds a particular place in the transnational imagination. Carnival of the present, however, is not the one that is so powerfully meaningful to returnees. It is a different Carnival that many, especially older, Trinidadians remember from their youth. That was the era of the famous and elaborate fancy masquerades of George Bailey and Harold Saldenah; those were the glory years of the steelband and the calypso, before the advent of massive sound systems, before the "wine" and "jam" Carnivals.[3] Those were also the years of massive military and sailor bands. For Trinidadians returning home, there is a quest not simply for Trinidad, but also for a place of memory, a place lodged in a particular time. To invert David Lowenthal's well-known title, "the foreign country is the past."[4] At the same time, the past is where the state locates its authentic national culture. The celebrated costumes and portrayals from bygone eras are the source from which the state draws its examples of a viable, unique national culture, a culture that is marketable. There is, then, a confluence of two factors: on the one hand, a desire stemming from a reproductive imagination that requires authenticity, memory, legitimation; on the other hand, there is a generation of commercially viable cultural forms, national culture, and cultural authority.

REASONS FOR THE STEELBAND-ON-THE-ROAD CONTEST

For Carnival of 1996, the National Carnival Commission inaugurated a steelband-on-the-road contest. The prize was announced as TT $100,000. The NCC had been concerned about the loss of the steelband presence on the road, as steelbands over the years slowly but surely had been left behind on Carnival Monday and Tuesday as sound systems took over. In addition, the NCC and Pan Trinbago, the steelband organization, were worried about the possible "theft" of steelband craftsmanship and innovation by other nations. The history of the pan (commonly referred to as the "steel drum" outside of Trinidad), many were afraid, would be forgotten and therefore the memory of its origins in Trinidad would be lost as well. If other nations were allowed to appropriate the instrument without having to give credit or pay homage to its roots in Trinidad, yet another piece of Trinidadian history, culture, and identity would be lost to the great anonymity of "Caribbean" identity. Worse, it might be lumped into some kind of Jamaican identity, or merely forgotten as regional in any way. It might go the way of the guitar, an instrument hardly associated with Spain any longer.[5] A related concern was that the performance of celebrated Carnival traditions would be lost too; there would be no performance, no culture, and no identity at home or abroad. By way of example, in 1996 TIDCO engaged in a massive self-promotion that included huge, multipaged advertisements in national newspapers. In one such advertisement in *The Express,* the headline read: "Reclaiming the Steelpan's Birthright—Born and Bred in T & T." The article went on to describe all that TIDCO was doing to let the world know that pan was a Trinidadian art form. Kathleen Pinder, manager of corporate communications, described a recent undertaking in which steelbands were brought to New York to distribute flyers, give concerts, and generally "boast of their Trinidad and Tobago roots." The group also sold pans and ended up returning with TT $38,000. But, as Pinder stressed "more important than the money" was the "re-affirming of Trinidad and Tobago as *the* creator and home of Steelpan in the eyes of the international community" (*Sunday Express*, February 18, 1996:26).

The NCC thus decided that one way to ensure the survival of steelbands at home was to encourage them to make a showing on Carnival Tuesday, as they had in the days before the mobile sound systems. The proposed competition rewarded the steelband that gave the best presentation. In addition to the musicians, there would have to be at least fifty costumed supporters walking with the band. On Carnival Tuesday, most of the large steelbands came out with their followers, many of whom were dressed in the sailor costume traditionally associated with steelband portrayals. A significant number of these sailors were from New York, Canada, and England. Their return and participation in a state-sponsored nostalgia competition highlights an important feature of the formation and continuation of the transnation.

The interaction of transnationals with their home countries nourishes both nationalist sentiment at home and ethnic identity abroad. The relationship is neither neat nor symmetrical. Returnees and locals, state representatives, culture brokers from Trinidad and from abroad, and the tourist industry: all have different agendas that are in part served by and in part undermined by the promotion of and participation in contests such as this one. Yet its presence supplies the reproductive imagination of the transnational community in ways that go beyond its purpose. For returnees do not merely consume nostalgia and commodified culture passively or in the service of a state–nationalist agenda. They also appropriate the raw materials of nostalgia for use in the ethnic political struggles of the metropole. What this implies, then, is that the success of the contest is only partly attributable to the efforts of the state.

THE IMPORTANCE OF NOSTALGIA: JASON GRIFFITH

The sailor is one of the most celebrated and oldest of masquerades, with roots extending back into the nineteenth century. As a working-class masquerade, it was perhaps the most commonly played mas by male Trinidadians who emigrated to the United States. It is also the mas most widely remembered, at least among my informants in Brooklyn, as the mas of their youth. Sailor bands, until their general demise in the 1960s, were routinely the largest bands on the road on Carnival Tuesday. One Trinidadian man, who has been involved with mas since the early 1950s, described sailor bands as being more than three thousand strong. On one occasion, he recalled, the Silver Stars Steelband had so many sailor masqueraders in its ranks that the front of the band was crossing the judging venue in downtown Port of Spain, while the rear was coming up French street in Woodbrook, a middle-class neighborhood about a half mile away.[6]

One of the last sailor band specialists still working in Carnival is Jason Griffith. I interviewed him in 1994 at his home in the Belmont section of Port of Spain. Belmont lies at the foot of the Laventille hills and is primarily a working-class neighborhood. Unlike other parts of the city, its streets are not arranged in a grid pattern, but wind gently up from the eastern side of the Queen's Park Savannah. Most of the land had belonged to the Warner family whose members included Charles Warner, the powerful attorney-general of the island from 1844 to 1870. The land was sold and finally incorporated into the city limits of Port of Spain, and the neighborhood was brought under the jurisdiction of the government, which provided for its development with the Belmont Improvement Ordinance of 1905. With the introduction of arc and incandescent lamps, many hundreds of new homes were built so that by 1907 Belmont was a thriving suburb.

The area has a long history of involvement with Carnival. Like the storied neighborhoods of Woodbrook and Laventille, and like the suburb of Barataria, Belmont has produced its share of notable mas men including Harold Saldenah who brought his band out from Oxford Street. Jason Griffith, whose name is practically synonymous with fancy sailor bands, began in 1946. He brought out his own band by 1949 after an apprenticeship with Jim Harding, one of the first fancy sailor masmen. Griffith worked steadily in sailor mas until 1955, when he shifted to historical and fancy mas. Throughout the 1960s, he freelanced as a

Fancy Sailors by Jason Griffith celebrating his twentieth anniversary of bringing out a sailor band on the stage at the "Big Yard," the Queen's Park Savannah, 1993. Photograph by Garth Green.

costume maker, but was not deeply involved in the sailor masquerades. It was only in 1969 that he stepped back into the role of masman, making sailor costumes and headpieces and bringing his own band from his home on Pelham Street.

When Griffith returned full time to costume production, the steelbands and their sailor masquerades were still quite popular. Michael Anthony reports that in 1967 Desperadoes played *Fancy Sailors from U.S.S. Spikenose*, Tokyo played sailor calling the band *In Harms Way,* and Invaders played sailors from the U.S.S. Wasp. With five thousand members, "Invaders had by far the biggest band of Carnival" (Anthony 1989:329). Yet a mere two years later, sailors were on the wane, even if steelbands were still a fixture on Carnival Tuesday. Carnival of 1969 reflected the deep impression made by Black Power politics on many mas men. There were at least fifteen bands that year carrying African-inspired themes, such as *Afromania '69, Psychedelic Afro, African Power, Tribute to Africa, Modern Africa,* and many others. Anthony notes of that year that "All these bands seemed to swamp out the usual sailor band and other military bands," with the possible exception being Winston Gordon's band *Sailor's Ashore in Africa* (1989:339, 341). The sailor band recovered, however. As steelbands became less and less of an option for masqueraders, other mas bands picked up the sailor portrayal. A steelband boycott in 1979 probably had some small role to play, but it was the advent of soca and massive sound systems that helped diminish the presence of steelbands.

In 1982 Jason Griffith brought out a band called *Old Fashioned Sailors Gone Fancy*, and in 1983 he designed one titled *Hats Off to Old Fashioned Sailors.* These bands were enthusiastically received but were not massive in the way the old sailor bands were. Anthony indicates that the latter band gave viewers an idea of what "old-time Carnivals looked like." The big bands that had taken the sailor theme, Anthony points out, had had to transform the basic costume to fit the expectations of the masqueraders who demanded contemporary styles and fabrics (1989:429). They were no longer playing sailor the way it had been played before; of all the sailor productions, only Griffith remained faithful to the styles and concepts of past masters. Griffith himself does not entirely agree with this assessment. He points instead to the many innovations he and his associates have made over the years, including the inclusion of historical and fantasy themes within the parameters of the sailor's basic structure. Yet this is not what he is primarily known for. By the late 1980s, Griffith's bands were an expected feature of Carnival Tuesday, but some felt that they should not be judged in comparison to the other large fancy bands (Anthony 1989:467). They were certainly not of the same size or magnitude, even though they provided some of most spectacular and finely crafted costumes.

As the sailor mas waned and as Griffith's portrayals became more and more relegated to the realm of "living history," his bands began to attract more and more Trinidadians from abroad. In my conversations with him, he mentioned that "at least two or three sections a year are made up of people from Brooklyn" (Griffith Interview 1993). This is not to say that the majority of people from Brooklyn who come to Carnival play sailor. But the sailor bands are largely supported by Brooklynites and older Trinidadians within Trinidad. The gradual supercession of the sailor by other types of portrayal reflects broader changes in Carnival. Griffith pointed out to me that his is one of the last types of masquerade in which men and women both play in relatively equal numbers. What is most remarkable about that fact is that the sailor is perhaps the last masquerade that men play in at all. The sailor bands carry more male participants proportionately than any other kind of mas band. They are the last bands that look and feel like old-time masquerade; this is due in large measure to the supporters from home and abroad who like to keep it that way.

THE ART OF NOSTALGIA, THE NOSTALGIA OF ART

Transnationalism, in a cultural sense, is a lived experience. In exploring the ways in which individuals who have returned from abroad, especially from the older generations, choose to play mas, I was able to recognize a source from which they were able to draw images of ethnicity, a sort of ethno-capital. Arjun Appadurai's notion of the ethnoscape is useful here, as he notes that

> even as the legitimacy of nation-states in their own territorial contexts is increasingly under threat, the idea of the nation flourishes transnationally. Safe from the depredations of their home states, diasporic communities become doubly loyal to their nations of origin . . . [A]s populations become deterritorialized and incompletely nationalized, as nations splinter and recombine, as states face intractable difficulties in the task of producing "the people," transnations are the most important social sites in which the crises of patriotism are played out. (1993:424, 428)

I would argue that transnations are only one of many important sites in which to view the crises of patriotism. What the example of Trinidad shows us is that the crisis of the nation's identity is not always the same as that of national identity. In the serendipitous confluence of official, state-sponsored nostalgia and the nostalgia of the returning migrant we can see such disparities at work in the formation of a global ethnoscape.

It has been said that nostalgia is a particularly powerful mode of cultural expression that emerges with great intensity in relation to the postmodern fragmentation of social life (K. Stewart 1988:229). Stewart maintains that nostalgia "rises to importance as a cultural practice as culture becomes more and more diffuse." Nostalgia is manifested as a kind of narrative of wholeness, which seeks to redress the disruptive nature of exile and dislocation. Nostalgia, the sickness for home, is a way of re-membering not only the past, but the cultural forms that presumably existed conterminously with the space and place of their occurrence. I am speaking here not only of a kind of personal nostalgia, rooted in the experiences of the individual, but of the production of a kind of nostalgic collective memory intended to capture the common ground of individuals with specific reference to public and national cultural forms.

Important in the formulation of the contemporary ethnoscape, especially in the Trinidad case, is the overlay, the imbrication, of the forces of cultural production and consumption. By looking at official, unofficial, and semi-official discourse it is possible to draw a relationship between the active construction of nostalgic identities and the growth of commodity aesthetics and fetishism in the service of national culture. In addition, these currents run towards a larger stream which is the formation of digestible identities which themselves become

A competitor in the Fancy Sailor Category "Fireman" at Viey La Cou, 1993. Photograph by Garth Green.

consumed in a marketplace of identity both at home and abroad. In previous chapters we have looked at the official discourse of nostalgia as it relates to other issues such as national culture, sovereignty, and economics. This chapter has been much more concerned with the ways in which nostalgia figures into the transnational imagination. Jason Griffith is both a "national treasure" from the state's perspective and a "transnational treasure" from the point of view of returning migrants, yet he is a private individual who works in an independent capacity. The competition in 1996 was an attempt to further capitalize on the sailor nostalgia and to create a version that the state could organize and benefit from, at the same time it was an implicit recognition that the nostalgic forms are the very symbol of the forces of diffusion that threaten the nation state itself.

THE CURRENT STATE OF THE SAILOR: SAILOR AS NOSTALGIA

I have mentioned that the disappearance of the steelband from the road and the subsequent passing of the elaborate sailor and military bands that accompanied them were due largely to a combination of the oil boom, emigration, and the rise of sound systems. In addition, the changing demographics in the festival had enormous impact and resulted from the increasing role of the middle and upper classes and their state-mandated carnival organizations (precursors to the NCC). Steps were taken by these organizations to limit steelband violence through the formation of a steelband association in 1960. The national Panorama competition was instituted a few years later, in 1963, to channel steelband rivalry into less violent outlets. Corporate sponsorship of bands, combined with new developments in mobile music technologies, ultimately rendered the steelband obsolete on the road on Carnival Tuesday. Steelbands no longer required large portrayals to help them with revenue due to corporate involvement. Mobile sound trucks became the musical choice of most other types of masquerade bands.

Ironically, the very class that helped to bring it about later lamented the passing of the steelband from the road. Once the steelband had been appropriately tamed through competition and sponsorship, it was reintroduced to society as an example of bona fide cultural heritage. In 1996 many of the older, more established steelbands emerged to vie for the TT $100,000 prize, quite a few of them playing sailor. The masqueraders were no longer the rowdy youths of the 1940s and 1950s, but an older set, playing nostalgia mas. In a sense, they were playing a masquerade of the masquerade of another era. The presence of the steelbands brought with it the possibility of experiencing something like the Old-Time Carnival. However, one thing that Jason Griffith could not provide was the steelband presence. The true sailors were not the elaborate fancy ones of Griffith's band, but the old sailors on shore leave whose era had passed nearly twenty years before.

SAILOR MAS 1996: THE "UTOPIA OF USE VALUE"

The steelband competition made the Carnival seem exotic to returnees. In presenting it, the state established a crucial separation between the past and the here-and-now, privileging the former over the latter. Yet the state, in general, sees this process as a form of recovery. For the state, recovery carries with it the promise of product differentiation; in the objectification of the past, the state trades on the power of "use-value" as a form of marketing. The object's caché as artifact becomes its attraction in exchange such that its use-value (imagined, in this case, as the sailor masquerade's existence outside of the commercial and degraded Carnival and therefore capable of restoring and supplying authenticity to, ironically, the returning consumer) is its exchange value. Susan Stewart (1993:145–151) treats this connection between use-value and nostalgia and concludes that what she calls "the souvenir's" power is not only its separation from the present, but also its ability to figure into a narrative of restoration: "The souvenir must be removed from its context in order to serve as a trace of it, but it must also be restored through narrative and or reverie. What it is restored to is not an 'authentic,' that is, a native context of origin but an imaginary context of origin" (1993:150).

Stewart points out the importance of context for the nostalgic object. It is this that makes the crucial difference in the success or failure of state-sponsored cultural forms. She claims that such narratives relate to an "imaginary" context of origin, which I would suggest implies, again, the "invention" of a context, a fabrication. If we take her meaning to be that the context is imaginary in that it is no longer the immediate context and must be supplied by the imagination, then I would certainly agree that the context is part of the reproductive imagination, in that its presence is vital in reinforcing ideas of identity.

The growth of a thriving Carnival industry between Trinidad and the United States today relies not only on the presence of Trinidadians in the foreign metropole but also on the persistent desire on the part of dislocated nationals to want to cultivate and perpetuate a cultural heritage. This requires two interconnected, yet distinct circumstances: lack of—or more accurately, resistance to—assimilation, on the one hand and adaptation to local identity politics on the other. Lack of assimilation is marked not so much by a maintenance of radical difference, but by a conformity to the general shape of difference required by American-style multiculturalism. By looking at the sailor mas as it developed in Trinidad, we have been able to see the unstable and fluid relationship that masqueraders have to the state and state-sponsored institutions there, as well as to the ways in which players in masquerade bands have been partially successful in negotiating a political identity terrain that has expanded to include more than just the neighborhoods, city and national boundaries. Traces of Brooklyn, and the United States in general, hang over the actions of Trinidadians in Trinidad, sometimes in ways that are clearly perceived and sometimes in ways that are only partially understood or understood not at all.

The creation of a Trinidadian identity by that country's transmigrants abroad must negotiate the fragmented and dislocated nature of the transmigrant experience. To that end, Trinidadians in New York frequently draw upon essentialized cultural forms from which to imagine a concrete social identity. Such forms are frequently found in the nationalist cultural mythologies of the "homeland" from which the transmigrants have come. These mythologies take the form of cultural and historical narratives that serve to legitimize Trinidadian sovereignty and autonomy within the global family of nations. But such narratives must be relevant and must resonate with the other versions maintained in the minds and practices of the transnationals themselves. And this often carries the production of meaning away from that which is envisioned by the state. Thus, even as the state counts its projects successful by seeing them played out on the streets of Port of Spain, it may be watching those very projects slipping from its grasp.

NOTES

1. Jean Grugel (1995:180), for instance, notes that even with the oil boom, foreign investment slowed down in Jamaica and Trinidad, with disinvestment occurring. Prices for other main exports fell at the same time as agriculture and food production declined.

2. A radio program in Trinidad cited this trade as a possible area for expansion for the Trinidadian economy. Local scholars from the University of the West Indies pointed out that as Trinidadians have established a presence in New York and other foreign locales, they have carried with them their culture and have exposed foreigners to cultural products such as Carnival, soca music, and West Indian foods. It only remained for the government to seize upon these opportunities to both make profit and promote national culture abroad (Breakfast Club Radio Program, Trinidad, December 1993).

3. Wining and jamming are descriptive terms for dancing. They are especially erotic and symbolize to many the downfall of the Carnival, its loss of craftsmanship, and its defeat by the forces of debauchery and commercialism.

4. This is a reference to David Lowenthal's *The Past is a Foreign Country*, 1985.

5. The fervor over pan reached a peak during my stay in Trinidad. Articles appeared routinely in the newspapers that seemed to contribute to the "pan-ic" or "steal-band" as I began to think of it. Innovations in pan design by Canadians or the Swiss, that were being patented, Americans instead of Trinidadians teaching pan in Japan, steel orchestras being founded in Europe without Trinidadian input or expertise were all sources of anxiety. The final controversy surrounded a debate over the teaching of the pan versus the harmonium in schools. Many Trinidadians, especially those of African descent, considered the pan the logical choice of instrument for musical instruction in the schools because it is the only instrument to have been invented in Trinidad and is routinely cited as the *only* new acoustic instrument to have been invented in the twentieth century, anywhere. The harmonium, championed especially by Indo-Trinidadians as an example of their cultural heritage, is rejected as a colonial instrument, introduced by the English into India and therefore not even "authentically" Indian, let alone Trinidadian. The positioning of Indians within Trinidad as ethnic minorities, no matter what their numbers in the population, has been a feature of Trinidadian cultural negotiation. Indo-Trinidadians have often emphasized their separateness from Trinidadian culture and their con-

nection to India, leaving, by default, African Trinidadians as the bearers of the national culture in their capacity as "Creole." This has emerged historically both by conscious withdrawal from national culture and by exclusion from it. The trend changed dramatically when the majority Indian party, the UNC, came to power. There now seems to be a greater interest in demonstrating the Indian contribution to Trinidadian culture and society.

6. This story was related to me by Winston Carr, son of the well-known Trinidadian folklorist Andrew Carr.

5. Reading Caribana 1997: Black Youth, Puff Daddy, Style, and Diaspora Transformations

Lyndon Phillip

"It was all about the Benjamins, baby," when Puff Daddy "mash up de Lake-shore" for Caribana 1997. This was the disruptive moment that changed the way people imagine Caribana—one of North America's largest Carnivals over the last three decades.[1] Watching Puff Daddy, a superstar rap musician, record mogul, producer, and sometime Hollywood celebrity, "jamming de session" and "moving the crowd" signaled a clear change that Caribana in Toronto no longer resembled the Trinidadian model organizers have copied for years. Pejoratively referred to as "Puffybana," "Rapabana," or the very ambiguous "Ameribana," the festival, primarily its Saturday parade component, appeared to be born from something quite different and distinctive of the version masquerade-makers relied upon for inspiration. "Where was the Carnival in that?" casual observers begged to know. Opinions lamenting the presence and dominance of urban music in general and rap in particular flooded talk radio programs and newspapers in the black community. Most fingers were aimed at Puff Daddy, marking him as an American villain intent on increasing record sales. Toronto's longtime Carnival purists and traditionalists defenders of Carnival's pillars—calypso, masquerade, and steelband—mocked Puff Daddy's performance as culturally weak, capitalistic, and a "flash in the pan." More astute critics, some belonging to the festival's organizational body and mas camp groups, rightfully removed the focus from Puff Daddy and posed a series of cultural concerns. Foremost in their minds was the issue of cultural retention and what they saw as a problem among black youth. A shortage of properly trained youths in the idealized truths of Carnival jeopardized the longevity of this festival more than a "fly by night artist" could.

Organizers also posed the problem as a moral cultural responsibility that black youth should be exposed to legitimate Carnival arts and not a "watered-down North American street festival" devoid of black historicity in general and Carnival's essence in particular. Fuelling their sympathetic yet denigrating critique of black youths' assumed de-culturalization of Caribana were political and financial factors crippling the organization's tenuous foundations. Responding to the unique situation of 1997, organizers and their traditional supporters in the black community maintained that Hip-Hop's ascendancy was incidentally produced through a series of financial abnormalities. And once economic woes were resolved, Hip-Hop's encroachment would safely return to its non-threatening and controlled place as tangential to real Caribana. At fault with this logic, however, was the sense that the economic could rescue, remedy, and fix the cultural in view of it promoting simple cultural reproduction. That what organizers had framed as processes of de-culturalization among black youth would cease to exist following economic restructuring. This was a misguided assessment. Economic restructuring of any sort could only ensure the idealized, essentialized, and objectified notions of Carnival art and not reduce the exuberance with which black youth contest and rewrite the boundaries of Caribana. Solving the problem was termed in view of the business of managing Caribana. Chair of Caribana's organizing committee, Henry Gomez, projected this philosophy well, emphasizing that "there is no-show without the business," stressing the ties between economics and culture. But this rigid economic determinism neither impressed upon nor diminished the ways that black youths uprooted the Carnival pillars and attempted to invent a relationship between urban and Carnival cultures.

This chapter addresses the way in which black youth contest and contradict traditional notions of Carnival in Toronto by tapping into their diasporic sensibilities. I argue that what initially appears as a total rejection of Carnival culture is rather the product of a mediating relationship combining aspects of Carnival and other cultural styles shaping young black lives. Black youth in Toronto engage their diasporic sensibilities through forays in and out of traditional performances of Carnival. Through their Carnival practice in Toronto, black youth move between and within cultural boundaries, take up new subject positions, create new meanings, and express their desires. Through a series of ethnographic jaunts, interview notations, and cyberspace debates, I unpack the complex ways in which black youth are reading and performing Carnival in Toronto.

CALYPSO CARNIVAL

Anthropologists and social scientists have produced a vast literature on the effects of migration in shaping black Caribbean populations in Canada in general and Toronto in particular (Henry 1994; James 1989). Their work identifies various push–pull factors directing the flow of migrants to urban centers such as Montreal and Toronto. Black Caribbean migrants rapidly shifted the racial and ethnic make-up of these cities, before changes to Canadian immigration law in 1962 curtailed the flow (Satzewich 1989). Black Caribbean communities developed the Canadian Carnival tradition in Montreal and Toronto. The origins of Carnival in Toronto, while not to overlook the parental roots of the Trinidadian Carnival, also has some roots in official Canadian multiculturalism and a little known black women's organization of the 1950s. But it is the former that scholars and lay historians most often remember. A group of hard-working black women put down very important tracks, which unfortunately are rarely acknowledged in current depictions of Caribana's history. This absence of rec-ognition for ancestors has cut off the memory of black Caribbean and black Canadian relations. This break has historical significance for the youth under discussion here.

Caribana began as a joint venture between black Caribbean communities in Toronto and the federal government's new stance of multiculturalism. Though official multiculturalism did not appear as stated policy until 1971, the centenary celebrations at Expo 1967 in Montreal marked the seed of the program. Eager to display a new-found sense of nation and nationhood, the federal government solicited communities throughout Canada to display ethnic arts marking one hundred years of nationalism. The goal was to have ethnic arts occurring throughout the country all tied to the grand celebration in Montreal. For the black Caribbean community the pavilion hosted by Trinidad and Grenada on Montreal's St. Helene's Island at the behest of the Canadian government emphasized blackness as contributing to a revised national picture. It is noted, however, that blackness was and remains quite distant to any historic and present conceptualization of Canadian nationhood. Nevertheless, the black Caribbean pavilion, which ran from April 28 to October 27, 1967, celebrated Caribbean food, music, and dance. In support of this event, an equally grand event was hatched in the basement of an abandoned fire station on Bathurst Street in Toronto. This aspect of the "idea for Caribana" beginning in a basement on a cold evening in February 1966 has been mythologized in the black Caribbean community as indicative of the hard work and racial struggle this festival and black Canadian peoples in general have endured. By deploying this factual event as a constitutive myth of origin, organizers effectively mark this event as an essence. I saw the impact and use of this myth during membership meetings and other informal gatherings. Organizers recalled the notions of hard work and solidarity in speaking against youth they deemed as subverting Carnival history in favor of the easily attainable urban culture imported from the United States. The myth, fully deployed, serves as subtle political censure in the discourse of "moral responsibility" active since Caribana's inception.

Unacknowledged in this dominant origin myth is the work of a largely unknown group of black Canadian women crucial to Ontario's black history. From 1951 to 1976, a group of Canadian-born black women, the Canadian Negro Women's Association (CANEWA), initiated the first black history celebrations in Ontario, supported the final stages of desegregation in some southern Ontario schools, and provided the first academic scholarships for black students. From 1952 to 1964, CANEWA members produced, funded, and hosted annual events they called Calypso Carnivals. Largely serving as fund raisers for scholarships, the calypso Carnivals attracted attention for a one-day event of Caribbean food, dance, and music. While highly successful in terms of presenting a positive public image, CANEWA women were often chastised for their middle-class values and lack of street-level politics (for a brief history of CANEWA, see Hill 1996). Unfortunately, not much is known about the role CANEWA played in Canada's Carnival tradition, nor does there seem to be a desire to cultivate such memory. The oral historians I consulted in 1997 vaguely remembered the connections between the two celebrations.

CANEWA women came from the community of black Canadians who trace their roots in the northern movements of black Americans during the nineteenth century and early part of the twentieth. These women were part of the black Canadian experience that was not Caribbean, a point that is often misrepresented in social histories. Yet their interest in Caribbean arts speaks to the diasporic sensibilities that shape the black Canadian experience, in terms of the border crossings, both real and metaphorical, that mark the black Canadian experience. As Hill (1996) points out in his short history of CANEWA, very few of the women had direct Caribbean roots. What I am suggesting is black youth contesting Carnival are advancing our understanding of the diasporic transference that shapes Canadian blackness in ways not unlike CANEWA some fifty years ago. The imaginative ways in which black youth cross boundaries and *play* with different notions of blackness draws from a history of such moves, like those of CANEWA. Reading their moves in this way, I suggest, begins to strip away at problematic conceptions of subversion as corruption and deculturalization and reattaches them to the history of cultural crossings that have shaped black Canada. For Caribana, it means imagining new possibilities that live through the losses and gains of figurative and real crossings.[2]

EMANCIPATION DAY PARADE TO JUMP UP

Black people in Toronto celebrated the liberation of enslaved Africans throughout the Americas before the first mas band ever jumped in 1967. Each November in the west end of Toronto in the old fashion district, black people celebrated the Emancipation Day Parade marking the 1838 liberation of slaves throughout the British Americas. Archival newspaper photos from the *Toronto Telegram* indicate that the parade occurred around the same time period as the CANEWA Calypso Carnivals, 1952–1964. The parade was a military-style affair symbolizing black victory over British Empire. As such, military regalia, marching bands, and drum corps were heavily featured. The descendants of fugitive American slaves and other northern black travelers who settled in the rural communities of southern Ontario started the parade. The Emancipation Day Parade was the most visible black event in the city. This role was eventually relinquished to Caribana.

Contemporary Caribana organizers forget the importance of the Emancipation Day Parade. Except for a few of the founding members I interviewed, not much about this parade has been worked into Caribana's social history. The Emancipation Day Parade provides historical threads between recent black Caribbean immigrants and the older black Canadian community and suggests a larger social historical framework within which to analyze current conflicts within Caribana and the black Canadian community. Caribana's development may be best situated within the larger social history of black Canada. The Emancipation Day Parade and Caribana suggest the historical complexity of black expressive arts. I suggest that the subversive activities of black youth can be linked to the diasporic flows that produced both the largely black Canadian Emancipation Day and the black Caribbean Caribana celebrations.

DEVELOPMENT OF CARIBANA

Caribana began in 1967 as the West Indian contribution toward Canada's centennial celebrations. In 1965, the federal government began approaching ethnic communities, partly in search of centennial contributions and also to give face for a future multicultural vision. Across Canada, representatives such as Mark Blevins were explaining to ethnic community leaders the federal government's desire for racially and ethnically diverse centennial celebrations. Blevins contacted emerging civil rights lawyer Charles Roach in Toronto. Roach had come to Canada in 1955 from his home in Port of Spain in Trinidad. He came to study at the University of Saskatchewan, and after completing his undergraduate studies, he enrolled in law school at the University of Toronto. Roach was called to the bar in 1963. It was during his time as a civil rights lawyer that he made tremendous strides within the growing West Indian community. During his early days in Toronto, Roach experimented with the music business. Before 1967, he served as a music promoter at a nightclub called the Little Trinidad Club. He brought in popular calypsonians like Mighty Sparrow, Lord Ryner, Kitchener, and Lord Superior. Roach would later convey his experience at the Little Trinidad Club into organizing the first Caribana.

Many of the people Roach contacted were young students, nurses, domestics, workers, and professionals. There is an inspiring story that has achieved mythlike status if only because at this point verifying it is difficult. But documenting the factual truth of the claim is less important. It is much more significant to understand how the story stands alone, separate from the sole sense of a newly emerging West Indian community providing a "gift" to Canada. The following story is important for conceptualizing a fork in the road of Caribana's development. By *fork* I mean two things: first Caribana's centennial connection is primarily captured and boiled down to the bureaucratic language of folk multiculturalism; and, second, the emergence of Caribana is a distinctive moment in the broader development of West Indians living in Canada.

On a cold evening in February of 1966, Charles Roach and a group of West Indian students, professionals, and workers came together in an abandoned firehouse on Bathurst Street to discuss what they were going to do for Canada's birthday. The challenge was twofold: doing something for Canada, but also for the thousands of West Indians who were pouring into the city. The *West Indian News Observer* (WIN) in 1968 reported that the group wanted to showcase "what constituted the West Indies, their way of life, their joys [and] their struggles" (WIN July 1968:3). All present that night agreed that staging a celebration based on the Trinidad Carnival would be the best model to display West Indian cultural arts. Charles Roach told me that the group (which also included fellow founders Peter Marcelline, Elaine and Alban Liverpool, Sam Cole, Romain Pitt, among others) talked for hours well into the night. The Caribana founders spoke about how they were going to transport a never before seen Carnival to Toronto. In addition to the traditional parade of the bands, their Caribana (a name that joins Caribbean and bacchanal) was to include a fancy Ball, catered boat cruises along Lake Ontario and an island picnic on Toronto's Olympic Island. Charles Roach remembers that there was great community support for Caribana at that time. Soon hundreds of volunteers rallied behind the idea, meeting in church basements, West Indian clubs, and people's homes to further strengthen the plans. Getting people on board was not a difficult challenge. In 1995, Peter Marcelline remembered that "there was a great sense of euphoria . . . you could feel it in the atmosphere and people were very excited about coming out to participate" (Foster 1995:30). Community support for the inaugural Caribana was tremendous.

In 1967, Caribana was a joint symbol of multiculturalism and ethnic pride. The *West Indian News Observer* described the initial event this way: "Caribana invaded Canada for the first time, bringing with it the joyous levity that is so symbolic of the West Indies" (WIN July 1968:4). Charles Roach remembers the first Caribana as a grand celebration with few overtly political goals. Politics came in the form of thousands of black and Caribbean people parading on the streets. Roach described 1967 as "really magical" and a "watermark kind of year." "It was the year," he recalls, "the Black community really made its presence in Toronto." The first Caribana was intended as a one-time "gift." A small parade was held on Yonge Street, a main downtown thoroughfare. Seven masquerade bands took part. The parade of the bands was judged at Varsity Stadium on the University of Toronto campus and proceeded to dance eastbound along Bloor Street. The seven bands then turned south onto Yonge Street and jumped until they reached the recently erected Toronto City Hall, where the celebration continued. Caribana's nine-day festival celebration brought in a record crowd of 80,644 people onto Toronto's Centre Island, which at that point was the single largest gathering Toronto Island had witnessed. Ferry services carrying masqueraders, spectators, politicians and media were busier than at any other time of the year. City Hall, the Province of Ontario, and the Federal government immediately recognized the draw of Caribana. "The government of Ontario was so pleased with the venture that they included it as an added tourist attraction in their tourist brochures" (WIN July 1968:4). The city of Toronto was so delighted with the spectacular show of color, costuming, music, dance, art, and food that the mayor of Toronto, William Dennison, suggested "that the affair should be an annual event." The first Caribana had the support of all three levels of government.

By 1968, the centennial committee led by Charles Roach and Alban Liverpool had renamed itself the Caribbean Cultural Committee for Cultural Advancement and was institutionalized as a not-for-profit volunteer organization. Caribana 1968 was conceptualized with different intentions than the multicultural notions that had delivered the inaugural event as a gift to Canada. This time, Roach and company looked toward using Caribana as a foundation for harnessing and developing infrastructure. George Miekle, chairman of the Social Committee 1968, explained the goal as a cultural endeavor "to acquire, maintain, operate, and conduct a Caribbean-Canadian community center and to give donations for charitable and educational purposes" (WIN April 1968:4). The need for a community center was urgently felt as newcomers continued to pour into the city. "Many of whom," Miekle noted, "felt unsettled and lost during the first years of their lives in the new environment" (WIN April 1968:4). "A centre," the *West Indian News Observer* wrote, "would be the place where West Indians could get together for social programs and entertainment [and] where newcomers meet those familiar with the Canadian scene to obtain advice and assistance" (WIN April 1968:4). Furthermore, children would come to hear and learn about the West Indies and foster "a strong sense of identity with their own culture . . . while learning to live with the larger [white] community." Alban Liverpool, as the newly elected president of the Cultural Advancement Association, spearheaded the move to run a financially successful festival with an eye toward the stated goals. The interesting irony is that the community center would replace Alban Liverpool's dentist office, in the College-Spadina Street area, as the formalized place to receive community information. His office had become an informal information outlet. One local source spoke about Liverpool's office as "a sort of unofficial information service . . . about where to go for jobs, housing and other related problems of a strange society" (WIN April 1968:4).

Caribana 1968 was different because it took on the challenges and problems of community politics. Responding to the challenge shifted organizational sensibility toward financial and fiscal responsibility. This meant that President Liverpool was now responsible for creating and managing festival events that would enable and generate a surplus. For the first time and only in its second year, Caribana was testing an ability to be financially lucrative. And why not, as all the previous year's indicators and reviews seemed to suggest that the parade and festival events enjoyed wide support. However, the crucial difference was that Caribana 1968 was operating without the backing of the Centennial and the full support of the federal government. It meant that Liverpool's stated goal of generating between Cdn $20,000 and Cdn $40,000 would severely test Caribana's ability to draw crowds minus the centennial fervor. In order to fill in the partial financial support that the federal government was offering for the second Caribana, Liverpool and his group approached respective Caribbean governments. The Cultural Advancement Committee was seeking financial assistance, essentially in order to have a community center built.

The agenda for Caribana 1968 included ferryboat cruises, picnicking, and a Miss Caribana pageant. There were two ferryboat cruises scheduled, for July 31 and August 1, 1968. A local account described the cruises as "essentially West Indian, as Lake Ontario substitutes for the blue Caribbean Sea wafting the stimulating rhythm of the steel-band across her waters" (WIN July 1968:4).

For three hours on both nights, the ferry took people on an imaginative trip back to the Caribbean. The boat's restaurant served the best in West Indian cuisine as Caribana enthusiasts released pent-up nostalgia and longing for home. The cruises were the warm-up parties for the festival highlight. The parade of the bands was held on Saturday August 3, and included eight bands competing for prizes. The route out of Varsity Stadium remained the same, which had revelers dancing towards Nathan Phillips Square at City Hall. During the week of picnic festivities on Olympic Island, there were two organized musical shows. Island revelers were treated to the high-tuned pans and ringing tones of the Antigua Hell Gates. From Trinidad, the BWIA Sun Jets displayed a true steel orchestra, and from Jamaica the world famous Blues Busters played the wafting sounds of rock steady and ska. Additionally, local Caribbean artists such as calypsonian Andy Nichols from Guyana and King Ricardo from Grenada, who held the title of world's greatest limbo dancer, made the island festivities of Caribana 1968 one of the best. These top performers underscored Caribana's 1968 "accent on entertainment and fun."

From its inception, Caribana's festival music was pan-Caribbean. Although modeled around ideas drawn from the Trinidad Carnival, it appears that early committees sought to appeal to the diversity within Toronto's West Indian community. However, even these formative years clearly defined the parade and the festival as hosting distinct music. In a simple though not easy sense, calypso and steelpan music reign during the parade of the bands, leaving other Caribbean and diasporic music to the festival. There was black music that ranged from the traditional calypso to reggae to the sounds of U.S. rhythm and blues. In coming years, the nature of the pan-Caribbean musical focus would be contested, as constituencies within the community spoke against the dominance of calypso music. For instance, local reggae music promoters have claimed that Caribana organizers have made it difficult to include reggae artists in the festival. This debate intensified around 1974 and culminated in 1981 when reggae became a central Caribana theme. These differences later emerged as pivotal nodes that shaped Caribana's cultural development.

Early in Caribana's formation, the issue of financial responsibility and accountability emerged as a recurring theme. The failure to generate the necessary funds for a community center in 1968 was the first kernel in discussing Caribana's economic successes and frustrations. For example, the failed venture raised questions about whether Caribana should be used for financial or cultural ventures, an argument that poses an opposition between the two. Nevertheless the prevailing sentiment seemed to indicate that overtly financial objectives would compromise the *true* nature of Caribana. Complaints were levied against Liverpool and his group's ability to manage Caribana. The idea of building a center became a source of continual frustration in the ensuing years. Different ideas for Caribana began to surface, albeit each retaining traces of the traditional aspects of the Trinidad Carnival. Whereas Caribana had begun as a gift to the Canadian centenary celebration, it had quickly moved beyond that gesture. The desire to fulfill the dreams of West Indians in the city led organizers to pursue a cultural endeavor that put them ahead of their financial resources. These financially strained differences persisted throughout the 1970s as groups vied for control over the idea of Caribana. The struggle for administrative and ideological control defined Caribana's development throughout the 1970s.

Caribana: 1972–1980

After 1967, community support for the parade wavered. Controversies emerged over how Caribana was administered. The support of the organization was left almost entirely up to the small community of organizers, players, and producers forming around Caribana. Also the expense of renting halls, warehouses, office space, equipment, booths, ferries, artist fees, tables, security, and insurance were becoming more difficult to sustain. Caribana was becoming a logistical nightmare and financial burden.

By 1969, the Caribbean Cultural Association–Caribana had incorporated itself as the Caribbean Cultural Committee (CCC). This newly named organization was responsible for running the business of the festival, managing all its aspects. One area stressed by the CCC was "the integrative functions of Caribana within Toronto's various Caribbean communities" (Jackson 1992:133). These functions were contested by at least one segment of the community. The year 1971 saw questions arise in Caribana's role in the community. In the *Contrast* newspaper, The Black Student Union of the University of Toronto criticized the CCC for not doing *enough.* They wrote:

> The organizers undermined any serious effort to articulate grievances of Black people in Toronto. The people who continued to expose Canadian racism in all forms of discrimination in housing, lack of jobs, racism in education and police harassment seemed like the lunatic fringe, when, every August the petite Black bourgeoisie put on their show for white people. (Jackson 1992:133)

Part of the frustration of the Black Student Union had to do with the fact that the CCC did not make good on their promise to build a community center. The students felt that the CCC could do *better.* They were concerned that the CCC did not have a political focus and that too much emphasis was put on the "dance" and "not the struggle."

By 1972, there was a dramatic change in the way Caribana was celebrated. In a few years the event had become increasingly politicized. Some of the organizational difficulties of the early years had led to the defection of some members. For analytical purposes, this period was characterized by the struggle to take control of the production of Caribana. This struggle was mainly internal, as organizational members became increasingly dissatisfied with the festival's direction. But, as the Black Student Union noted, talk of division and difference is always implicated within a larger set of social circumstances. During the 1970s, the future of Caribana was in trouble. Financial difficulties had forced the committee to appeal to governments for help. However, governments were reluctant to offer assistance. Another issue was brewing in addition to these fiscal concerns. This problem was taking place inside the organization over the meaning of Caribana and how it was celebrated.

By 1972, questions of race and class had emerged within the debates of what Caribana was all about. These debates were fractured along lines of ethnicity and Caribbean nationhood. Some members within the community were dissatisfied with strong Trinidadian influences in the festival, as Trinidadians assumed the right to control production. They claimed ownership: "We're born into it. It's our blood" was a common position. This put the non-Trinidadians in an uneasy position. As a result, two rival organizations emerged: the Carnival Development Association (CDA) and the Caribbean Cultural Committee (CCC), with each group fighting for control. Their split largely had to do with trying to express a West Indian Carnival that spoke to the "Canadian experience." By this I refer to the different ways in which *Canadian* may be conceptualized. It is worth quoting at length Frank Manning's discussion of this split:

> The non-Trinidadians therefore insisted that the name Caribana was meant to indicate a distinctive type of festival in which Carnival items—chiefly street masquerading, calypso shows, and steel band music—were only one component. The festival as a whole was to have pan-Caribbean scope and significance, and an overall emphasis on black racial identity. They sought to broaden Caribana as much as possible, introducing ferry cruises, fashion shows, picnics, art and craft exhibits, dramatic presentations, group singing and dance performances, merchandising displays, beauty contests, dance balls and various other social and entertainment events that had little or no direct connection with the Carnival genre. (Manning 1983:189)

This was the *idea of Carnival* that the CCC was producing, and it was an attempt to articulate the Canadian experience by grafting onto traditional notions of Carnival other experiences. This process created tension. The CDA formed their own ideas of what Caribana should celebrate. Again a lengthy description offered by Manning is helpful in gauging the response by the Trinidadians, who were more closely associated with the "authentic" and "real" Carnival:

> The Trinidadians formed the Carnival Development Association, which ran what it called Carnival Extravaganza. This included the masquerade parade, a contest for king and queen of the masquerade bands, the display of prizewinning costumes from the Trinidad Carnival, a children's Carnival, and a number of dances featuring calypso music played by steel or brass bands and highlighted by top name calypsonians from Trinidad. Events were promoted in the Trinidadian argot. Dances, for example, were announced as "jump ups," and the public encouraged to "jump," "jam," "wail," and "wine." Appropriating the Trinidad Carnival calendar, the night before the masquerade was termed jouvay, a patois term abbreviating jour overt (daybreak) and referring to the Trinidadian practice of revelling until the sun rises on the night before the first day of Carnival. Similarly, the concluding day of Caribana, like the concluding day of Carnival, was described as "las lap"—an occasion of reckless, unbridled abandon. (Manning 1983:189)

Manning raises the question of islandism and the resulting insularity. He notes that even under conditions of migration and travel Caribbean peoples retain a strong sense of connection with their island countries. This is despite the opportunities for connections that the condition of diaspora creates. In his essay, "Carnival and The West Indian Diaspora," Manning writes: "Jamaica lacks a carnival tradition and has stigmatized that genre by associating it with smaller islands. Jamaicans have had virtually nothing to do with Caribana" (1983:188). However, what we do not hear is that from the beginning Jamaicans were also actively involved in bringing Carnival to Toronto. Founding member Eric Lindsay, a Jamaican, strongly influenced the leadership of early Caribana festivals. Furthermore, poet and journalist Clifton Joseph, in a scathing article, continuously stresses that the idea of Caribana was "pan-Caribbean" from its inception(1996). Manning notes that the virtual neglect of Caribana by the Jamaicans "is dramatized on Caribana weekend when the Jamaican-Canadian Association runs an alternative celebration," marking independence in 1962 (1983:188). Granted that some of Manning's presentation of the differences may lack some of the constructivist nuance found in more recent cultural critiques, his work does hit on key schisms that fueled development of Caribana throughout the 1970s. Manning argued:

> The non-involvement of the Jamaicans left the Caribbean Cultural Committee, organizers of Caribana, to the Trinidadians and those from the smaller eastern Caribbean islands. The Trinidadians, many of them masquerade band leaders, insisted that the festival should preserve the format of the Trinidad Carnival, and that they should have the upper hand in running it. (Manning 1983:188)

Extending Manning's argument is to notice the sense by which a convergence is producing Caribana as something uniquely Canadian. Convergence via the conditions of diaspora immediately troubles the pursuit of tradition. Likewise, convergence casts the maintenance of Caribana as an exercise in difficult preservation: the very idea of Caribana is up for grabs. So, for example, the differences that Manning clearly outlines can be a measure for pointing to new conceptualizations and negotiations of what it might mean to produce and practice the "authentic" and "real" Caribana. Caribana emerges as uniquely Canadian in terms of its cultural conundrums. Thus, the popularly held stereotypes of islandism can be dismantled as more nuanced ideas of difference are worked, such that ethnic closures are subject to the various cultural flows at play within diasporic communities.

Caribana's structural arrangements were also contested. Structuring Caribana has primarily been figured around two broadly construed camps: the *cultural purist* and the *business minded*. There has been much overlap between camps. In service of preservation, both positions compete and propose mergers that ensure the success of the general celebration. Peter Jackson (1992:133) has noted as follows, that the

> Carnival Development Association (CDA) . . . emphasis was on making Caribana into an economically successful event, and the Caribbean Cultural Committee (CCC) . . . vision of the scope of Caribana was more political.

Attempts to ideologically arrest control of Caribana pit the CDA and CCC on opposite sides of what largely was the same debate. Their products were very similar, particularly in the eyes of mainstream observers. Although the CDA's Carnival Extravaganza and the CCC's Caribana Festival displayed similar shows, both groups continued to attack each other. For example, the CCC criticized the CDA for its inability to successfully negotiate with the police to provide sufficient time for the bands to parade (Jackson 1992). In spite of the criticism, each group continued to organize shows. There were competing celebrations, which took place at the Ontario Harbourfront area. The CCC continued to organize the parade of the bands. Each group attempted to put on a good public face, not airing the dirty laundry in public. Each would try to deny that there was a split. Jackson writes that "CDA officials accused the CCC of trying to manipulate the masses, arguing that the success of Caribana was more important than the internal politics of some private little club" (Jackson 1992:133). Despite attempts to keep the rift private, however, public outbursts such as the one above were typical of the way that the groups argued. Their attempts to gain more hold of the idea of Caribana were heavily dictated by their financial capabilities. Each group could only do as much as their financial resources allowed. The financial pots of each had slipped worryingly into the red. Eventually, financial difficulties constrained resources such that for the first time organizers appealed to the Province of Ontario in search of funding to help produce the festival.

In writing about this first appeal, Patrick Shepperd notes that the "situation deteriorated to the extent that in 1974 the chairman Mr. Elmore Daisy, presented to the province a brief" (Shepperd 1984:137). In his briefing note, Elmore Daisy (of the CCC) explained Caribana's financial condition and its organizational split:

> The Caribana festival is our major source of revenue. While we can justifiably claim that the past six Caribana events have been culturally successful, we have been able to realize only minimal amounts of net revenue. The 1970 Extravaganza experiment left us with a deficit of some $16,000, which we have reduced to some $2,500 total indebtedness.
>
> In brief then, net profit from each year's function was barely sufficient to enable the organization to keep functioning on a year-round basis. We therefore, request that you consider favourably this application for a grant of $25,000 in support of general activities and to finance in part our planned community activities on a continuing basis. (Shepperd 1984:138–139)

The province denied the request. However, Daisy and his group were not to be completely shut out. Plans were already underway for the following year's celebration. To secure enough money, Daisy and the other board members "signed personal loan guarantees to obtain the needed funds" (Shepperd 1984: 138–139). Two years later in another funding application, "the province awarded a rival group of Carnival band leaders, called the Carnival Development Association, $20,000 to stage a Carnival parade scheduled for Caribana week" (Shepperd 1984:138–139). Government has always had an interest in Caribana. Or as Charles Roach told me, anywhere in the world where there are two or more Trinidadians, there will be some kind of Carnival, as long as government wants it. Government interests have shifted along a continuum of vested interest and passive acknowledgment. In this example, the decisions by the provincial government significantly dictated and set the terms of Caribana's celebration. Not only do groups like the CDA and CCC exert pressure on each another, but they are also subject to the disciplining power of the government of Ontario. The government's decision to grant one group money and not the other put the festival in jeopardy and effectively controlled the interest of both groups. Referencing the exercise of power in terms of cultural products becoming part of an ideology for projects such as multiculturalism, Arjun Appadurai notes that "nation-states do this by exercising taxonomic control over difference by creating various kinds of spectacle to domesticate difference. . . . By seducing small groups," Appadurai further claims "that with the fantasy of self-display on some sort of cosmopolitan stage nations more easily regulate difference" (1990:13).

From 1976 to1981, Caribana continuously came up against financial and imagined cultural limits. Patrick Shepperd notes how the "essence and spirit of carnival" were gone and the "impact of colour" suffered (Shepperd 1984). Peter Jackson indicates that by 1977 the question of island insularity had resurfaced and despite claims for a "real West Indian carnival," the "very foundation of the Caribana organization" was in question (*Contrast* August 3:1978, as quoted in Jackson 1992). Furthermore, Jackson tells us that still in 1978 there were "seriously unresolved conflicts." These kinds of tensions produced lackluster celebrations. Caribana was increasingly becoming a bothersome disappointment. It was not until 1980 that the CDA and CCC ended their split. It finally became apparent that both groups were working toward similar goals. A *united* effort was far more productive in terms of addressing the pressures exerted by the government and, increasingly, the police. "The rift," writes Manning, "had seriously eroded the efforts of both groups and . . . neither the West Indian population nor the city of Toronto were willing to support two competing festivals" (Manning 1983:193). Caribana had survived a rocky period in its development, but at much expense. It suffered from poor shows, largely due to lack of money and threatened walkouts by bandleaders. It was subject to the plague of islandism, as cries of "Small Island thing" and "Small Island men" were announced to ridicule Caribana as just some little pretty show.

The 1970s are a crucial era because virtually every financial and cultural threshold that contemporary Caribana currently experiences was first brought to light in the years between 1972 and 1980. But this period also begins the process of Caribana's institutionalization as an imagined pillar of community politics. Encapsulating successes and failures, the 1970s bore witness to the institutionalization of Caribbean culture in the city of Toronto. For example, Caribana is always held the first holiday long weekend in August, which Ontario residents more popularly know as Lord John Graves Simcoe Day, celebrating the first Lieutenant Governor General of Upper Canada who had ruled in 1791. However, during the 1970s the desire to produce "bigger and better" celebrations mounted as the beginnings of Caribana became more closely associated with the August long weekend than was Simcoe Day. Institutionally, Caribana became a foil whereby black and Caribbean Canadians debated issues of the day. Caribana became more than just a "once a year thing." Its politics stretched far beyond its performances.

Caribana's emergence as a sounding board for the politics of race, racism, and other discriminatory practices meant vetting these discussions in a manner that challenged the accent on "fun and entertainment." Specifically, it entailed pushing the advent on fun in favor of a Pan-African discourse that achieved what Caribana founder Charles Roach described to me as an agenda of "ethnocentric economics." However, Roach's desire for an inwardly focused economics was forced off the agenda somewhat during the 1980s as Caribana confronted the racialization and criminalization of its parade. Contesting representations by mainstream media became the CCC's principal public relations task between 1980 and 1988 as confrontations between black male youths and Toronto police served to hype Caribana as a haven for criminal activity.

CONTEMPORARY CARIBANA: A CLASH OF CULTURAL STYLES

Visitors to Caribana's more recent celebrations, particularly those of the 1990s, have witnessed an increasingly divided parade that features two distinct kinds of music. On the one hand, spectators and masqueraders will be familiar with the traditional sounds of calypso, soca, and steelpan, which make up the majority portion of the celebration. On the other hand, rap music and Hip-Hop cultural influences are fast becoming a minority influence that is difficult for festival organizers, participants, and spectators to ignore. Throughout the 1990s, Caribana celebrations were marked by debates about these two musical styles that focus on culture and cultural representations. Emerging from these debates are two broad ways of speaking about Caribana.

The first discourse is familiar and accepted as official by organizers, members, and sponsors as it resonates with many aspects of official multiculturalism. It is about Caribana the "real" and "authentic" Carnival. This discourse showcases and discusses Caribana as a "real" example of Trinidadian Carnival; moreover, it features representations of symbols traditional to Carnival such as calypso and masquerading and associated competitions. This notion of Caribana is readily attached to its financial benefit and reward through ideas about multiculturalism. Caribana is deeply tied to Ontario's tourist industry in this discourse. Ideas about sponsorship for multicultural arts in Canada are in collusion with ideas of the authentic and items construed as indigenous. Caribana "the real" becomes more attractive and valuable than Caribana "the other," as it is captured in the second discourse.

This other way of speaking about Caribana highlights the subversion of authentic and real performances of Carnival by alternative cultural influences. Its discourse draws strength and legitimacy around the hybridization and creolization of meaning within Caribana. By signaling the ways in which the performance has always been about hybridized form, ambivalence, and irony, rather than about certainty and essential ways of participating, Caribana, in this discourse, emerges as a mixed celebration constituted in and through prolonged intercultural movements. Here rap music and Hip-Hop culture can be grafted and blended with traditional celebration not as a denial of roots but as a recomposition of them. In this way, Caribana becomes less an exercise in locating the real than it does in recognizing the complexity shaping the performance. I suggest that rap and Hip-Hop are imagined as more than supplemental to the real Carnival but rather are part of the cultural text used to get to something retained as part of Caribana. The nature of participation filters through different, yet familiar, sets of references. For some black youth Caribana 1997 was being translated through Hip-Hop culture not simply as a contravention of the norm. In fact, what I demonstrate here raises questions about the moves that appear to pose little, if any trouble at all, for the black youth who participate (un)comfortably between old and new ways of playing Caribana.

What is critical about this other discourse is that those who lament and condemn Hip-Hop cultural forms and practices within Caribana must recognize and come to terms with them as something produced inside blackness and marking a terrain of diasporic complexity. This is to say that Hip-Hop culture, despite its global dimensions, is transported and translated along lines of black urban culture. And given the attachments that scholars of Hip-Hop studies, such as Tricia Rose (1994), offer with regard to the role of the transportation of Caribbean sound system culture to metropolitan New York in the early 1970s, eagerly dismissing Hip-Hop's Caribbean roots is not easily achieved. These two ways of thinking about the politics of Caribana identity characterized the 1997 parade. I want to share with you my experience of Puff Daddy "Jamming de Lakeshore," and the particular way I see black youth challenging the predominant sense of Caribana and blackness by taking up contested subject positions.

How It Go Look? Rap Music Meets Calypso

I enjoyed the parade. I did not have definite plans to meet the youths I was "kickin' it" with, but many of us had said we would "check out" the Caribana fete at the St. Lawrence market on Front Street. Going to at least one Caribana weekend "Jam" was just as, if not more, important than attending the parade for some of the youths I was around. Attending any of these dance clubs, like Infinity, Studio 69, Fluid, the Colony Hotel, the King Street Hotel, or parties hosted by the Soca Boyz, Dr. Jay "de soca prince," DJ Rhiyad, Baby Blue, or the All-American boyz requires enormous patience if one expects to "reach inside the dance." It was explained to me that in spite of the enjoyment of going to a dance, often the high prices charged by promoters eager to stuff the venue, sometimes Cdn $35 or Cdn $40 at the door, was enough to send people home or at least to congregate in the parking lot. Spurred on by the lure of doing more research, I packed a small writing pad in my back pocket and headed for the subway and eventually for the Lakeshore. As in my other Caribana experiences, the buses were densely packed with black bodies, an otherwise infrequent occurrence for Toronto's Transit System. The sounds of blackness were all around me. By this I mean black Canadian youth were slipping in out of Caribbean, American, and Canadian speech patterns.

Two black women next to me were "cussing each other off," in Trinidadian patois peppered with black American Hip-Hop slang. They were intensely discussing the differences between Bajan and Trinidadian calypso between sips of their champagne cola. They were intent on "jumping up" at the parade, but as one woman put it, the parade "is only a prelude, Atlantis is the lick" (Atlantis is a massive nightclub partly projecting over the Toronto Lakeshore with a revolving dance floor). This was an interesting moment for me because it highlighted a series of cultural signs in the way these black women were "getting on." Exchanges like this mark for me the way some black youth move between and within cultures. Their oratorical switching and sliding between Caribbean patois (one woman blasted the other for talking too much brango [gossip]) and black American slang was an invitation for me to think about the possibility of reading Caribana through the lenses of hybridity. And also as an encounter and interruption of the dominant discourses of Carnival and to figure the place of U.S. blackness.

Much of what I'm suggesting above is in light of Toronto rapper Kardinal Offishal's release of a song called *BaKardi Slang.* Brandi Costain (2002) writes "BaKardi slang . . . compares American slang developed in African American communities in cities such as New York and Chicago, with that of T-dot slang.[3] The result is an amusing but sophisticated single about Toronto's unique lingo and its Jamaican/Caribbean cultural influences." My concern with *BaKardi Slang* is not to expand Costain's sense of "Toronto's unique lingo," but rather to borrow from its comparative structure in support of this chapter's discussion of the relationship between Hip-Hop and Caribana. *Bakardi Slang* may be an instance of what Rinaldo Walcott, writing in *Rude: Black Canadian Contemporary Culture* (2001). references as "Black Canadian creole utterances." Walcott arrives at his point through a sense of the diasporic crossings, which shape Toronto contexts as a cosmopolitan and global city. In the verse that follows, Kardinal uses a dualistic structure that positions black Canadian urban vernacular as a creolization and response to what is essentially constituted as a product of U.S. slang:

> We don't say, "You know what I'm sayin'."
> T-dot says, "Ya dun know."
> We don't say "Hey that's the breaks."
> We say, "Yo, a so it go."
> We don't say, "You get one chance."
> We say, "You better rip the show."
> Before bottles start flyin' and
> You runnin' for the door.
> Y'all talking about Cuttin' and hittin' skins.
> We talkin' bout "beat dat face."

For another example, readers may be familiar with Trinidadian calypsonian Ronnie McIntosh. In 1998, he released a hot calypso called "How it go look?" on VP Records. The song is a brilliant social commentary spiced with the humor, jokes, and put-downs of a skilled calypsonian. In a series of vignettes describing sexual relations, masquerade and dancehall politics, masculine bravado, cooking and social relations, McIntosh asked his listeners to "mind their ways" and think about "how it go look." McIntosh focused his attention on Caribana in the following verse, making light ridicule yet all the while offering serious social satire.

> Ah pack my bags heading for Caribana,
> 'cuz ah hear down in Toronto have Carnival,
> now I going down on de Lakeshore looking for mas,
> but ah only hearing hip-hop / Ah can't hear brass / How it go look?

McIntosh's verse is interesting because it demonstrates the knowledge of Caribana that globally circulates. Decoding this verse is to encounter a perception about Caribana 1997 that traveled among the world's Carnival enthusiasts. McIntosh's verse captures the sense of travel and evokes notions of diaspora that point to the historical relationship Caribana holds to Caribbean Carnival, primarily to Trinidadian mas. What is it that McIntosh expects to meet in Toronto Caribana as he "packs his bags"? As the next line goes, McIntosh is hearing that "Toronto have Carnival." This line demonstrates further Caribana's stature as a worthwhile and important destination in the development of Carnival art forms out of the Caribbean region. It also puts into play certain logic about what a traveler ought to expect but differently encounters at Caribana. In "looking for mas," as the third line of the verse states, McIntosh prepares us for his pay-off by referencing a two-tiered structure of Caribana. "Looking for mas," a perception read as falling within the traditionalist camp ends in disappointments because Hip-Hop has split Caribana from what ought and should exist as real masquerade. Because the expectation, as interpreted in the overall logic of the verse, is a satire favoring authentic Carnival Trinidad-style and Caribana's attempts to replicate the model, disappointment is preordained. McIntosh communicates a sense of the split in terms of a musical disruption whereby brass, a stand-in for traditional calypso music, is subverted and eclipsed by Hip-Hop. In terms of the ascendancy of the latter, in 1997, the song's hook is applied: How it go look? Hip-Hop in this verse is treated as an anathema and is consequently framed in opposition to real Carnival. The song is suggestive of many questions that can be asked of Caribana.

How will it look to others making a similar journey to McIntosh's? How will the international tourist interpret the diminished presence of brass? *How it go look* is a gem phrase because it gets to the issue of perception, which was firmly on the mind of Henry Gomez, chair of the Caribana Cultural Committee in 1997 when he made this statement just a few short weeks ahead of the parade: "If indeed American music dominates this year's event, the CCC will be forced to limit the inclusion of hip-hop, rap and R & B floats in the future" (Sharrif 1997).

The measures, which Gomez gestures toward, that will limit the presence of Hip-Hop in Caribana are in service of protecting and shoring up aspirations of purism. Protecting pursuits for pure depictions of Caribana becomes an institutional issue for Gomez. He suggests that given the potential of American music overriding the normalized sound, then a suitable recourse is for the CCC to mandate rap and Hip-Hop out of the parade. Institutional techniques of this kind are further flirted with, as in the next example: "The CCC can certainly stipulate a limit to the number of hip-hop bands on a first-come, first-served basis" (Sharrif 1997).

Timeliness aside, youths competed to get in bands primarily playing Hip-Hop. In my experience of CCC membership meetings in 1997, this idea for managing the amount of Hip-Hop acts received little serious consideration. Seeking to regain a more suitable level of control over the content of the parade purely as a quantitative exercise contributed little to addressing the qualitative issue of the absence of pomp and flair supplied by the traditional bandleaders (masmen and women boycotted the 1997 parade).[4] And as long-time Caribana advocate and past president Lennox Farrell states, "there's never been a hard-and-fast rule as long as what you bring in can be identified as Carnival" (Sharrif 1997). Yet, while Farrell concedes that historically Caribana has operated without explicit rules describing the look of a band, there remain what he suggests are tacit agreements. These implied agreements have provided the scope of Caribana in terms of a desire to replicate its parent. However, because of the planned boycott of the festival by established bandleaders who typically supply a traditional masquerade, the issue of legislated institutional constraints, rather than tacit agreements, was promoted as a better guarantee against potential incursion.

Ali Sharrif, a journalist writing for Toronto's *Now Magazine* the week of July 31 to August 6, 1997, demonstrates the effects of McIntosh's insistence on "How it go look?" Sharrif writes about the change and the continuities that Hip-Hop ushers and problematizes. Sharrif's article entitled "Calypso Hangs on by a Thread as New Rhythms and Hard Times Hit Caribana" operates along the lines I suggested in the above reading of Ronnie McIntosh's hit song, "How It Go Look." Sharrif's article is useful because it touches on a number of issues that operate along the tiered structure that set the terms for Caribana 1997. Essentially, what Sharrif describes are the tensions produced by the presence of two competing ways of performing Caribana within a single event. Significantly, he also documents the way in which the United States is implicated in the discourse of the "other" Caribana.

Rap and Hip-Hop culture in Sharrif's argument is figured as a specifically U.S. entity, one that exploited an economically embattled Caribana 1997 for capital gains. Promoting celebrity rap artists and their albums, U.S. record companies are cast as beneficiaries with regard to the economic fallout and its subsequent consequence for the demise of Caribana tradition. All of this was made possible because Caribana 1997 underwent rapid, eleventh-hour unplanned changes as part of an attempt to manage the economic risk and the CCC's mandated commitment to produce the celebration. Without the traditional sounds of calypso and soca, "star-studded flatbed trucks featuring a cast of top American hip-hop and rap artists" headlined the parade. In the extract that follows, Sharrif indicates that for the first time in Caribana's history traditional music "may be eclipsed" overwhelmed by rap and Hip-Hop.

> In the lineup of the 20 bands listed for the parade, only 11 will feature some form of costumed mas band. The major attraction in this year's parade may well turn out to be the number-one hip-hop star in the U.S., Sean "Puffy" Combs, a.k.a. Puff Daddy, who is on the cover of the current issue of *Rolling Stone.* The magazine dubs Combs "the new king of hip-hop." In addition to Combs, another flatbed truck will feature Luther Campbell, formerly of the controversial 2Live Crew, a Florida rap group who made themselves memorable by offending the politically correct with raw lyrics. And the American celebrities taking part in this year's parade are introducing an element of commercialism that Caribana has, in the past, managed to keep at arm's length. Campbell comes here to promote his solo career following the breakup of 2Live Crew. And similarly, Combs comes to the parade to sell his new album, *No Way Out.* "He's bringing everyone that took part in his new album, and they will all perform his new stuff on a float," says Sol Guy, head of hip-hop marketing for the Canadian subsidiary of BMG, the giant American music label that's sponsoring his trip to Toronto.
>
> The fact that record companies are putting money down to pay for floats is new, but there are no CCC rules to prevent anyone who can afford to rent a

> truck and put more than 50 band members on the road from participating in the parade. "There's never been a hard-and-fast rule as long as what you bring in can be identified as Carnival," says Lennox Farrell, Toronto teacher and former chairperson of the CCC. The American celebrity presence at the parade is sure to excite the younger generation of hip-hop and rap lovers in Toronto, who will stream out to this year's parade not to sway to the sounds of the amateur calypso and soca bands but to gawk and dance to the hip-hop rhythms.
>
> "I expect the quality of the bands will diminish," says dub-poet-at-large Clifton Joseph. "And it is pretty embarrassing, actually, for the 30th anniversary of Caribana for them (the CCC) to have probably the worst Caribana in terms of the splendour and the spectacle."

The interesting issues here are the notions that culture, as Caribana traditionally imagines it, can be guaranteed and economically preserved through proper funding. Short of this, guarantees disappear with the emergence of Carib-ana as "the other." Elaborating on this topic, Sharrif writes:

> Chris Celestine, a Toronto music promoter whose truck will feature Skywalker and a leading American actor from the television series *New York Undercover*, agrees. He says the problem can be solved by forcing the bands featuring American artists to play calypso in between the rap and hip-hop. He says people on his truck will play a few minutes of calypso to accompany the lyrics of Skywalker. "That's all they can do, because you just can't stop hip-hop from influencing Caribana," Celestine says. "The younger generation wants hip-hop."

The sense that resolving Caribana's economic pitfalls will solve and prevent its cultural shifts is further confirmed by an international think-tank of Caribbean Carnivals. This example also appeared in Sharrif's article:

> The real problem we have is mainly economic, and if the economics can be addressed then other problems can easily be solved," says Henry Antoine, president of the International Caribbean Carnival Association, an umbrella body of Carnivals spanning the two continents of the Americas.

However, contesting Antoine's trust in the ability of economic guarantees to control the problems is Charles Roach's conciliatory view of cultural shifts despite the crucial role that funding and sponsorship hold. It is significant that Sharrif uses Roach to explain the change that rap and Hip-Hop represents given that Roach is a noted Caribana founder. Quoting Roach, Sharrif notes the following:

> "When you have stronger trends like rap and so on at the parade, that's to be expected," says Charles Roach, the Toronto lawyer and activist who was involved in shaping Caribana when it started in 1967. "This is a unifying force, and everything is going to be thrown in there, and eventually new forms of music will come out.

Lennox Farrell confirms that managing the risk of alternative music entering the parade has never been a clear process. The rule of fifty band members accompanied by a rented truck is not set up as a deterrent. These minimum criteria are easily attained. Instead of providing the guarantees that Gomez suggested would be needed if the "American celebrity presence" did take over the festival, it the rule conceptually allows that opposite and implicitly invites greater heterogeneity and wider interpretations of Caribana play. The rule of fifty plus a truck works in reverse and is tenuous at best. It does not stamp the authenticity that Gomez desires; nor does it protect tradition. And it certainly does not dissuade or admonish would-be alternatives. Rather, the strength of the "rule" is its appeal for re-negotiating meanings of emergent forms of Caribana play and participation. Thus, drawn from Sharrif's account of the relationship between Hip-Hop and Caribana in 1997 is the way in which U.S. record companies are seen to exploit the softness of the rule. Financially these record companies easily acquire a flatbed truck. And based upon crew members and requisite entourages, which BMG representative Sol Guy hints at, these companies also attain the necessary fifty members.

In the extracts above, the role given to U.S. record companies is one of a challenger to the Caribana tradition. But this is not the end of Sharrif's position. The interesting twist is an example that shows how U.S. record companies financially support a group of Toronto youth that wanted to bring a band to Caribana 1997 but could not secure Canadian funding after many appeals to local corporations for support. The example that follows is useful because it shifts issues away from the celebrity status of Caribana 1997 toward that of understanding the everyday issues of ordinary black youth desiring to play Caribana but struggling to find funding to get the fifty plus a truck. In locating the "new forms" that are "involved in shaping Caribana," Sharrif shows that

> [I]n some ways, the American presence has been good for some of the local bands in the parade, like the group of 150 university, college and high school students who, under the banner of the Black Students Association, have entered to bring a message of hope to their peers. The students will deck themselves in graduation gowns to spread the message of staying in school. Had it not been for American music industry sponsorship of their float, they would never have had a chance to participate in Caribana this year.
>
> Keidi Ann Graham, spokesperson for the group, says the students contacted about 34 educational institutions in Ontario and as many as 24 corporate organizations for sponsorship, but they were turned down each time. "They more or less told us that they didn't want to be part of Caribana," Graham says. Having no luck with the Canadian corporate world, the students turned their attention to the United States. The association sent delegates to a conference of American musicians taking place earlier last month in

> South Beach, Miami. There they found hip-hop artists to sponsor them for the parade.

Although Sharrif does not do much with this example to expand possible meanings for the role that U.S. record companies offer in fulfilling the desires of some black youth to participate in Caribana, he nevertheless points toward an important reordering of a stronger sense of opportunistic and harmful U.S. commercialism that popularly explains the 1997 celebration. It is quite understandable why less, as Colin Rickards shows below, might be said of the ordinary and not the celebrity components of U.S. record company involvement in Caribana, because developing a stronger counter argument to the celebrity status must on some level deny agency to those youth actively seeking a financial way into Caribana. This means that the celebrity discourse of U.S. commercialism is the only allowable interpretation of the role contributed by record companies. Furthermore, this discourse stipulates that black youth were negatively acted upon and directed into particular forms of play. Paying greater attention to the discourse of the ordinary aspects of U.S. record company involvement demonstrates the way in which black youth sought and initiated the support to act upon their desires. The difference is crucial because it locates reordering and shifting meanings inside Caribana 1997 rather than as strict external occurrences. Acknowledging a shift in perspective makes this a useful and promising example for understanding the disciplinary response developed by Colin Rickards in his critique of Caribana 1997.

1997: CARIBANA IS IT DEAD?

In the days immediately following the end of Caribana 1997, a senior columnist for *Pride,* a Toronto black Caribbean newspaper wrote:

> When veteran band leader and mas' player Errol Achue warned the Caribbean Cultural Committee that holding the Caribana Parade without the boycotting bandleaders would make for changes he certainly knew whereof he spoke. For 29 years, the annual Caribana Parade was a joy to behold: A riot of colour, an explosion of creativity in costume design, a delight to the ear, with a festival of Calypso, Soca and steelband—and latterly, a bit of Reggae, too—a joyous, sweaty, exuberant family occasion. Last Saturday, as monster trucks ground along Lakeshore West—their flatbeds loaded with blasting, bass-heavy, almost unintelligible sounds and massive amplification—it was clear that the Caribana Parade, as fans knew and loved it, was a thing of the past. Gone was the West Indian verve and energy, the Caribbean zest for life. Instead, North American Rap—some of it Gangsta—and Hip Hop, by the hour. Instead of the cut and thrust of Calypso, standing on the grass near the concession stands, I heard lyrics about "Niggas" and "bitches" and "hos." Hold

> it. There's something wrong with all this. The Caribana Parade is supposed to be a family occasion. . . . The Committee will have to determine whether the public wants their old Caribana Parade back—or whether North America's largest street festival is going to now become a "Rap and Hip Hop convention down on Lakeshore." (Rickards 1997)

In this account, Rickards celebrates what he believed Caribana once was: "a riot of colour, an explosion of creativity," "a festival of calypso, soca and steelband," which with a "bit of reggae too" made for "a joyous, sweaty, exuberant family occasion." But then the writer laments what it has become: North American rap, Hip-Hop "by the hour" with the lyrics of "niggas, bitches and hos." Caribana 1997, in this account, is no longer an "exuberant family occasion." It strayed from its roots because of the participation of superstar rapper Puff Daddy, otherwise known as P-Diddy or Sean Combs. It was Puff Daddy's participation, which for many was an overwhelming statement on how Caribana had changed.

I remember watching Puff Daddy as he performed his then-latest hit, "The Benjamins," on top of the cab portion of a flatbed truck, wearing his trademark white tank top, diamond-studded crucifix, and wrist watch. I wondered if he felt awkward performing between two traditional Caribana bands. How it go look? As it was, his float, called "Crush," which was supported by WBLK, the black American radio station in Buffalo, New York, and local Toronto urban music producers, all but drowned out the Panatics pan players in front of him and the mas band behind him. He was nestled between two long-time Caribana participants, and he was an unusual newcomer who for some was 180 degrees outside Caribana's imagined tradition. McIntosh's question is important because the "look" or the visual is often the most disturbing, particularly so when one considers the time bandleaders spend constructing prize-winning king and queen costumes. The look is essential in this sense. But the Puff Daddy Crush float did not resemble Carnival. It did not dazzle with spectacular color, nor did it feature above-the-shoulder costumes (a development in mas-making that some Tor-onto designers attribute to the spaciousness of playing mas on the Lakeshore). It simply featured Puff Daddy as the emcee, surrounded by his bodyguards, crew members, and some local Toronto celebrities. Neither the Panatics players nor the masquerade were instrumental in the way the young people around me were celebrating Caribana. They barely heard the brass as suggested in McIntosh's verse. For them, the attraction was not the sounds of steelpan or the glamour of the Kings and Queens; rather, it was the opportunity to see Puff Daddy perform.

I found a spot on the parade route between police officers on horseback and a man hustling tee-shirts, hats, necklaces, and food. It was a crowded spot, and some of the overanxious youth had begun worrying that they had arrived too late and missed the Crush. Others were disappointed that his scheduled concert the previous Friday night had been canceled. As I listened, I was soon co-opted as a salesperson for the tee-shirt guy. I wondered to myself whether or not these young people found the small bits of calypso and soca disappointing. They did not jump and wave when the "Faces of the D' Americas" band passed. They clearly had their minds set on Puff Daddy and not, as it appeared, on aspects of the traditional Saturday parade. However, they did not have to wait for the Crush float to hear or even see Puff Daddy. Other floats playing urban music featured images of Puff Daddy and played his jams. There was a noticeable hysteria each time the deejay mixed in a Puff Daddy or Notorious B.I.G. beat. I noticed how the deejays were chatting over break-beat records to promote their dances and vibe with the crowd. The really skillful deejays were able to tease the crowd by spinning enough of the song but pulling back the instant the heavy bass lines were ready to drop. The teasing would continue for about three or four times and then finally the record would drop, "yuh wanna be a baller, shot caller." These kinds of bands earned the loudest cheers from the youths. The other bands passed relatively unnoticed, as much as could be possible in a Carnival environment. Even old school Hip-Hoppers, like myself and the tee-shirt guy, were jamming as the deejays mixed 1990 hits with the banging joints from the mid-1980s.

Sponsorship, advertising, and commercialization have long been an aspect of Caribana play. However, the image of a blinged-out Puff Daddy and his crew members flinging CD singles into the crowd must be treated and measured against insidious marks of commercialization. One mark closes in around Caribana and measures U.S. cultural flows as overbearing and as a threat that upsets the traditional logic of the celebration. However, as a spectator and sometimes reluctant participant in the show, one is hard-pressed not to consider the power in the music business that Puff Daddy, now P-Diddy, commanded and the way this overshadowed all the 1997 bandleaders. Bearing this in mind, harsh sentiments about the ill effects of perceived U.S. cultural imperialism in the form of the "Bad Boy" Family Record label taking over Caribana, congealed around an objectified Puff Daddy. Thus, a fallout of Caribana 1997 was a re-invigorated sense of an ever-present U.S. cultural machine forcing rap and Hip-Hop culture onto Caribana. The sense by which this sentiment is communicated to Caribana enthusiasts comes through in editorials found in local Caribbean newspapers such as *Share, Pride,* and the *Caribbean Camera.*

The parallel in this sentiment about perceived U.S. cultural aggression is eerily familiar in another context. The similarity here is to the continuation of metaphors of Caribbean nation-state politics present in the pejorative rhetoric of Small and Big Island peoples. The identity politics that these metaphors evoke are returned as a parallel that works to sharply close borders along issues broadly construed as representatively Canadian or American. However, the piece of the issue that most clouds one-way perceptions of U.S. cultural might is the way that local, at home, disruptions are totally ignored. Missing from the issue is the bulk of local rap and reggae sound crews who deejayed and played mas long before Puff Daddy. These local crews, including Black Supreme, Black Reaction and the Ebony Sound Crew, brought their sound systems and played Hip-Hop and dancehall reggae music. Like Puff Daddy in 1997, Black Reaction, for example, did not play costumed mas. There were no Kings/Queens/Individuals or sectioned masqueraders. Rather, like Puff Daddy, these Hip-Hop and reggae sound crews played atop a flatbed truck typically lined with flags of the Caribbean and promotional sound system banners. The flatbeds usually carried some of Toronto's finest black male and female celebrities drawn from dancehalls, clubs, and local court and street basketball lore.

For example, these Hip-Hop and dancehall reggae deejays would call out for the crowd to respond with a scream here and a chant of "ho" there. They would also ask the crowd a familiar Hip-Hop question such as, "Where my West Side peoples at, Mississauga, Brampton, Malton, where you at?" or one of its competing questions, "Are they any East Side heads in the house, Scarborough, 416 where you at, Jane/Finch show your love?" How strange, I thought, for deejays to be asking which side these black youth represented. Did it really matter for Caribana if they were from the east side or west side of metropolitan Toronto? The issue of Hip-Hop sides representin' and showin' love for T-dot subverts the more familiar calls during Caribana for Dominicans, Antiguans, Kittians, and Lucians, among others, to show national affiliations. The interesting issue, of course, is that either call does not openly preclude those assumed to be more active participants in the acrimoniously named "Rapabana" from identifying with traditional Caribana. My point is simply to cast doubt that it can be known ahead of time where participation, particularly in terms of desires and yearning, will reside. Participation in terms of a traditionalist discourse, which for the most part remains Caribana's strongest voice, may demand and tolerate less movement between forms of play. This is not to suggest that ambivalence is a tendency present only in this "other" discourse of Caribana. But I frame the issue generally so as to further question the assumption that black youth regaling Puff-Daddy were not the same persons jumping with the Return of the Dread I mas featuring the AfroPan Steel Band. Both discourses run together. The more traditional deejays were asking a very different question. They wanted to know where the Trinis, Grenadians, Bajans, Guyanese, and Jamaicans were. Responding to the question was to gather round and get something and wave like your flag. This was not so with the Hip-Hop deejays. Instead of a flag, black youths responded with an emphatic fist or by "raising the roof' (two flat hands palms open extended above the shoulder in an action resembling pressing a heavy object.) But what does the flag symbolize that "raising the roof" might not?

Reaction against the Puff Daddy performance was fierce. I followed the debates on the official Caribana Web site. This message board was an important site for contesting the representation of Caribana. Many volatile reactions were posted; interestingly, some of the more abrasive comments were removed. One person wrote:

> It was a real shame to see such few trucks and floats and the majority that performed were rap acts. We are not crazy about rap we will admit but to see rap performers as a main attraction instead of Caribbean bands defeats the purpose of going to Caribana. (Caribana website 1997)

Another said:

> I go to Caribana to see my country represented, as most others do. Please, Please, do not let hip-hop take over a great event like Caribana. (Ibid.)

And speaking about expectations, another person wrote:

> My wife and I come to Caribana to see the costumes and hear the music of the islands. If we want hip-hop we can get that at home. I realize these people invested their money to keep Caribana running, but if necessary, I'll go to islands to get the real thing. (Ibid.)

But others spoke differently:

> As far as Caribana goes it was my first, and I don't know what all the controversy was about. Whether you're an American or a Canadian doesn't matter. How we choose to celebrate be it Carnival, reggae, hip-hop, soca is not an issue, as long as we can all come together share, enjoy, converse and keep it on a positive tip we have done a good thing. (Ibid.)

"Carnival," as Philip Kasinitz (1992) noted, "refuses to speak with one voice: the mass participatory nature of the event both attracts and frustrates those who seek to make of it a political statement."

IS ONLY HIP-HOP: RAPPING ON THE LAKESHORE

Referring to the parade as "Ameribana" served to diminish the contribution of Hip-Hop music by black Canadian youths. Beat Factory records, a rising local record company in the urban music industry entered a band into the parade along the lines of the Puff Daddy float. In 1997, this record company was enjoying local success from their CD releases of *Rap Essentials* volumes one and two. Coupled with the rising stars of Toronto rappers Saukrates, Choclair, Ghetto Concept, Thrust, Red Life, Dan-E-O, Kardinal Offishal, and West Coast Vancouver crew the Rascalz, has been Beat Factory Records' support for the "northern touches" of Canadian Hip-Hop.[5] The Toronto rap scene for the most part has an ambivalent relationship with the Caribana parade and its organizers. This is despite the promotion of Los Angeles rapper Ice-T and New York lyricists Kool Moe Dee back in 1990. Caribana organizers attempted to include these two rap stars as part of a "music of the Americas" concert at the newly erected Skydome entertainment complex, but the idea failed and was scrapped amid a sea of controversy.[6] Since then, Caribana organizers were reluctant to showcase rap music as part of the festival, despite the fleeting attempts to include the title of "best rap" alongside the traditional crown of "best calypso." However, among the new breed of Canadian rappers chipping away at this ambivalence has been local Scarborough suburban rapper, Infinite. His 1997 video was the first, in my memory, to blend images of traditional Caribana with that of Hip-Hop culture (i.e., images of the street, the hood, and the crib). The video featured quick stylistic shots of masqueraders such as Infinite and his crew rapping alongside them wearing a traditional Hip-Hop look of baggy shorts, tank tops and iced-up jewelry (diamond-studded necklaces and wrist watches). Watching this video on MuchMusic ("the nation's music station") was a defining moment for me, as it brought together different constructions of Caribbeanness and blackness that embellished ideas of hybridity, contestation, irony, and ambivalence. The video director's control of images of blackness inside the Carnival with those of the hood speaks to the persistent complexity, slipperiness, and mixture against which identifications and identities are constructed. Reading this video for what it suggests about making diasporic moves supports the opportunity to think more deeply about the way in which black youth regard Carnival in Toronto. The video inscribes the complex ways that Caribana comes into representations of Carnival and blackness. At least in this video Carnival traditions and Hip-Hop culture combine to say something important about the politics of black youth culture in Toronto.

Another example of mixture is found by looking at Toronto rapper Choclair and his relationship, through his record company, to Caribana in 1998 and 1999. In 1998, Choclair became the first Canadian Hip-Hop artist signed to a major U.S. record label. In addition to an aggressive street-marketing campaign and the usual media teasers, Virgin specifically targeted Caribana as niche audiences for his debut CD *Ice Cold,* scheduled for release in 1999. The association that Virgin imagined between Hip-Hop and Caribana was made primarily in terms of the idea of blackness Caribana represented in popular imaginations. This is why "during Caribana '98 for example, Choclair had a float in the parade," which was, "followed by a double-decker bus emblazoned with a banner announcing his debut album was 'coming soon'." Additionally, Virgin created an "impressive web site, with a photo album, online gaming and loads of information" about Choclair. "During the '99 Caribana, they [Virgin Records] tossed out 10,000 freezies emblazoned with 'Choclair.net'." This example shows the way in which rap and Hip-Hop generate associations with Caribana by virtue of the celebration existing within something framed as blackness. Blackness in this example is invoked as the pivotal link that forges relations between Hip-Hop and Caribana. What the Choclair–Virgin Record Company example allows is for the possibility of thinking about expanding ideas of Caribana's involvement within broader notions of Canadian blackness.

Television Tourism and the Consumption of the Real

For the better part of the 1990s, Citytv, Toronto's premier television station for local news, aired post-Caribana recap shows on Channel 7 and more recently on City Pulse Cable 24. The shows highlighted special moments of the parade, often showing behind-the-scenes footage of mas camps, shots of the King and Queen shows, Panorama, and the boat cruises. Harold Hosein, a Citytv employee and six o'clock news meteorologist, was the long-time host, but in 1998–2000, the younger and more hip entertainment correspondent Tracey Melchor took over. Usually the one-hour show aired within two weeks after the end of Caribana. The show was important for two reasons. It gave those unable to attend an opportunity to view Caribana, an important aspect of the public consumption of Caribana. Moreover, many people I spoke with approached this as a viable option given incompatible employment schedules and the growing hysteria due to the sensationalization of crime at Caribana. Second, the show contributed to official Canadian multiculturalism as an example of ethnic folklorism. That is to say, the show contributed to the objectification of the three tenets of Carnival culture and washed clean the subversiveness associated with black youths.

The 1997 recap show was an explicit example of how this rinsing preserved the idea of real Carnival; it did its best to present "Caribana the real" and not "Caribana the other." Most of the footage featured the sprinkling of masquerade bands, steelbands, and calypsonians. It seemed to me that a concerted effort was made to overlook the Puff Daddy performance and instead focus only on elements of real mas. It was a deceptive maneuver meant to write Puff Daddy and the black youth he attracted out of any sensible understanding of Caribana. This was an odd move because all anyone could think about was Hip-Hop, yet Citytv only obliquely referred to it. Their unwillingness to engage in a critique of Hip-Hop, except in a minimal way, silenced, controlled, and disciplined the black youth interested in Puff Daddy. Citytv dismissed black youth as insignificant and erased them from Caribana history in obedience to their "normal" expectations of Carnival. Their marginal discussion publicly confirmed that Hip-Hop can only properly exist on the periphery of Caribana. Citytv's represented traditional and purist strains of the Caribana discourse that sanction and control Hip-Hop and those who enjoy it. This particular Citytv recap show and its depiction of "Caribana" falsely projected Carnival as an easily replicated and an unproblematic event. Citytv shamefully filled in portions of the show by airing footage of masquerade bands from the 1996 parade. Such a projection necessarily closed down moments of black complexity and difference in which Caribana was inscribed and most explicitly displayed by black youth. Moreover, in this instance it presented blackness as uncomplicated and without difference. Like official multiculturalism, the show was not intended to provoke critical conversations about Caribana, and by extension black–Canadian identity. This was quite clear given how marketing, economics, and tourism agreed in determining what counts as useful material for the show.

Much of the exuberant defense of Caribana as simple ethnic folklore is tied to the trinity of marketing, economics, and tourism. Protectionist discourses, such as the above example of Citytv, safeguard true representations of the performance. The sense of ethnic folklore to which Caribana organizers very much play into was toppled by black youth's exuberance for Puff Daddy. I want to use this to point out how ways in which economics, sponsorship, multiculturalism, and the activities of black youth are viewed as undermining this. Since inception, Caribana has struggled to define itself financially. Partially relying on government grants, corporate sponsorship, and special one-time-only loans, the festival has been able to subsist. Underwriting the granting of monies has been a relationship that dictated "ethnic authenticity" and not the "corruption" witnessed during 1997 parade. Historical symbioses exist between Caribana, its corporate sponsors, and the way in which official multiculturalism has been used. Recalling for the moment *Pride*'s view on the "Rapabana," one is reminded of the importance of this relationship by the plea, "the committee will have to decide whether the public wants its old parade back." This plea is an indication that the "old" parade bears financial rewards in several senses, whereas other ways do not. A Caribana that features Hip-Hop did not figure in official definitions of ethnic folklore. As a result, Caribana's historical sponsors withdraw their support.

RECONCILING TRADITIONALISM AND THE SEARCH FOR REPRESENTATIONAL SPACE

Discourses of traditionalism are called upon to stabilize the messiness within contemporary forms of celebrating Caribana. Traditionalism is invoked as a healing agent for problems. An appeal to true Carnival cooperates with the logic of Canadian multiculturalism and its funding arrangements. The assumption is that traditionalism also works at the level of repairing the "problems" related to black youths' desire to exploit the parade as an opportunity for Hip-Hop. Traditionalism, as used in the *Pride* newspaper example, delivers a stern warning and a knock-out blow to any contradictory representations of Caribana. But tradition as it is critiqued here is flawed; it is never that easy. There is always an aspect of the Caribbean diaspora that invokes a more essential than defensive thesis in hopes of containing the syncretic activities of youth (Gilroy 1993; Mercer 1994). I saw this working during the CCC membership meetings I attended. It was my sense that some Caribana folks view their parade as most like the Trinidad Carnival, and that Toronto is thus seen as producing the most Trinidad-like Carnival in North America. There is much pride in this assertion, and maintaining it requires a convincing supporting rhetoric. On two occasions, I was present for grand speechmaking that pinpointed Toronto's uniqueness in continuing the tradition. While this sort of rousing is important for the symbolic and sentimental politics important to Carnival, this chapter has suggested where gaps in the logic of such a rhetoric of traditionalism and verisimilitude might be found and how we can begin to debate seriously the issues about black Canadian identity that Hip-Hop provokes; or to suggest following Hebdige (1987), Hall (1991, 1992), and Gilroy (1996) that there can never be certainty in the overlapping cultural spaces that are fashioned in diaspora. To bring in Paul Gilroy is to say the following:

> Contrasting forms emerge to create new possibilities and new pleasures where dispersed peoples recognize the effects of spatial dislocation as rendering the issue of origin problematic and embrace the possibility that they are no longer what they once were and cannot therefore rewind the tapes of their cultural history. (1996)

But it is the desire to recreate a pristine history without difference and contestation that troubles Caribana purists and against which black youth are reacting. A key ingredient, then, is the reinvention of Trinidad Carnival as unproblematic. But this denies consideration of the ways in which Trinidad's Carnival has changed. The Trinidad Carnival has been changing in ways attributed to North American and other Caribbean influences. Re-presenting tradition without difference in Caribana requires a logic of erasure and manifestations of Carnival as an uncontested space in terms of notions of blackness (Cohen 1982; Manning 1983). Many examples abound, feeding a reconstitution of a pristine Carnival. The following was taken from the official 1997 Caribana website:

> If you enjoyed reggae and rap and R&B, then you don't know what Carnival is; you don't know what Caribana is all about and is supposed to be. Never in my life have I experienced such rubbish under the guise of Carnival. I think some people need to 'take themselves back to their roots' to discover (or rediscover) what is Carnival. (Caribana Web site 1997)

Traditionalism is ordered up and invoked as a stand-in for continuity and used to pathologize the new ways of celebrating pursued by black youth. Dick Hebdige (1987) reminds us that "roots don't stay in one place, they change shape, they grow up . . . there is no such thing as a pure point of origin." It is the slipperiness of identities that troubles the traditionalists the most. At another level, the appeal of traditionalism is not entirely lost on young people. What I am seeing happen is the way traditionalism is a canvas for relational and contextual readings of Caribana. Rather than an outright rejection of Carnival pillars, black youth construct their Carnival performance through the interplay of several themes. Marking the tensions this interplay produces, one person wrote:

> I can't say that the hip-hop portion of the parade was not appropriate. I think it added a little flavour to the parade. But I agree calypso, reggae, and the like should be the primary music focus. (Caribana Web site 1997)

These kinds of moments of feeling inside and outside, Daniel Yon (1995) tells us, demonstrate how discourses marking differences between and within cultures can be encountered in ambiguous and ambivalent ways. Placed at the center of Caribana's 1997 struggle for representational space, black youths effectively opened the question of what it means to play Carnival in Toronto. Whether it was the "Benjamin's" or "jamming de Lakeshore," black youth showed something of both, begging purists to ask, "where was the Carnival?" and to think about "How it go look." Puff Daddy returned to Caribana for the 1999 parade on the heels of another album and promotional tour. But his second round of Carnival was less disruptive. As the only thing that interrupted real mas was the rain, not the Hip-Hop.

NOTES

1. "The Benjamins" was a popular rap song during the summer of 1997 by black U.S. rap musician Puff Daddy. I understand "Benjamins" as black U.S. slang, referenc-

ing the faces of U.S. presidents on their dollar bills. In Hip-Hop culture it is used to signify the pursuit of making money, through various kinds of hustles—macking, drug selling, rapping (see Gilroy 1993, 1996; Rose 1994). My interest in the term is for its metaphorical possibilities in framing broad distinctions between Hip-Hop culture and Carnival culture. I am careful not to overemphasize the economic focus of the term and to assert that Carnival as not interested in making money. I am more interested in reading the possibilities for cultural difference in the term.

2. Exemplary treatments of black Canadian movements are found in literature by Austin Clarke (1996), Lawrence Hill (1996), and Dionne Brand (2000). These authors write critical fictions that invoke real and imaginative narratives constituted in the movement and crossings of black Canadian lives.

3. T-dot is a Hip-Hop pseudonym for the city of Toronto, also known as T.O. When spoken, it is referred to the T dot O dot.

4. A boycott by twenty-nine established (traditional) bandleaders, following unpaid prize money and insufficient seed-money to underwrite the cost of producing mas bands, undermined the possibility of CCC organizers staging a lavish 30th anniversary celebration. In their place were a number of junior and less experienced bandleaders. The political turmoil, coupled with a financial crisis, jeopardized the festival. At the general meetings I attended, some members linked the political and economic demise with the opportunistic ascendancy of Hip-Hop as an unlikely feature of the Caribana parade. My position is to not rely on the economic opportunism, as it were, for an explanation. Rather, I am interested in the kinds of cultural questions opened as a result of the boycott.

5. "Northern Touch" was a popular song released in 1998 by Vancouver Hip-Hoppas the Rascalz. It featured fellow Canadian rappers Choclair, Checkmate, Kardinal Offishal, and Thrust. The song signifies an important development in Canadian rap and Hip-Hop culture. The real and metaphorical "northern touch" contests the traditional play of East Coast and West Coast Hip-Hop familiar to U.S. rap music. Northern Touch is first a spatial remapping and then an imaginative rethinking, marking Canada as a distinctive Hip-Hop territory, which disrupts the traditional East–West spatiality of U.S.-based Hip-Hop. The "touches" also reflect the particular diasporic transformations that help write Canadian Hip-Hop.

6. The official concert name was Caribana Skydome Concert: A Celebration of Black Music. It was sponsored by the *Toronto Star,* radio stations Power 94 WBLK from Buffalo, New York, and CFNY FM 102 in Toronto. In addition to Ice-T, Kool Moe Dee, and Toronto rapper Maestro Fresh Wes, the lineup also included Jamaica artist Frankie Paul and Trinidadian calypsonians Charlie Roots and David Rudder. The concert was canceled following poor advanced ticket sales.

6. Carnival in Aruba: "A Feast of Yourself"

Victoria M. Razak

> The heat begins, we goin' jam and sing
> Its carnival, lots of bacchanal
> Jouvert morning we goin' grind, grind, grind
> Break a day, carnival all the way.
>
> I feel so crazy, don't look for me
> I too busy, busy
> It's carnival, we don't give a damn
> Drums them beating, bradam, bradam
>
> —Mighty Heads

The official start of Aruba's pre-Lenten Carnival is the eleventh hour of the eleventh day of the eleventh month (the Fool's magic hour). Public festivities begin after the New Year with the evening Torch Parade (known in Dutch as the *fakkeloptocht*). Costumed *carnavalistas* carry flaming torches through the streets of the capital, Oranjestad—jamming and wining to the music of Asambeho brassbands, disco vans, and live music bands. The torches symbolize the heat generated by the festivities—several weeks of competitions, parties and parades that take place all over the island.[1]

Aruba's Carnival is a time for excess, fun, and self-indulgence stretching from mid-January to the beginning of Lent. The festival marks the pre-Lenten season for Catholics, picks up the slack between Christmas and Easter for commerce, and provides a celebratory opening of the new year for everyone. In Aruba, this time is known also as the "hot season." This does not refer to the climate, but rather to the fever generated by the celebrations. The island "cools down" on the eve of Ash Wednesday with the fiery sacrifice of Momo, the Spirit of Carnival.

Carnival in Aruba has been called "a feast of yourself"[2]—a phrase that signifies the deeper meaning of the festival as participants explore, reinvent, and elaborate themselves for representation to the outside world. For these *carnavalistas,* the Carnival is indeed a feast—a glorious, indulgent celebration of ethnic identities.

This chapter describes the origins and structure of the Aruba Carnival and explores the way in which it provides a frame for the construction, display, and play of island identities. Trinidadians who came to work at the American-owned oil refinery in the early 1940s introduced the Carnival into Aruba. With no public carnival of their own, Arubians embraced the festival with enthusiasm and striking creativity. In the decades since, although retaining many of the original masquerades and competitions, continuing immigrations and transnational flows have gradually introduced features from other carnivals into the celebrations, especially those of Venezuela, Brazil, Holland, and North America. Of more significance for this paper, however, is the way in which the Carnival has been consciously appropriated and nativized by the native Arubians.

Aruba still maintains a significant, but much diminished, British West Indian community, some of whom assert that their Carnival was "stolen" by native Arubians. Even after fifty years of capable management under the native Arubians, some older British West Indian mas players still dispute their ability to run the festival because "they do not have Carnival in their blood." The Arubians strongly counter this by asserting that Carnival is an Arubian thing—a generation of children has grown up within the festival's embrace, and therefore it *is* in their blood.

THE PAST IN BRIEF

Some historical background is needed to understand why the relationship between native Arubians and the English has been competitive and antagonistic since the 1940s. Of central importance is the way insiders and outsiders of Aruba are constructed around notions of relative indigeneity as well as around the question of who has the right to control and represent Aruba's cultural history and resources—including the Carnival.

Aruba is a Dutch Caribbean island situated off the northern shores of Venezuela. Its spheres of cultural influence include the Caribbean, Europe, North America, and Latin America. First the Ciboney, then the Caiquetio and Jirajara Arawaks, settled from the nearby Paraguayan peninsula. The Spanish arrived after 1499, but were ousted by the Dutch in 1636. In the centuries that followed, a diversity of immigrants arrived as farmers, laborers, and merchants, including Sephardic Jews from Curacao, Venezuelans, Colombians, Portuguese, and Europeans. Some later settlers brought African slaves with them to work as house servants (Aruba had no large plantations). Over time, these settlers intermarried with the Indians, creating a hybrid population with many biological, cultural, and linguistic influences. Papiamento, the much-loved native language developed from this mix—a melodic potpourri of Spanish, Portuguese, African, Arawak, and Dutch. By 1863, the last of the "pure blooded" Indians had been absorbed into the population; and in the ensuing decades, so too were many of the 758 newly manumitted African slaves (although many Arubians still deny this).

Aruba has had a difficult economic history. Before the twentieth century, its parched landscape was dotted with *cunucus* (farmsteads) and simple cottages built from mud and cactus stems. Sparsely populated, the island's few families grew maize and kept small kitchen gardens protected by goats and sheep by stone walls and cactus fences. Scarce rainwater was caught in barrels or earthen reservoirs. Economic activity was limited, and erratic and endemic poverty eventually forced men into wage labor on the plantations of Venezuela, Colombia, and Cuba.[3] With little industry and an unforgiving climate, the Arubians were increasingly dependent on the outside world (Hartog 1961).

In 1928, the American Lago Oil and Transport Company established a large refinery on the southern tip of the island near the small village of San Nicolas.[4] This began a new era of infrastructure growth, prosperity, and an end to hardship for the Arubians. This was also the beginning of the Americanization of Aruba and the increasingly complex question of indigenous identity.

NATIVES, ENGLISH, AND EMIGRES

The oil industry radically affected the island's environment and cultural composition over a remarkably short period of time. In 1900, the population stood at 9,702; by 1951, Aruba boasted a thriving community of 53,000 people (Hartog 1961). Today, the islanders fall into three main groups: native Arubians, Afro-Arubians, and Emigre Arubians (Razak 1998a).

The Natives

The native Arubians are those who are descended from the original founding families of the Dutch and Iberian settlers, Sephardic Jews from Curacao, and other West European migrants who arrived in Aruba in the seventeenth and eighteenth centuries. This group has retained the pattern of endogamous marriage through the Sephardic tradition of cross or parallel cousin marriage. The Sephardics converted to Catholicism through marriage with Latin Americans; this reflected an interest in establishing and securing commercial relations with Venezuela. Another reason may have been to mark themselves off from the Curacaon Sephardics who retained the Jewish faith, and from the Protestant Dutch on Aruba. The Catholicism of the Arubian mestizo Indian population may have also been an influence.

The eventual sharing of language, religion, sociocultural ties, and an appreciation of relative isolation from Curacao and its Dutch control and focus all served to consolidate these groups into a native Arubian population with an endogamous Sephardic-descendant elite and a mestizo Indian-descendant base (Phalen 1977:218–220). While native Arubians as a whole occupy the median of somatic characteristics, some individuals exhibit higher levels of Indian or African biological traits (Rife 1972). However, emic descriptions of the ideal Arubian specify "light to white skin, sparse freckles, hazel eyes and Auburn hair" (Kalm 1974:79). Nonetheless, most individuals are brown skinned, with dark hair and eyes, resulting from intermarriage between later non-Sephardic nineteenth-century immigrants and the "predominantly Indian, black, and mulatto offspring of the first settlers" (Kalm 1974:78). The white category is reserved for the self-definition of Sephardic-descended elite Arubians.[5] These comprise a few extended families (the so-called "top ten" founding families of Aruba) who tend to hold dominant positions in government, banking, and commerce and are, regardless of economic status, the social and political elite of Aruba (Kalm 1974:80). This group has also remained relatively socially and culturally segregated from the English and other Afro Arubians who are considered "black" in native terms. After the 1970s, with increasing nationalism and a call for separation from Curacao and increased autonomy from Holland, many native Arubians expressed a concomitant hostility toward Caribbean refinery workers and the emigres.

Who's Native, and Who's Not?

Given the complex biological and cultural identity of the native Arubians, a question much asked on the island is "ken ta Arubiano?" or "who is a real Arubian?" Whether you are native or of foreign descent is still of central importance to many native Arubians (Emerencia 1998, Alofs and Meirkes 1990). This question also presents a conundrum that pervades many aspects of secular life—in politics, in education, in social structures and relationships—and manifests in visual terms through public (Carnival) and semiprivate celebrations. In order to identify who is native and who is not, native Arubians tend to sort individuals into groups within the societal structure according to their degree of Arubianness (Razak 1998b). This is a challenging task given the hybrid disposition of their identity. Further, there are only a few symbols of relative indigeneity that are associated primarily with natives: the native lingua franco Papiamento, Indian ancestry, old family names, certain foods, the festival of *dera gai* (Arubianized festival of San Juan), and two localized forms of regional music—the tumba and the dande. Although both Papiamento and the tumba are shared with Bonaire and Curacao, there are small but important differences among their manifestations in the territories. Native Arubians also claim for themselves an ethos that appears as a set of ideal social behaviors and values embodied in expressive performances.

Based on these criteria, native Arubians order individuals and groups into a status hierarchy according to their distance from themselves. The degree of this proximity is defined by an abundance or deficiency of native characteristics (behavior, language, and somatics). In this way, each group is assigned a position within the social hierarchy, each with some kind of boundary between themselves and others based on certain claimed or ascribed features. Non-native islanders view this native construction of Arubian society with concern because such an ordering of the population establishes a principle of paramountcy for natives, creating exclusive spheres of social, economic, and political practices.

The English

The Lago Oil and Transport Company (USA) established an oil refinery on the southern tip of Aruba in 1928. An initial lack of industrial skills among the Papiamento-speaking native Arubians and the desire to hire an English-speaking workforce led the company to recruit thousands of foreign laborers from the British Caribbean territories.[6] Thus, between 1940 and 1950, workers arrived in large numbers from Trinidad, Jamaica, and British Guiana, with smaller numbers from Barbados, Antigua, St. Kitts, St. Vincent, and Grenada. Many of these employees had acquired industrial work skills through British or American corporations on the Panama canal or in the modernizing sugar refining industries. These new immigrants settled in the village of San Nicolas below the smoking chimneys of the refinery. Today, these workers and their descendents are included among the island's Afro-Arubian population, which comprises the so-called "English" from the British Windward islands, Guyana, and the Dutch islands of Saba and St. Eustatius; the "Antilleans," the Dutch-speaking Afro-Antillians from the islands of St. Maarten, Bonaire, and Curacao, and from Suriname; and peoples from the French and Spanish-speaking territories including St. Martin, Guadeloupe, Martinique, and the Dominican Republic.

The Emigres

The emigres are juridically Arubian, comprising primarily the Dutch (*macambas*), Surinamers, East Indians, Lebanese, Ashkenazi Jews, Chinese, and individuals from the rest of the Caribbean and the Dutch Antilles. Apart from the Dutch colonizers, the latter groups came to Aruba in the wake of the establishment of the oil refinery. Since the mid-1980s, other settlers have arrived from Columbia, Venezuela, the Dominican Republic, Haiti, and Africa. The Spanish-speaking population makes up the largest cohort of recent emigres.

ECONOMIC CHANGE AND THE BIRTH OF ANTAGONISM

The oil industry brought immediate tangible material and economic benefits to the island.[7] Handicapped by a lack of English, poor timekeeping skills, and work habits geared to the needs of horticulture, the Papiamento-speaking native Arubians were initially unable to participate in the ensuing economic boom. Although Afro-Caribbeans were excluded from the higher status jobs in the refinery, many took advantage of the vocational and U.S. college-bound programs initiated by Lago. As a result, they prospered economically and educationally compared to native Arubians. Because of these perceived inequalities, native Arubians developed antagonisms toward the English and other outsiders during this period. Moreover, the impact of the oil industry signaled the end of the dominant role of the few native Arubian merchants in the economy, and displaced the dominant cultural influence of Venezuela and the Spanish language with that of the United States and the English language.

However, within a few years, and with improvements in the general level of education, many natives were able to move into the new industry and its supporting service sectors. This provided the native population relief from their dependency on drought-prone subsistence horticulture and the necessary seasonal migration of family members to plantations overseas. Until the most recent waves of immigration (1986–2000), the English occupied the lowest ranks in the social hierarchy of the island, even though they by no means occupied the lowest economically.

When the automation of the refinery, and the dismissal of surplus workers, began in the 1950s, many of the original English workers repatriated to their places of origin.[8] The few who opted to stay consciously began to integrate socially and culturally with the larger Arubian population through marriages (few) and through music. Others were able to transfer their skills into the Arubian economy by starting businesses, joining Arubian-owned firms, and by entering the growing tourism industry—today the major engine of economic development on Aruba.

Overall, the residual "English" (i.e., the descendants of the original oilworkers) in Aruba are relatively skilled and educated. Many are professionals, and several occupy quite senior public positions, and each major political party lists Afro-Arubian candidates. This group is well-versed in Caribbean history and politics, and is keenly aware of its reduced numbers and sometimes-less-than-welcome status in higher social circles. Minimally educated English and other new immigrants from the English-speaking islands tend to occupy less menial positions than immigrants from other islands. But native Arubians have retained control of the tourist industry, and have consciously "Arubian-faced" the hotels intentionally by bringing in Costa Ricans, Filipinos, and others "that look like them" (Cole 1994), and a greater number from Columbia, Venezuela, and the Dominican Republic—another source of resentment for the English.

CARNIVAL IN ARUBA

The continuing high level of immigration (today the population stands at well over 100,000, representing seventy-nine nationalities and ten languages) has brought music and customs from various regions, some of which are liberally peppered throughout the Carnival. Thus the festival, which is still strongly based on the Trinidad model, has become an amalgam of local customs and practices, and elements absorbed from other carnivals—most notably those of Venezuela, Brazil, Holland, and New Orleans. Although several ethnic groups have contributed to the festival in different ways, it is the native Arubian elite and the first generation Trinidadians who have shaped the Carnival.[9]

The first era of Carnival spanned the period 1921 to 1944 and consisted of private indoor European-style carnival parties in and around Oranjestad. The social elite also held European-style balls, debutante balls for the daughters of Aruba's most prominent families (until the 1950s), Halloween, Christmas, and New Year parties, and participated in public street parades to celebrate the Dutch Royal family's coronations and birthdays. Native familiarity with masquerade parties and street parades allowed the Trinidad Carnival to be adopted so easily and enthusiastically. An elite native Arubian social club, the Aruba Tivoli, held (and continues to do so) European-style carnival parties in which members wore costumes representing Pierrots, Sailors, Arabs, ballet dancers, conquistadors, pirates, matadors, African kings, old hags, Mexicans, Mariachis, cowboys and Indians, and Chinese Mandarins. From 1946, the Tivoli *carnavalistas* rode through the streets on floats fashioned into flower gardens, giant swans, and the like, accompanied by *conjuntos* (folkloric music bands).

The Tivoli once held a formal elite ball called the *Luhoso* or Lux Ball, on the eve of the grand Carnival parade in Oranjestad. It was such an elegant affair that the public would stand outside the club just to watch the guests as they arrived in their sumptuous costumes. Guests danced throughout the night and flirted behind their masks and played jokes upon one another in the tradition of the French and New Orleans elite carnival balls of the nineteenth century (Hill 1972; Orloff 1981; Kinser 1990). On this night also, the Dutch governor or the commander of the Dutch marines crowned the Tivoli Carnival Queen-elect.

The second era or sphere of festival activity took place between 1944 and 1954 in the oil town of San Nicolas. During the Christmas period of 1944–

Trinidadians bring their Carnival to Aruba (ca. 1957). From the author's collection.

1945, a group of Trinidadians, accompanied by music, paraded in public in San Nicolas.[10] Some native Arubians were somewhat shocked by this "noisy rabble" and referred to the Trinidadians as "a bunch of monkeys"—a taunt that has never been forgotten. But in the following year, 1946, the Tivoli Club itself took its private Carnival celebrations onto the streets of Oranjestad for the first time. In February 1947, a group of Trinidadians obtained permission and again held a public Carnival parade in San Nicolas:

> We had a little group that we confined to San Nicolas. It wasn't something elaborate; it was just to keep up the tradition of Carnival that we knew. A lot of elderly people helped sew the costumes, and we passed in the streets in front of their houses so they could see their work. The costume was "Arab Sheiks." They were cheap, but colorful—yellow, black, red—and each Arab had a sword. To us we were just duplicating a group very common in the Trinidad Carnival. (Mas leader Calvin Assang, Aruba, April 13, 1991)

In 1949, the Tivoli Club again paraded in the streets of Oranjestad and chose a Carnival queen.[11] By 1951, district and social clubs all over the island were holding regional Carnival parties and queen elections.[12] Aruba had developed Carnival fever.

The third era of the Arubian Carnival began at the end of 1954 when the native Arubian and English groups joined to organize an island-wide Carnival. The Aruba Tivoli Club began the drive toward the realization of an organized public Carnival with the following announcement made on November 10, 1954:

> Carnival 1955! That is our immediate goal! Allow us to inform you of a wonderful plan, in a few words: Forming a committee to further carnival celebrations at our individual clubs and possibly throughout Aruba.

The response was immediate and enthusiastic, and by the end of that year, representatives of several native Arubian, English, and other Afro-Caribbean social clubs and associations agreed to coordinate their efforts towards a single grand Carnival parade in Oranjestad.[13] In February 1955, the newly established Central Carnival Committee of Aruba organized the first coordinated public Carnival on Aruba. Out of 120 contestants island-wide, the first official carnival queen, Eveline Croes of the Tivoli, was crowned in San Nicolas. However, because San Nicolas residents boisterously contested the election outcome (too boisterously for the conservative native Arubians), the election final was moved to Oranjestad the following year, where it has remained ever since. It was this incident that instigated the custom (beginning in 1957) of having two Grand Parades—one in San Nicolas and one in Oranjestad, and began the long-standing Carnival rivalry between the two towns. In 1964 calypso and roadmarch music became a part of the Carnival season when the calypso competitions and the titles of Calypsonian and Roadmarch King or Queen were introduced. In 1966, the present Carnival committee was formed—Stitching Arubaanse Carnival (SAC).

When Lago downsized in the 1950s and 1960s, the resulting repatriation robbed the San Nicolas Carnival of its most important and committed English mas players. After their departure, the control over the development of the Carnival passed wholesale into the hands of the native Arubian middle class, with the dominant participation of the Tivoli. Since the beginning, and throughout the ensuing years, the role of the Tivoli has been indispensable to the Carnival's success. In 1994, the Tivoli's pride in its achievements was evidenced in its Carnival program:

> Forty years ago carnival was celebrated for the first in Aruba at the Tivoli Club and as such our club is proud to be the place of birth of carnival in Aruba . . . In Tivoli carnival blood runs in the veins of the youngsters but certainly also in those who over 40 years ago initiated carnival in Aruba. (Tivoli Club Program 1994)

Today's Carnival still embodies the distinct cultural styles of both the Trinidadians and the native Arubians, a dichotomy revealed through the performance of music, events, and languages that counter one another (for example, the calypso versus tumba, Jouvert Morning versus Cocoyoco Jam, and English versus Papiamento). But the most important factors shaping the festival today are the issues of native versus alien island identities. The kinship structure of the native Arubians provides the basis of the strong social and economic networks that have consistently and efficiently managed and supported the Carnival. However, under their competitive patronage the carnival has become a largely spectator event. Their larger and ever more luxurious costumes and road pieces have long discouraged any truly spontaneous or broad public participation.

PRINCIPAL CARNIVAL ACTORS

The Carnival season in Aruba revolves around a set of principal actors: the King or Spirit of Carnival, Momo; his Queen of Carnival, her Prince of Carnival and his Fool, Pancho. Also important, and responsible for the music that rouses the spirit of Carnival from his sleep, are the kings and queens of calypso, tumba, and roadmarch. The central figure of the Carnival is the Carnival Queen. She presides over the season and leads all the street parades, making public appearances that promote the Carnival and representing Aruba at home and abroad during the year of her reign. The format of the elections is based on the early Tivoli Club celebrations and on those of the New Orleans Mardi Gras.[14] SAC organizes the district Carnival queen elections while social and sport clubs arrange their own. Large amounts of money are invested in these elections; districts and clubs are particularly competitive in trying to outdo each other in costume design and construction, presentation show, and their ability to rally community support. Support means a large group of family, friends and community supporters, all wearing tee-shirts printed with the candidate's picture, a hired brassband, self-advertising posters, sirens and other noisemakers, balloons, and costumes for her stage-show dancers who are part of a candidate's self-presentation to the judges.

The King or Spirit of Carnival is Momo (Papiamento *popchi disfrasa:* a disguised doll) derived from the Greek god of censure and mockery, Momus or Momos. The model for Momo comes from Spain's *Rey Momo.* Aruba's Momo appears as a gaudily dressed effigy with a painted mustached face, a glittering rag-a-tag assortment of clothing, and a golden crown upon his head. To mark the end of Momo's reign over the season of excess and indulgence, he is symbolically put to death. This is called the "burning of Momo," or in traditional European phraseology, "burying the carnival" (Frazer 1959). The custom of putting kings to death at the end of a set term has prevailed throughout history in many lands and has long been a central feature of carnivals. Burning, drowning, stoning, or decapitation (Frazer 1959) carries out the burlesque death. On Aruba, Momo is paraded through the streets and taken to a public stadium. There at midnight, he is tied to a tall pole and set alight by the Queen and her royal court. As the flames envelop him, Momo (packed with firecrackers), explodes violently, sending a shower of sparks into the sky. It is the dying embers of his pyre that symbolizes the cooling down of the island at the close of the "hot season."

Aruba's Prince of Carnival is modeled on the Carnival Prince from the south of Holland (formerly a part of Catholic Spain). The role of the Prince is to present his Queen to the people on her election, and to accompany her wherever she appears. The reign of the royal court officially begins when the prime minister hands over the keys to the island to the Prince of Carnival. This takes place at a televised public ceremony in front of the government building. On this occasion, the Prince reads a proclamation that outlines the new rules by which his citizens will be governed for the festival season. The Prince takes this opportunity to vent the Arubian peoples' opinions on a range of subjects, but with some limits of propriety. Government officials and their deeds are rudely lampooned to the delight of all Arubians.

Pancho is the Prince's sidekick; his role is to tell jokes and to accompany the Prince in all his royal functions. The character of Pancho originates from the Fool of the European festivals of old. The sobriquets that the Prince and his Fool devise for themselves derive from common phrases, which they split and combine in playful ways. For example, there are Prince Bud and Pancho Weiser; Prince Dollar and Pancho Rent-a-Car; Prince Gordo (fat) and Pancho Flaco (skinny); Prince Lenga (tell) and Pancho Largo (tale). The name *Pancho* was adopted from Aruba's first Carnival Fool, who chose to use his nickname as part of his sobriquet, "Pancho Morris." Prince and Pancho competitions in Aruba play off the legendary qualities of the fools. The pair performs a comedy routine in which they must demonstrate their mastery over buffoonery and wit—essential qualities for holding such important positions in the royal court. Scoring is based on originality, comedy, educational content, personality, and audience popularity. Candidates who use bad or vulgar language will be disqualified, and occasionally they are.

The emcee, or master of ceremonies, is chosen for his or her knowledge of local issues and popularity within all communities. Roger Abrahams (1983) identifies the emcee as a verbal trickster, or in West Indian celebrations, as a "man o' words." Like the calypsonian, he gets away with saying what others cannot say without fear of retribution. The popular emcees currently active in Aruba (2003) are Reuben "Scorpio" Garcia and Juby Naar. Both have an intimate knowledge of social and political life in their country, and both are welcome in many doors. Because of the small size of Arubian society, however, they do not take too many liberties with the goodwill of the community. In this way, they remain popular and effective in their roles. Scorpio has a popular radio program that runs throughout the Carnival season. Through his daily broadcasts, he keeps everyone informed about the myriad events that are taking place all over the island. He conducts on-air interviews with popular musicians and would-be queens, and of course, dispenses all the latest carnival gossip (and there's lots of it) with great relish and wit.

CARNIVAL MUSIC IN ARUBA

The music that accompanied the first Tivoli Club Carnival parades of the 1940s was performed by small groups of musicians or *conhuntos*. Costumed Tivoli members rode on decorated floats together with conhuntos that played folkloric or *tipico* music such as the waltz, tumba,[15] meringue, danza, and mazurka. The Trinidadians introduced the calypso into the festival complex in 1964. It transplanted well, partly because it was similar in some respects to the local music of the tumba, the tambu, and the dande, in the sense that these genres also embodied social commentary.

The steelband was also a part of the Aruba Carnival from the beginning. Trinidadian Leonard "Shoo-Shoo Baby" Turner introduced the steelband into the oil refinery town of San Nicolas in 1945.[16] Since the 1960s, Carnival has also danced to the beat of the Arubian brassband music known as *Asambeho*.[17] Traditional brassband music had been played on Aruba since 1930 but was not considered well suited for dancing in the parades.[18] Two San Nicolas musicians, Arnold Beyde and his colleague Samuel Hodge, experimented with different rhythms to develop a sound for the brassband that would provide a fitting musical accompaniment for jump-ups and parades. Blending samba, calypso, and marching band music, they created a new sound with a rhythm and beat suitable for dancing. The melody of the Asambeho is carried by wind instruments—the trumpet, trombone, and saxophone, while the beat is carried by a bass drum, a light drum, and a snare drum. The infectious music made its Carnival debut in 1967 and was soon embraced by Arubians of all ethnicities as an integrative symbol of national identity.

Musical road bands riding on flatbed trucks (belching toxic diesel fumes) became popular in the 1960s. Unlike the pan men who had to travel on foot and take regular rest stops, the mobile roadbands could play for much longer periods. And, with their electric instruments and giant speakers, they could also play much louder. This development contributed to the decline of the steelbands in the 1980s. It can be linked also to the unsuccessful attempt to merge the steelband music with the Latin American rhythms so favored by native Arubians.

Today, the roadbands dominate the parades, together with the popular Asambeho drum and brass bands. The disco vans with their disc jockeys, sound systems, and taped soca roadmarch music are also common—mainly because they are much cheaper to hire for the less affluent carnivalistas.

After taking root, the Trinidad calypso was subjected to local cultural influences. However, its integral elements have been retained—including the convention that singers should adopt sobriquets like Mighty Spoiler, Lord Melody, and Mighty Sparrow, which have continued in Aruba with names such as Lord Cobashi, King Paul, Lord Boxoe, Mighty Talent, Mighty Gold Teeth, and Lord Cachete. In line with its origins, the Arubian calypso pokes fun at local figures and national politicians. It is still the unofficial voice of the people, expressing social, economic, and political concerns through wit, words, and music in both serious and comedic ways. The ability of the Arubian Calypsonian to sing extemporaneously is admired and appreciated as it is in Trinidad. Although no true *picong* tradition has ever existed in Aruba, Calypsonians frequently mock or respond to each other in song. For example, this is the response of Mighty Talent to Mighty Hippie's boasting calypso in which he (Hippie) compared the size of their respective anatomies and sexual prowess with women, while brandishing beef sausages of varying sizes at the audience:

> Now Mighty Hippie won't you please tell me There's one thing I don't understand The only way you would know how my hot-dog go 'Cause you are playing with it in your hand!
>
> You like the sauce, hmmm . . . finger lickin' good The secret's out now Hippie, publicize you never should People asking who's the boss. He tell you, Talent is the man with the pepper sauce! (Excerpt from the calypso "We" by Claudius "Mighty Talent" Phillips, 1993)

In the ethnically diverse environment of Aruba, the calypso is a dynamic art form, absorbing lexical items from other language groups on Aruba, notably from Spanish, Dutch, and Papiamento. With the increasing social and professional integration of the island's musicians, and the fact that the new generation of calypso singers is island born, there is some tension between the first and second generation of English calypsonians, and between these groups and the native Arubian singers who try their hand at the English calypso. The Arubian calypso is being shaped by these contradictions and influences and by other music genres inside and outside the island.[19]

> The feelin' is not there. If the natives sing tumba, the feeling is there because it's in their native tongue, Papiamento. They would not fully understand what the real Trinidadians sing, because of the expressions. Calypso is tongue, it's the accent, the way of "pronunciatin" the words. (Lord Cobashi, Aruba, February 26, 1992)

In recent years, the Arubian calypso has become more Latinized under the cultural influence of the native Arubian musicians, despite the resistance of some older, traditionally inclined calypsonians. Innovation is discouraged through the application of strict rules for performance in the calypsonian competitions. These include the correct accent, palate, and feeling standards that are impossible to attain for Papiamento speakers. This is not to say that there are any serious rifts between musicians; on the contrary, the island's musicians are well integrated, and in turn integrate the Arubian society as a whole through a shared love of Caribbean and Latin rhythms. However, music cannot be prevented from innovation and development over the longer term and is always a reflection of the altering sociocultural environment. Because Arubian society has changed significantly since the 1930s, the island's music has similarly undergone transformations. With respect to Arubian calypso, for example, popular second-generation calypso composer Claudius Phillips infuses his lyrics with a mix of English, Spanish, Papiamento, and Dutch, reflecting the island's diverse ethnicities. He incorporates traditional instruments into his compositions, such as the Indian *calco* and *wiri*, while consciously maintaining the traditional function and structure of his calypsos as a reflection of his own British West Indian cultural heritage. But as a product of two cultural spheres of influence, Phillips is attuned to the music of both worlds. While responding through song to the contemporary political, economic, and social problems around him on Aruba, his music also reflects his own generation's mixed aesthetic of cross-cultural music flows and languages:

> Aids it don't care if it's he or she
> So you women please beware
> and you men use a *handschoen* down there[20]
> On every local radio
> In Courant and Diario
> You read about the same old crime
> *Muher a worde viola*[21]
> *Menor di edad abusa*[22]
> Can we solve this problem in time
> These dirty men putting us to shame
> Give Aruba a nasty name
> If they feeling so damn horny
> Let they go spend they money in some *hanchi*[23]
> It's a shame to be out raping
> It's a shame, please stop child molesting.
> All this crime go me in shock
> If I was judge I cut off their _____
>
> (Phillips 1991)

Representing "native" culture and history in the Aruba Carnival. From the author's collection.

In the above calypso, Phillips includes other commonly used languages: Spanish, Papiamento, and Dutch.

A CHANGING AESTHETIC: NATIVIZATION OF THE ARUBA CARNIVAL

After fifty years of innovation and change, few of the events and masquerades that originated in Trinidad have any meaningful connections to their antecedents for native Arubians; neither do they have much meaning for second-generation English. But they have been maintained for a variety of reasons. The most common of these is that they were already familiar fare in the private Carnival festivities of the native Arubian social clubs before 1944; were in tune with local aesthetic taste; or were simple to replicate and inexpensive to produce. The masquerades that still follow the Trinidad model are the Historical, Original, Luxurious, or Fantasy masquerades. These include African tribes; Indians (Fancy, Indigenous, North American); the big bands that depict Historic themes and popular Hollywood films, Sailorboys and Combat groups; and Bats, the Devil, Pirates, Midnight Robbers, and Mavis Clowns. For the older English players, each of these masquerades once embodied a semantic complex and incorporated a characteristic dance or pantomime. However, all of these events and masquerades have been subjected to a native reinterpretation of form and meaning since their introduction.

The native aesthetic sensibility has long looked toward Brazil as a model for many of the luxurious road pieces. A strong affinity with all things American has imparted a Disney World feel into costumes, especially in the children's parades. The comedy is decidedly a "Dutch thing," but elaborated and localized with much talent by native Arubians. Historical bands from a 1950s Trinidad are used to elaborate and re-present local and regional history. In addition to depicting events from the distant past, most notably *The Conquest of the Americas* (1992), the recent Arubian past is portrayed in critical terms. In particular, after the abrupt closure of the Lago Oil refinery in 1985, the carnival brings together themes that include the nostalgic: *Aruba before Lago,* and the optimistic *Our Brilliant Future.* The Status Aparte[24] relationship with Holland, achieved in 1986, resulted in several carnival groups bearing celebratory neonationalistic themes such as *Star of Status Aparte, Aruba Our Paradise, The Sky is the Limit, Shield and Flag,* and *New Aruba.*

The Indian masquerade has also been enthusiastically adopted from twentieth-century Trinidad, but rather as a potent visual symbol of Arubian Indian ancestry. The groups creatively explore, redefine, or reinvent their Indian heritage through serious or playful frames. Whereas the shared native American and African experience of New World colonialism and enslavement is sympathetically linked in the aesthetics of the costuming in some Trinidad masquerades (Hill 1972, Kinser 1990), in Aruba, the notion of "Indian" is loaded with local connotations alluding to political power, social status, class structure, and relative indigeneity. As part of the separation movement from the Netherlands Antilles in the 1970s, the Arubians began to re-evaluate the term *Indian* as a positive mark of social status and as a means of differentiating themselves from the rest of the Dutch Antilles, especially from Curacao whose population is mainly of African descent. Thus, in some of these masquerades, direct representation is made to the Jirajara and Caiquetio Arawak ancestors of the present native population. This representation occurs most frequently in the folkloric Carnival parade in Noord and in the Caribe Club group theme (every five years the Caribe Club celebrates its lustrum by entering the Oranjestad Grand Carnival parade with their signature theme *Original Indians*, led by a cacique [big chief] and the Caribe Queen.)

The insistence on the inclusion of symbols that are native rather than imported alludes to the process of appropriation, the continuing loss of native tradition, high immigration, and rapid social and cultural changes. After 1970, concerned about the dearth of native Arubian elements in the Carnival, SAC president Milo Croes encouraged masquerade groups to "portray things that are Arubian." In response, each new Carnival season brings myriad themes celebrating the island's traditions, for example, *Casamento di Antanjo* (old-time marriage) and *Nos Cultura* (our culture). The cultural institute in Oranjestad is similarly concerned with the maintenance of Aruba's cultural heritage and identity and believes it can help achieve this goal by sponsoring Carnival groups that educate the public about the island's social history. These carnivalesque enactments of the past, however, "exist somewhere between history and fiction" (Schechner 1985:38), this is because Arubian history, as told in performance, has been retold and reshaped through idealization and elaboration with aspects selectively included or excluded.

In addition to the calypso, roadmarch, steelband, and Jouvert Morning, and the already mentioned masquerades, other Carnival themes were created and added to the festivities by Arubians. These include the *tipico* and *comico* masquerade groups, the Tivoli Lighting Parade, and the Cocoyoco "Rooster" Jam. The *tipico* masquerades are often heuristic in nature, and deployed partly to show outsiders the "real" Aruba, partly to differentiate between insiders and outsiders, and partly to warn the younger generation that they are losing their cultural values and customs. *Tipico* groups often mobilize symbols of an idealized agricultural past with the island's natural surroundings providing a source of inspiration for costumes. Birds such as the *troupial* and *chuchubi*, local fish and insects, the tall *cadushi* cactus, the low-lying aloe plant, the natural bridge, and the vast rock formations with their Indian paintings have all inspired road and body pieces from the mundane to the spectacular.

These representations of place allude to a sense of "belongin" among native Arubians that relates to both legal and emotional (but not necessarily nurturing) ties to the land. A common assertion is that if your ancestors owned a piece of farmland, or *cunucu*, then you are the descendant of a "real" Arubian family. For most natives, the cunucu resonates with emotion; an ancient place associated with Indian origins, myths, and autonomy. Thinking about and using the land in the mode of the past helps Arubians achieve a profound sense of community. Although traditional farming activities have all but ceased, the old cunucus with their characteristic cactus fences are still maintained and valued as symbols of indigeneity. Traditional cunucu houses are often featured in the parades despite the enormous amount of work that goes into building them. Traditional aloe farming equipment is also displayed in the main parades. Popular folkloric festivities such as *dera gai* (San Juan)[25] and the native *dande* music (New Year celebration in which a group of musicians visit the homes of relatives and friends with a gift of song) are also presented in carnivalesque style.

As with most carnivals, Aruba has several comic groups that participate each year. The central focus of Carnival is humor that stems from the transgression and mockery of valid laws and normative social behaviors (Sebeok 1984). The native comico groups who turn the Carnival into a vaudeville theater of the streets exemplify this phenomenon. Their humor is direct, stinging, and political. Nothing escapes their satirical scrutiny—including the politicians, the police, the Carnival committee, and the tourists. They take their themes from local gossip, topical local news, and international issues, presenting them as theatrical set pieces to be told and retold as the parade progresses through the streets. Interaction with spectators is essential to a successful performance. Spectators are routinely invited to participate and play some role in the performance, much to the amusement of the onlookers. But the *comico* groups comprise insiders talking to insiders (in Papiamento), so you have to know the language, and be a local resident, to understand the jokes.

The spectacular nighttime Lighting Parade (formerly the Tivoli) is a major tourist attraction on the Carnival calendar of events and takes place in Oranjestad one week before the grand parade. This event epitomizes the conspicuous spending that has become associated with the middle- and upper-class players of Aruba. Tivoli members (in particular) invest a good deal of time, money, and effort into their costumes. They carefully research their themes, make detailed working drawings, and often produce scaled-down prototypes for testing. The level of financial investment, artistry, and craftsmanship in these masquerades is impressive. Influenced by the Walt Disney World light parades in Orlando, the Lighting Parade is famed for its sumptuous fairy light-covered costumes that give the parade its unique ambiance. The designers experiment with different lighting effects—including the use of neon paint, colored lights powered by small generators or batteries, twinkling lights, colored smoke, black light, and laser light. The body costumes are made from reflective materials and are covered with up to five hundred light bulbs. This illumination gives the Lighting Parade a psychedelic, dreamlike quality not easily forgotten. To jump in behind the Lighting Parade is to understand the compelling attraction of Carnival.

Public jump-ups are held all over the island throughout Carnival season. They are essentially street parties with soca bands held on an ad hoc basis that add to the general feverish atmosphere of the island. These street jams are popular with teenagers and are accompanied by plenty of parading, preening, and flirting. The northern town of Noord holds an early morning jump-up known as the Cocoyoco Jam. Held before sunrise on the day of the children's parade in Noord, it is the native Arubian counterpart to the Trinidadian-style Jouvert Morning held a week later in San Nicolas. Noord lies close to the northwest coast of Palm Beach where the majority of the hotels are situated, affording tourists and visitors to the island a chance to experience a joyful early morning jump-up with Arubian revelers.

Jouvert Morning begins at around four o'clock in the morning on the day of the San Nicolas Grand Parade. This event is the emotional center of Carnival for the English San Nicolanians, and is attended by all serious carnival revelers from other parts of the island. In earlier years, costumes were varied and amusing, including underwear worn as overwear, and jokes or social commentaries displayed on costumes or hand-held signs in the manner of the Trinidadian "ole mas." Today, most participants wear everyday clothes, although some do still practice the custom of wearing pajamas, nightdresses, and shower caps with some cross-dressing.

In 1971, the Carnival committee introduced a tumba contest into the program of competitive events. This was consciously done to balance the festival culturally by showing a native face to the tourists, one that represents and reflects the island's native culture. The custom of dancing to Trinidad-style soca roadmarch music in the parades has been retained, in part, because it serves to differentiate Aruba from Curacao whose own Carnival dances to tumba music. Interestingly, in the ensuing years, the tumba contest has come to serve the same function as the English calypso, that is, as a vehicle for gossip and information. The tumba lyrics (sung in Papiamento) have become increasingly embellished with sociopolitical satire and a Tumba King or Queen is chosen and crowned in much the same way as the Calypso King or Queen. Thus, the two music genres both complement and oppose one another:

> In San Nicolas, the people coming from Trinidad and the English islands had their own way of doing carnival. From them we have the calypso but the tumba is typical Arubian music. It's between a rumba and a meringue, but it has its own sound. We put the tumba into the carnival so we can play our own music. The people feel that the tumba is something of their own, with our own composed songs in our own words. (Milo Croes President, Carnival Committee, May 21, 1991)

The Carnival committee organizes the carnival season rather efficiently and tries to make sure that the more than fifty events are well policed and orderly. The Carnival brings a potential for disorder to the island at a time when the island is at its most vulnerable and at its most open (tourist high season). This generates a public spectacle of harmony and safety that is truly representative of a growing national identity—in fact, the Carnival *is* an important integrative mechanism for national unity. Both the Arubian government and the island's commercial interests want the carnival to be an orderly and safe affair that the visitor (and potential investor) can enjoy with a sense of security. The successful organization of the festivities, then, metaphorically displays to outsiders the

Arubian's ability to organize, adapt to, and control, the demands of the changing local and outside worlds:

> Our carnival is getting a good name. We are also known as the safest carnival in the world. We have no accidents, except one or two collisions, no fighting, no riots, no killing. Drunkenness yes, but just in a very decent way. Once a year they can drink publicly without being jailed, and the police don't arrest them. Even after such a big drinking party, where we have the whole of the population drinking, on Monday morning you won't see one person lying on the street. (Croes 1991)

Thus, Aruba sees itself as distinctive even though its Carnival shares most of the features of other Caribbean carnivals, particularly in the festivals's tendency to reflect the island's social and political structures through their temporary overthrow or their ardent reaffirmation through performance. And, as with other carnivals, the Aruba carnival offers a time and place for individuals, groups, and institutions to confront each other over social, economic, and political interests and actions through competitive challenge. Aruba's Carnival has also taken on a nativistic quality that serves to revitalize local culture and counterbalance the negative impacts of social change.

When the native Arubians formed a Carnival committee and organized the island's first "official" public Carnival in 1955, the Trinidadians of San Nicolas already had their own Carnival committee.[26] However, as a heterogeneous community, it lacked the strong kinship structures possessed by the native Arubians, which formed the bases of the social, political, and economic networks necessary for efficient development, management, and financial support of a successful Carnival. Because of this, the English players have long argued that native Arubians stole the Carnival from them at the beginning. This, some claim, has resulted in the erosion of meaning and the loss of authenticity, and any written or oral claims relating to this issue tend to heighten tensions between the two groups. A 1956 Carnival program illustrates an example of this dispute, with an editorial written by a Tivoli Club member:

> Tivoli has established that great Tradition of Carnaval in Aruba . . . upholding a tradition set by *themselves.* TIVOLI = The standard of Carnaval. Authors name withheld for the guy's safety. (Anon; Tivoli Club Carnival Program, 1956, Biblioteca Nacional, Aruba)

This self-serving taunt was fueled by a contentious relationship between the two groups, stemming from the fact that the native Arubian refinery workers had been displaced by British West Indians who had greater language and work skills.[27] Today, a marked (but less obvious) ethnic and regional dichotomy continues between the English Afro-Arubians and the natives, and although the island is relatively well integrated with all ethnic groups and social classes working well together, underlying tensions between them still surface from time to time.[28]

Although Carnival has been well managed by the native middle classes for fifty years, the English still dispute the natives' ability to run the festival.[29] Native Arubians strongly disagree with this view and assert that Carnival belongs to the island, that it is a part of Arubian culture—it is "an Arubian thing." Even the president of the Carnival committee boasts as follows:

> Carnival is an Arubian thing. The Tivoli Club started the carnival in their club before the British West Indians came in. The role of the carnival committee is to coordinate the whole carnival so that everything may be orderly . . . they [all participants] have to come through us. We want to make carnival a typical Arubian festival you know, that's why we have to handle it. Now when you say Aruba, you say carnival. We are *isla carnaval*. . . . (Milo Croes)

Although specific Trinidad imports did not survive past the 1960s—for example, stickfighting, Moco Jumbies, Devil Bands, Biblical Mas, Flag Women, and wars between rival costume groups and steelbands—these remain in the imagination and are passionately idealized as central to a "real" carnival. For the English players, these were authentic and exemplary models of, and for, Caribbean Carnival. Surviving masquerades, such as Sailorboy and Military groups, Amerindian and African masquerades, and large Original or Historical groups survived transplantation from Trinidad for different reasons. Either they were (in some form) extant in native social club celebrations, or they thrived because they were able to be successfully recoded with local meanings.

For the aged Trinidadian players, the reglossing in native Arubian terms has (for them) caused the loss of meaningful historic context, authenticity, and the embodied symbols these themes once generated. Gone are the narrative frames, the accompanying costume paraphernalia, and the characteristic dance steps that were associated with different Carnival characters. Today, the numbers of these original mas players are few, but their adult children and more recent English immigrants keep the contentious relationship alive (in part because of their marginal social position). They assert that the natives are "nibbling around the edges" of what is left of their original Carnival. Certainly there is a sense that Arubians would love to move everything up to the capital, and San Nicolonians say they are definitely fighting to "hang on" to their Calypso contest—especially since the native-Arubian town of Noord introduced their own version of Jouvert Morning—the Cocoyoco Jam. Many saw this as a hostile act. The establishment and location of a Carnival museum and theater are causing the most current antagonisms. Both San Nicolas and Oranjestad claim the right to locate the museum in their vicinity. No doubt, as past clashes have shown, Aruba will end up with two Carnival museums.

The continuing argument over the management and authenticity of Carnival is today fueled in part by the English and Afro-Arubians' relative social marginalization in a society where they are still referred to as "outsiders." Thus, despite the angst over the past and the contradictory claims over the festival's genesis, the continuing competitive nature of the festival is fueled by real social and economic inequalities. Aruba sees its Carnival as unique even though the festival shares most of the features of other Caribbean carnivals, particularly in its tendency to reflect the island's social and political structures through their temporary overthrow or their ardent reaffirmation through performance. And like other carnivals, Aruba's bacchanal has taken on a nativistic quality that serves to revitalize local culture and counterbalance the negative impacts of social change. It offers a time and place for individuals, groups, and institutions to confront each other over social, economic, and political interests and actions through competitive challenge (Manning 1977, 1984, 1990).

The birth and development of Aruba's Carnival provides insights into the history of relations between ethnic groups and social classes, between tradition and change, and between the local and the global. The distinct and primary focus of Aruba's bacchanal, however, is the continuing dichotomous discourse generated at its twinned birth that brings a dynamic subtext to the festival in the form of a power struggle for control over its future. However muted today, the question of "Whose Carnival is it anyway?" remains a potent issue and provides the Carnival with its festive dynamic and local identity. Paradoxically, however, although playing Carnival involves the assertion of individual and group identities, it also serves as an integrative social mechanism for the population as a whole. To play Carnival in Aruba is to feel Arubian, to belong. This sense of belonging is attained through play.

NOTES

1. The range of events that take place during Carnival varies from year to year, with new ones being added that may or may not become a permanent part of the celebrations (Jeep Parade, Costumed Roller Blades Parade, and Horse Parade, for example). But of the more than fifty contests and entertainments, several core events take place each Carnival season: costumed street parades, jump-ups in all barrios; grand all-comers Carnival parades in Oranjestad and San Nicolas; the Noord children's parade; and the grand children's carnival parades of Oranjestad and San Nicolas. The International Carnival Costume Festival takes place in Oranjestad with several regional carnivals participating, for

example, from Aruba, Brazil, Jamaica, Santo Domingo, St. Maarten, Tenerife, and Trinidad. There are also Old Mask parades in the major towns, including Noord, San Nicolas, Santa Cruz, and Savaneta, but these appear not to differ from other jump-ups. Jouvert Morning (also known as the Pajama Parade) takes place in San Nicolas, with its native northern counterpart, the Cocoyoco "Rooster" Jam, in Noord. The Calypso Festival and competition take place in San Nicolas, as do the roadmarch and Calypso King and Queen competitions, and the Jubu Happening where the island's most popular musicians perform and are honored by the San Nicolas community with the title of *e cantante di pueblo* (the people's singer). The tumba festival is held in Oranjestad and elects the island's tumba king or queen. The Brassband Jamboree is also held in Oranjestad. The Steelband competitions used to take place in San Nicolas but have not been held since the 1980s. The transfer of command by the prime minister of Aruba to the Prince of Carnival takes place at government house in Oranjestad. The Prince's motorized parade circles the entire island, passing through its main towns. Queen competitions occur in all barrios, as do Prince and Pancho competitions. The Mrs. Carnival takes place in Oranjestad.

2. The phrase is attributed to Carnival committee president, Milo Croes.

3. The gathering of cochineal and tannin, straw hat plaiting, and fishing all helped to sustain the people at one time or another over the centuries. Aloe grew well in the arid conditions, and small but ubiquitous aloe plantations were dotted around the island. A few deposits of phosphate and gold were discovered that provided income for some people until the beginning of the twentieth century. Nevertheless, the Arubians still suffered from periods of famine and near-starvation.

4. Lago Oil and Transport Company later affiliated with the Standard Oil Company of New Jersey, which subsequently became the Exxon Corporation. Today Coastal Corporation owns the refinery.

5. Even though the native Arubian elite assert that their white ancestry and endogamous marriage patterns set them apart from others, even these prominent families absorbed Indian blood. Records support this assumption, noting that in 1806 there were 256 heads of families in Aruba comprising 60 whites, 141 Indians, 10 mulattos, 35 lighter skinned admixtures, and 7 black. But by 1868, white heads of household had diminished to a mere 1.5 percent of the population (Hartog 1961:111).

6. The Lago oil refinery employed 2,074 British West Indians between 1930 and 1951.

7. During its peak in World War II, the Lago Oil and Transport Company was the world's largest refinery, producing aviation fuel for the allied forces, refining some 440,000 barrels per day, and employing some 8,300 workers (Green 1974:24).

8. Direct employment at the plant declined from 8,300 in 1949 to 5100 in 1960, 1,600 in 1972, and 1,000 in 1984, just before the closing (DECO 1984:17).

9. Dutch was only spoken by educated Arubians, and then only in conversation with the Dutch.

10. A two-page account of the Carnival's origins ("Carnival on Aruba" (Figaroa et al., n.d., National Library) reports that the Carnival dates back to 1939 when Trinidadians established it in San Nicolas. The first masmen, among others, were Calvin Assang, Elric Crichlow, Robert Murray, William "Woody" Woodley, Adolpho "Chippy" Richardson, and "Shakey" and "Tremble" Welch.

11. *Aruba Esso News* (February 22, 1949).

12. *The Aruba Esso News* reports that in February 1951, the Surinam Club sponsored a carnival in San Nicolas, and in March 1952 groups from the French islands of Martinique and St. Martin gathered for a French-style carnival at the Netherlands Windward Islands Club.

13. A meeting was held on November 23rd at the club to form a central committee to organize the Carnival celebrations. Aruba Tivoli Club member G. A. Oduber presided over this meeting in which seven of the twenty eight clubs invited were present. A temporary Aruba Carnival committee was formed, chaired by Oduber, with six male committee members: N. E. Henriquez, Jr. (Rotary Club of Aruba) was appointed secretary, A. A. Harms (Caribe Sport Club), Frans Croes (Santa Cruz Social Club), a Mr. Panne-flek (Netherlands Windward Islands Association), a Mr. de Kort (Commandeursbaai Club), and Harold Harms (American Legion). Committee members resolved to invite other clubs and associations to participate. Included were Watapana, Lucky Strike, T.C.C., Trappers, Golden Rock Club, Chinese Club, Lago Heights Club, Pova, Lions, Palm Beach Club, and the Country Club.

14. Carnival Queen elections in New Orleans are associated with debutante balls and coming out parties in which the daughters of the social elite are formally introduced into society. Rex, New Orleans's Mardi Gras King, was escorted by a Queen for the first time in 1873. The carnival season in New Orleans begins on January 6, with parades and balls. Secret societies called Krewes organize the festivities; the best-known Krewes are Rex and Comus (Roman God of Joy).

15. Tumba is part of the generic rumba complex including macumba and tambo; it is secular party music, with its own style and instrumental formats for interpretation.

16. Trinidadian Leonard Turner, a Lago refinery worker, recruited a group of young men to form a steelband. They crafted pans from Lago oil drums and learned to play increasingly fluent renditions of the sambas, rumbas and other popular music of the day. By 1948, Turner had put together his first professional steel orchestra, the Invaders, which performed at both public and private venues. In 1950, Turner teamed up with San Nicolas resident Naldo Brown to form another steelband, Shoo-Shoo Baby and the Aruba All-Star Boys. "Shoo-Shoo" was Turner's stage name. Naldo Brown eventually took over the group and changed its name to the Aruba All Stars. San Nicolas calypso singer Lord Cobashi sang with this band. One young pan man in the band, Edgar Connor, went on to form his own steelband in 1952, called the Aruba Invaders. The two bands competed against each other in the first Carnival steelbands competition in 1964. Eight steelbands competed: the Merrymakers, the Devils, the Curacao Heroes, the Long Gun Boys, the Paradera Steelband, the Silver Stars, the All-Stars Steelband, and Edgar Connor's, group The Aruba Invaders; the latter won with their rendition of the theme from *Exodus*. By the 1960s, a proliferation of steelbands was providing music for Aruba's Carnival parades, and continued to do so for thirty years. Although the original panmen of the 1950s and 1960s were predominantly of British West Indian descent, today the bands are fully integrated with Arubians of all ethnic origins and cultural backgrounds.

17. The name for this novel music derives from a combination of the authors' names —Arnold SAMuel BEyde Hodge.

18. The formation of the first Arubian brassband took place at the Pan-Am Club, San Nicolas, on March 7, 1930. The Aruba Refinery Brassband contained between twenty and twenty-five musicians. Source: *Pan Aruban* newsletter (February 15, 1930),

weekly mimeo of the Pan American Petroleum Corporation (part shareholders in the Lago Oil and Petroleum company).

19. The Trinidadian calypso has been influenced by Spanish music from Venezuela, the Dominican Republic, some French, Irish, and English music forms, and more recently, East Indian and Chinese melodies.

20. Dutch for *glove*.

21. Papiamento for *women wait for rape*.

22. Papiamento for *young ones are abused*.

23. Papiamento for *alley*.

24. Aruba is no longer part of the Federation of the Netherlands Antilles (with Curacao, Bonaire, St. Maarten, Saba, and St. Eustatius). Aruba opted out of the federation in 1986 and became an independent entity within the Kingdom of the Netherlands. Aruba now has its own parliament and council of ministers; the Netherlands remains responsible for Aruba's defense, foreign affairs, and justice.

25. *Dera gai* means "to bury the rooster." The curious custom of burying a rooster and hitting it with a stick three times is associated with two Catholic feast days, those of St. Peter and St. John.

26. Although the Trinidadians accounted for the majority of the mas players along with some Guyanans, the "English" San Nicolas population was rather heterogeneous and included peoples from Jamaica, Grenada, St. Vincent, and Dominica, two of whom later became prime ministers on their home islands (Green 1974).

27. When Vera Green was studying on the island in the 1970s, the social distance between the two groups was still considerable (Green 1974).

28. For example, the hosting of the Calypsonian and Tumba King and Queen contests by San Nicolas and Oranjestad respectively epitomizes the ethnic, linguistic, and regional divisions of the territory.

29. Ironically, in Trinidad too, the Carnival is controlled by middle-class Creole leadership rather than Afro-Trinidadians (J. Stewart 1986).

7. Creativity and Politics in the Steelband Music of Ray Holman, 1957–1972

Shannon Dudley

Ray Holman was born in Woodbrook, a western neighborhood of Port of Spain, Trinidad, in 1944. His cousin Leslie Holman played guitar with several prominent dance bands, but as a young boy Ray showed no inclination toward a musical vocation, nor did his family encourage it. Then one day in 1956 he and his friend Roy Rollock got the chance to experiment with a set of steel pans that were kept at the Little Carib Theatre belonging to Rollock's aunt, Beryl McBurnie. At the time, playing in a steelband carried a stigma of danger and vulgarity; but in Trinidad they say "pan is a jumbie," a spirit that possesses people. Perhaps this is why, just a few months later, Holman and Rollock defied the warnings of their families and teachers and joined the Invaders steelband, the first boys from a middle class Woodbrook family that had dared to play with an established "grass roots" steelband.

In 1962, having become one of the Invaders' most respected players, Holman left to arrange for Starlift, another Woodbrook band, and many younger members of Invaders went with him. The move to Starlift coincided with Trinidad's independence from England and, more importantly for Holman's musical career, the beginning of the Panorama steelband competition. Between 1963 and 1973 (while working during the day as a humble Spanish teacher at Fatima College) he established himself as one of the premier steelband arrangers in Trinidad, winning Panorama with Starlift in 1969 and 1971, and helping to define a whole new approach to steelband music. In 1972 Starlift abandoned the convention of arranging popular calypsoes for Panorama, and instead played Holman's original composition, or "own tune" in the competition. This was a momentous event in the history of Panorama, which led to the end of Holman's association with Starlift, and the beginning of new possibilities for the steelband.

This article relates the experiences and ambitions of Ray Holman to a pivotal period in the history of the steelband.[1] The dates in the title mark important moments in Holman's own career: his start with Invaders and his first Panorama own tune. The same dates frame a period during which Trinidad became an independent nation and the trajectory of the steelband art form was dramatically altered: Panorama became the premier performance venue for steelbands, leading to changes in repertoire and style as well as steelband organization and economics. The parallel between Holman's career and these developments is not drawn to suggest that Holman was primarily responsible for these changes in the steelband movement. Indeed there were many other influential musicians during this time, and the art form was impacted by powerful forces of history, politics, and ideology that could not be attributed to a single person. However, the most active period of Holman's career coincided with certain dramatic changes in the broader steelband movement. His musical decisions responded to these changes, but also helped to shape them.

My decision to describe this period of the steelband's history through the prism of an individual musician's experiences responds to a concern that many Trinidadians have for scholarly documentation of their artists' achievements. Trinidadian journalist and steelband historian Kim Johnson, for example, urges researchers to pay more attention to the histories and experiences of particular steelbands and musicians, and expresses dismay that the steelband, unlike Trinidadian calypso or masquerade, "fell to the social scientists by default, as if beating pan was some quaint folk practice, an aspect of ethnicity or national identity or pluralism—anything but a serious, modern art form" (1996:4). To be fair to social scientists, Johnson's concern has parallels in much social science scholarship that looks at the way individual actions are not only conditioned by larger cultural forces, but may also change or constitute those forces (Ortner 1984). Nonetheless, it is true that a lot of scholarship on the steelband has foregrounded the (admittedly fascinating) issues of class, colonialism, and nation (e.g., Aho, Diehl, Dudley, Elder, Hill, Stuempfle), effectively stressing group interests and identities over individual artistry.

The very unlikeliness of the steel pan's invention compels us to ask what individual genius could have conceived of something so novel: pounded out from a discarded oil drum, a metal bowl with individually shaped and bounded areas which, when struck with a rubber-tipped mallet, produces a brilliant, ringing, rippling sound—pieces of junk metal that have been so transformed, they can be mistaken for an organ when playing together. The instrument is a testament to the creative vision of men like Neville Jules, Winston "Spree" Simon, Ellie

Mannette, Allan Gervais, and Bertie Marshall,[2] who imagined something hidden in the metal and brought it out for the world to hear. At the same time pan is the product of intense competition, class conflict, and the need to win respect through improvement—the cultural "politics," broadly speaking, that are referenced in the title of this article. I will begin by reviewing the steelband's early history and proceed to recount several stages of Ray Holman's career, relating his musical experiences and choices to the political issues that impacted the steelband generally.

THE CHANGING STATUS OF THE STEELBAND, 1940S AND 1950S

When pan was first invented, and by whom, are topics of enthusiastic debate.[3] But while accounts may vary in their claims for different neighborhoods, individuals, or dates, they are consistent in the stress they lay on the steelband's lower class origins and its subsequent transformation into a respectable art form, culminating in the official proclamation of pan as Trinidad and Tobago's national instrument in 1992. This transformation is at the heart of what folklorist Steven Stuempfle calls the "steelband master narrative" (1995:3), a view of Trinidad's cultural history that stresses the triumph of oppressed people over repression and derision. The steelband's status changed partly as a result of concerted efforts to promote the art form in the 1940s and 1950s, a pivotal event being the 1950 formation of a Government Steelband Committee. The most important accomplishment of this committee (whose convening was motivated as much by concern over violent steelband clashes as by interest in the new instrument) was the formation of the Trinidad and Tobago Steelband Association, with representatives from all the major bands.

With help from the government, the new Steel Band Association put together the Trinidad All Steel Percussion Orchestra, or TASPO, which provided tuners and players from different bands their first opportunity to work together. It was also the first opportunity most of them had to work with a formally trained musician, police lieutenant Joseph Griffith, who helped them develop a repertoire of music that included classical pieces, Latin music, and calypsoes (Stuempfle 1995:96). In 1951 TASPO was sent to London to represent Trinidad at the Festival of Britain, and astonished reviews in the English press greatly enhanced the status of the art form at home in Trinidad. In the following year, a steelband category was introduced in the annual Music Festival, which was primarily a venue for classical music. Through these opportunities steelband musicians received greater exposure to formal musical training, broadened their repertoire, and played for diverse audiences.

During the same time middle class Trinidadians began to identify themselves more and more with what had previously been regarded as a pastime of shiftless and dangerous young men. In a climate of increasing cultural nationalism, the steelband began to be seen as a potent symbol of local creativity. Middle class youth also got involved as performers around this time.

As early as 1950, with the formation of Dixieland steelband, middle class school boys began to play pan. In 1951 a group of boys from the prestigious St. Mary's college formed a steelband in the backyard of Ronald Chan, on Picton Street in the middle class neighborhood of Newtown (Inniss 2000). Though they first had to hide their pansticks to avoid expulsion, the Silver Stars were later asked to play at the St. Mary's commencement ceremonies (Pouchet 1993). Silver Stars also brought out a masquerade band and developed a huge middle class following, even winning Band of the Year in 1963 with the theme of *Gulliver's Travels* (the only steelband ever to win this masquerade title). Other so-called "college boy" bands also provided Carnival entertainment for middle class communities who embraced the music enthusiastically, once their own children were involved. The social stigma attached to pan was thus rapidly breaking down during the 1950s, as more middle class people became involved playing, listening, and dancing to the music. At the same time, however, Trinidadians of different social backgrounds began to stake their claims to an art form that was still claimed with a fierce pride of ownership by its lower class originators, setting the stage for heated debates over the steelband's role in Trinidadian culture.

INVADERS

While college boy bands like Silver Stars played an important role in popularizing the steelband among the middle class, the first "established" band of lower class panmen that developed a middle class following was Invaders. The Invaders' panyard was located in a vacant lot behind the house of leader and tuner Ellie Mannette on Tragarete Road, to the west of downtown Port of Spain, and at the edge of the middle class neighborhood of Woodbrook. Their ties to a middle class constituency began when they were invited by folklorist and dancer Beryl McBurnie to play at the Little Carib Theatre in 1948. By the mid-1950s the Invaders had a following that included many residents of Woodbrook, and the band attracted people of all walks when they played on the road at Carnival.[4] When Ray Holman and Roy Rollock joined Invaders in 1957, however, they were the first people of middle class education and status to actually *perform* with the band. As in the case of Junior Pouchet, Holman's association with Invaders was initially frowned upon by his teachers and administrators at Queen's Royal College. In the panyard, on the other hand, he recalls being treated "like a prince" from the start (Holman 1993).

Invaders provided Holman with important role models and an invaluable musical education. Ellie Mannette was the most influential pan tuner in Trinidad during the 1950s, and through watching and listening to him Holman developed a keen appreciation of timbre. He learned not only how to judge a good pan, but also how to strike it so as to get the best possible sound. Emmanuel "Corbeau Jack" Riley, Invaders' greatest virtuoso and improviser, was another player who made a deep impression on Holman. "He was our mentor," Holman remembers, "All of us following. We used to worship at the temple of Corbeau Jack. Right? Everybody wish that someday they could play close to Jack" (1999). People would come to Invaders' rehearsals just to hear Corbeau Jack solo, and his solos also spiced the tunes that Invaders played on the road. Invaders left room in many of their arrangements for solos, so Corbeau Jack and other leading players, like Holman, also got experience improvising. This model of arranging was also followed in Holman's second band, Starlift, where in parties or on the road someone could call out "'round the world" or "syncopation" and everyone in the band knew what chords to play while one player soloed.[5]

In Invaders, Holman also began to learn about arranging, but the position of the arranger was less well defined at that time, and certainly less exalted, than in the modern steelband. It was relatively easy for an ambitious and talented young player to have some input into the arrangement; yet, at the same time, no-one could presume to be completely in charge of a tune. Holman remembers a communal process of arranging in Invaders:

> You would come in the yard and Jack would be playing, people playing informally then. I would go on the second pan, Roy and them fellas on the bass, so we backing Jack, Jack was the soloist then. Then in the night now, we're learning a tune and Ellie might come and he would call out . . . Ellie might play it on the tenor pan, then go on the second and play something—nothing elaborate like it have now. He might do one or two tunes and Zephrine[6] might do a couple of tunes. I think for carnival Ellie used to do one or two tunes because he was tuning, and Zephrine would do some others. (1993)

This informal musical leadership was undergirded by a keen sense of style, particularly phrasing and rhythmic ensemble, that everyone in the Invaders shared. Holman credits Ellie Mannette's playing on the iron (a vehicle break drum) as the foundation for Invaders' rhythmic style, and even for other steelbands in the "West" (meaning the neighborhoods of Woodbrook and St. James). This rhythm was also the foundation for the sound of Starlift. "We had a good rhythm. You see everybody from one yard, it's like a culture. All I have to do is start the tune and they just bring it alive. The iron fellas, boy" (ibid.).

REPERTOIRE, STYLE, AND STATUS

The concept of Invaders' unique and cohesive style stands in interesting contrast to the extraordinarily diverse range of genres that Invaders and most other steelbands played. The late 1950s were a time when steelbands were revelling in the eclecticism of their repertoire. In stage shows and dances, they played a variety of music that included Latin popular songs and American film songs. The biennial music festival provided a consistent venue for the performance of classical music. On the road, steelbands played the mambos of Perez Prado, and a rivalry between Trinidad All Stars and Crossfire in 1956[7] spawned a competition called the "Bomb," in which bands secretly rehearsed foreign tunes—especially classics—and played them in calypso rhythm on j'ouvert morning. The more Trinidadians came to identify with the steelband, the more intensely they debated about the value of the different genres of music the steelbands played—both as music for carnival dancing and masquerade, as something that represented their nation symbolically. After Trinidad and Tobago's independence from England in 1962, debates about the relative value of calypso versus foreign music became particularly heated.

The steelband musicians themselves were generally agreed upon the desirability of a diverse repertoire. They were interested, for one thing, in proving their instrument's legitimacy through the performance of the "classics" and other internationally recognized music (Dudley 1997:44–53). Perhaps just as important to them, though, was the diversity of melodic and harmonic ideas that "foreign" tunes offered them, relative to calypso. Trinidadians tend to judge calypso by its text and verbal wit, and it is often noted that singers recycle many stock chord progressions, melodies, as they concentrate their creative efforts on wordcraft. This was most true of the 1910s and 20s when many calypsoes were sung in the standard "Sans Humanité" or "Old Minor" chord progression and form; but even in the 1950s steelband musicians found that foreign tunes provided them with a broader palette of harmony and melody. More ineffable affective qualities no doubt also influenced a panman's decision to arrange any given tune. For example, steelband musicians had an extraordinary affinity for the mambo, especially those of Perez Prado—in the words of steelband pioneer Carlton "Zigilee" Constantine, "That music was just definitely like [Prado] make it for pan" (Constantine 1993).

While in stage and festival performances steelbands often rendered foreign compositions in a style that was relatively faithful to the original, on the *road* all these "foreign" genres were interpreted with a "local" calypso musical sensibility. Classical pieces like Beethoven's *Minuet in G* (performed in Carnival by All

Stars in 1957) were rendered in duple meter, the melody syncopated, and harmonic accompaniment provided by chords strummed on the cuatro and grundig pans in fixed rhythmic patterns. The syncopated bass lines of Cuban mambos were replaced by a walking calypso pulse, and everything was driven by the "*tingi licki, tingi licki, tingi licki*" of the steelband irons. Despite this "indigenization" of composers like Beethoven and Prado, however, there was concern in some circles that the steelbands were increasingly abandoning Trinidadian calypso in favor of foreign melodies.

Official promotion of calypso started at least as early as 1944, when concern for the "improvement" of the calypso was expressed in a government-sponsored study of the genre by Charles Espinet and Harry Pitts. This work reflects a growing nationalism, through the prism of which calypso was viewed simultaneously as a valuable cultural asset and also as being somewhat crude and undeveloped. For example, Espinet and Pitts begin with the statement that "No study of a people can be complete without reference to their folk-music" (1944: 13) and go on to observe that, "hope is held by local musicians for further musical development of the calypso along classical lines (ibid.:22). By the 1950s concern for the advancement of the calypso was linked to a sense of alarm that the steelbands, which by this time were the most popular musical ensemble for masquerade, were favoring foreign tunes over local calypsoes in their carnival repertoire. When the five most popular road marches of 1955 turned out to be foreign tunes, "the preference of the public (or the musicians) for foreign melodies was the subject of much commentary after carnival" (Rohlehr 1990:437). A number of newspaper commentaries in the 1960s document debates about the merits of "indigenous" vs. "foreign" music (e.g., Simmonds 1964, Rouse 1966), a topic on which middle-class intellectuals had many differing opinions.

After independence in 1962 steelband musicians experienced increasing pressure, in the form of competitions and prize money, to promote calypso music at Carnival time (Dudley 1997:134–37). Disapproval of the steelbands' foreign music at Carnival was most vehemently expressed in relation to the practice of the Bomb, a steelband arrangement that would be rehearsed in secret and unveiled, or "dropped," on the road on Jouvert Morning. This tradition began with All Stars' performance of Minuet in G in 1957, and remained popular through most of the 1960s. Sociologist and cultural activist Pete Simon, the most vocal opponent of the Bomb in the 1960s, wrote:

> Isn't this preference for the classics by steelbandsmen during this tempo-setting period of our National Festival a clearcut attempt to downgrade the calypso? To relegate it to second choice? To give it an inferior place? (Simon 1970)

Simon's argument that European classical music is inappropriate for carnival suggests that, at a time when Trinidadians were trying to affirm both their cultural and political independence, the panmen's deference to colonial cultural standards was unseemly.

Certainly the panmen did measure themselves against the standards of European classical music, and took pride in their achievements, and in their *knowledge* of classical music. It is still true that when a steelband musician says someone "knows music" he is referring to a knowledge of musical notation, and perhaps theory. Ray Holman remembers one occasion when a display of such musical "knowledge" significantly boosted his status in Invaders. He was arranging a tune for Invaders when a question arose about whether his harmony was correct:

> Ellie come on the pan and he play and he say well that is A minor, how you playing D? He couldn't understand it. G, and you playing D. E minor and you playing D. So they call Mr. Pierre. Big thing, you know, when he say send to call Mr. Pierre. So they call Mr. Pierre, Mr. Pierre come in the yard.
>
> But in the meantime now I say listen, I jump on my bicycle, eh? And I head down Petro St. It had a fella called Blackman, they were music teachers and the fella used to go to school. I say listen, I want you to help me with something, tell me what this is, and I play for him, we going on the piano now (*sings the tune*) I say what you call that, what it is I doing there? And he go and he bring out his sister. He didn't know. When I play it she says that is a pedal point. I say what it is you say, a pedal point? What is that? She say just what you're doing there, playing one note, even if the chords change. I say, uh-huh, well they dead now! I gone now boy!
>
> I jump on my bicycle man, and I gone up in Invaders yard. I have my two sticks in my pocket. When Mr. Pierre start to talk, he say he can't understand this thing, "but Ray . . . " I say, "Mr. Pierre, you don't know what is a pedal point?" boy, all the young fellas in the yard, they watching me like I know this amount of music! That was kicks, boy! I feel like a big, big man now, because I teach them this thing. I say Mr. Pierre, you don't know what is a pedal point? Well you see that? Mr. Pierre lost all credibility then. Because some other man who was in the yard listening, a gentleman came, and he say what the boy saying is correct—and he speaking proper English, eh?—what the little fellow said is correct, it's a pedal point. (Holman 1993)

This story of one-upsmanship vividly illustrates the power associated with European musical repertoire and knowledge. Nonetheless, it is important to note that, while Holman defended his decision after the fact by resort to a classical music precedent, he initially used the pedal point simply because he liked the sound. Indeed, many steelband musicians, like Holman, may have been guided more by aesthetics than by concern for status in their choice of repertoire and of particular musical devices.

This is not to say that, in the context of colonial Trinidad, a Beethoven composition might not be more useful as a musical weapon—a "Bomb"—than a calypso by the Mighty Sparrow. Aside from the issue of rivalry, one can also imagine that the popularity of the Bomb at Carnival time was related to the prestige that steelbands acquired through stage performances of classical music. However, the application of colonial cultural standards was not the same on the road as in the concert hall—the Bomb was also judged by standards of Carnival festivity that were relatively independent of colonial hegemony. Frederick Street on Jouvert Morning did not have the impressive decorum and formality of Queen's Hall, nor did the governor and other important people attend, as they did at the Music Festival; but the Bomb was a chance to play all this great music in a context where people could dance and sing and *participate,* as Ray Holman explains:

> There was a great respect for classical music. So if a band play that in the road, it used to sound nice. You know this tune, and you could dance to it; because in the Queens Hall you can't dance to it. So the same nice tune, the same nice melody and chords, you're getting it that you could dance. And Trinidadians love to dance. So it was more appreciated. (8/99 p.15)

Holman chose Bomb tunes not only for their familiarity, or for the novelty of hearing well-known classics in a dance setting—he was also guided by a sense of how certain melodies worked well for arranging in calypso style and for dancing on the road at Carnival. His previously quoted remarks make it clear that Holman's sense of style is firmly rooted, as one might expect, in the rhythmic sensibility he absorbed through playing with Invaders. He also asserts, though, that "groove" and danceability have to do with melody and with a quality of sweet sadness that some songs have:

> I would look for a nice melody. That way I could make them groove. The Bomb was to groove. Or to make you feel in heaven—"Hallelujah Chorus" wasn't a groove, that was heavenly (*sings*). But when we play "Accelerations Waltz" it was groove (*sings*). . . . Melody, and a certain feel that people would want to cry when they hear the song. It is a certain feel, I don't know how to describe it. The tune must have a certain melancholy in it. That is the important thing, for the Bomb. When they played "Leibestraum" people used to cry.[8]

The socially constructed status of European classical music, calypso, and other genres in 1950s and 1960s Trinidad surely influenced Ray Holman's taste, but he and other steelband musicians were not just making a calculated appeal to someone else's standards of beauty and value—they were making music that they and their audiences *enjoyed.* For Holman, a certain affective quality that he found in Listz's "Liebestraum" or the Beatles' "Penny Lane" was missing in calypso, and this is one of the reasons he liked to arrange European art music, popular music, and American film songs. His experience with this music, and his affinity for certain qualities of melody and harmony, continued to inform his music long after the Bomb competition ceased to be popular.

PANORAMA

On August 31, 1962, Trinidad and Tobago became an independent nation. In the following year's Carnival the government's Carnival Development Commission in conjunction with the National Association of Trinidad and Tobago Steelbandsmen sponsored a competition called "Panorama." This new competition was intended to "give more prominence and status" to the steelbands,[9] giving them a share of the limelight alongside the Calypso Monarch and Carnival Queen competitions at the Queen's Park Savannah. Steelband musicians welcomed Panorama as a chance to take their place in a prestigious showcase of Carnival arts, and as another of several venues where they could vie for reputation and prize money. Only in retrospect could it be known how Panorama would eclipse other venues in importance and focus the musical energies of the steelbands much more narrowly than in the 1950s. Today Panorama is often discussed in terms of its constraints rather than its opportunities (Thomas 1986). Perhaps the most significant constraint of the Panorama competition, in relation to the preceding analysis of repertoire, was the requirement that steelbands play calypso.

Panorama did not at first diminish the panmen's enthusiasm for foreign tunes. Although the bands were judged at Panorama only on their calypso performance,[10] they maintained the same breadth of repertoire as always, and after playing in front of the judges many bands would strike up another tune to play for people in the Savannah grounds. The tune that Starlift was remembered for in 1963, in fact, was Leonard Bernstein's "I Feel Pretty" from *West Side Story*, and Ray Holman recalls that he "ruled the roost" with this tune (Holman 1999). While Starlift basked in the admiration of their supporters, however, it was Pan Am North Stars who won with the judges, playing Anthony Williams' arrangement of the Might Sparrow's "Dan is the Man." Starlift member Eddie Odingi remembers how Williams recognized what was different about Panorama and adapted before anyone else:

> The panmen didn't really take it that seriously, but North Stars did. Starlift played for the people, on the ground—"I Feel Pretty" and everybody ran over to the band, big favorite band, all right. Going down the straight,[11] Starlift played a Sparrow calypso, "Spend Your Money Wise." North Stars played

> "Dan is the Man in the Van," another Sparrow calypso. But Tony, being the man that he was, had an arrangement of "Dan is the Man in the Van" that was prepared for the competition, and he won.
>
> Everybody prepared but they weren't expecting that standard. He did things that people hadn't thought of. Just the way he arranged. Those days calypso was just verse and chorus. You play your tune, you might put in a rev, but just chords. Tony wouldn't play just chords. Our second pans would be strumming, right? But he wouldn't do this, he was running up and down, countermelody and thing. So they won, and everybody sat up and took note.
>
> By the following year, 1964, he won with "Mama Dis is Mas" . . . Tony changed 3 keys! First time ever in a Panorama competition. Before that they used to change keys in festival. Because we used to do calypsoes in music festivals. We used to change keys in music festival, but not on the road, because on the road is something you dance to, you just moving and dancing. But Tony changed 3 keys in "Mama Dis is Mas." Gone again. So he set the pattern. By then Panorama took a kind of classical outlook, because Tony was a sort of classical man. (Odingi 1993)

North Stars' success with the Panorama judges in 1963 and 1964 served notice to Starlift and other bands that they would have to develop a new approach to arranging. Form, in particular, became more elaborate, with variations on the original melody and modulations to new keys. Such pre-arranged variations required a much greater investment of rehearsal time on a single tune and precluded the kind of individual improvisation that Starlift usually made room for in their arrangements. The importance of the arranger in steelbands increased in proportion to the amount of pre-composition, formal complexity, and rehearsal time that Panorama required.

Ray Holman and other arrangers soon took aim at North Stars and applied their creative talents to the new challenge of Panorama. Holman's 1966 arrangement of Lord Kitchener's "Mas in South," in particular, was a groundbreaking model for Panorama music. Though the general model of theme and variation had already been established by Tony Williams, Holman strove for a more improvisatory quality in his variations, conceiving them in terms of a classical concerto. (Of course the "solo" sections were completely pre-arranged in Panorama, and played by entire sections, since an individual soloist would have been lost in a band of 100 players.) He also inserted a "jam" section just before the end: four times through the "round the world" chord progression (I–vi–ii–V), with a catchy bass line and melodic variations suggestive of an improvised solo. He changed keys with more elaborate modulations than Williams had used, and arranged the verse in the minor mode for one of his variations. Because of the improvisatory quality of his arrangement, and also because of phrasings and harmonies he used, Holman began to develop a reputation for using "jazz" in his arrangements.[12] Many of the devices that Holman employed in 1966—elaborate modulations, jam sections, minor variations, jazz-style chord extensions—are commonplace in Panorama arrangements of today, testimony to Holman's influence on the art form.

In 1969 Starlift won Panorama with Lord Kitchener's "The Bull," an arrangement that was remarkable for the way Holman transformed the original calypso's character. The "bull" in Kitchener's song is a blackjack (made from a bull's foreskin) with which he threatens to beat disorderly steelbandsmen: "Since they have no kind of behavior, I gon' lick them till they surrender. . . ." Not only are Holman's verse and chorus reharmonized with jazz-type chord extensions that Kitchener did not use in his version, they are also rendered with an extraordinary sweetness and lyricism that contrasts with Kitchener's belligerent lyrics. Notwithstanding his victory, the need to adapt songs that did not suit his taste frustrated Holman, even as he basked in the glow of success.

WRITING HIS "OWN TUNE"

By the early 1970s, Holman and other steelband arrangers were concentrating more and more of their artistic energy on Panorama, as steelbands started to lose ground in other performance venues. The Bomb had been eclipsed by Panorama in popularity and excitement. Steelbands had become less popular for masquerade generally because of their unwieldy size and competition from DJs. Even work in fetes, which Starlift had always had in greater abundance than most bands, was starting to wane as DJs became increasingly popular and many steelbands spent so much time preparing for Panorama that they could not maintain a significant repertoire of dance music. Panorama was emerging as the premier, and perhaps soon to be the exclusive Carnival venue for steelbands, narrowing the steelbands' choice of repertoire to the current year's calypsos. To make matters worse, the range of local calypsos to choose from was effectively narrowed to the recordings of two stars: the Lord Kitchener and Mighty Sparrow. Between 1963 and 1980, the only song by any other calypsonian to win Panorama was Lord Melody's "Melody Mas," played by Guinness Cavaliers in 1965.

By 1972 Holman felt that the well of local calypsos was running dry. After winning Panorama a second time in 1971 with Sparrow's "Queen of the Bands," he had had enough of arranging other people's songs.

> Whatever it was, by '71, tunes weren't . . . "Queen of the Bands"—I know that was the last for me. It was too much, to make something out of that song. I had no choice because, what I would have played? Kitchener had what? "Play Mas"? A million bands playing. I had nothing to play! So the man wrote the lyrics of "Pan on the Move." (1999)

"The man" was Holman's friend Alvin Daniell, and in 1972 "Pan on the Move" became the first original composition for steelband performed at Panorama.

In the short run, Holman and Starlift had no success with the judges. Moreover, Sparrow and Kitchener sounded alarms in the media, portraying Holman's own tune as a threat to the culture of Carnival. Even many fans criticized Starlift for not playing popular songs. Behind this opposition to the own tune lay a variety of motivations. Sparrow and Kitchener, and perhaps some other calypsonians, obviously saw the own tune as a threat to their role as providers of Carnival music. The own tune also contradicted the ideology of a unified Carnival, in which calypso, masquerade, and steelband should be united. This was the ideology that had undergirded the Panorama competition when it was established nine years earlier, and its proponents saw the own tune as a divisive and unhealthy development in Trinidad's national festival. Finally, many people who objected to the own tune did so neither on the grounds of vested interest nor political ideology; they had been attending Panorama for nine years and had simply come to expect inventive and exciting interpretations of songs they were familiar with. The own tune, in their view, deprived the audience of this pleasure, since it was not well-publicized ahead of time on the radio (Dudley 1997: 195–198).

All of this pressure only fueled Holman's determination to establish the steelband's musical independence:

> So, I say well look . . . when you go in a Calypso tent you hearing what Kitchener singing and what this one singing and what that one. When you come in a panyard, you hearing the same thing. Why when they come in the panyard they don't hear something distinctive of the pan? That was my philosophy. It should be so. We invent this instrument going—it's . . . nothing unique to it. I say that have to change. (ibid.)

Some members of Starlift, however, were less able than Holman to ignore the slings and arrows of public disapproval, and the pressure of being mavericks created dissension in the band. Holman left Starlift after the 1973 Carnival, and was never again associated so strongly with one band, arranging in different years for Pandemonium, Exodus, Tokyo, Hummingbird Pan Groove, Phase II and others.

Despite their lack of success with the judges and the censure of calypsonians and fans, the boldness and the integrity of Starlift's music did not go unnoticed. One measure of the impression they made is that they were attacked by jealous members of Invaders during the 1972 Carnival and many of their instruments were ruined. Holman came back the following year with an own tune titled, "Pan on the Run." The 1970s also saw several new calypsonians make their marks in Panorama: Shadow's "Bass Man" was popular with the steelbands in 1974, and Maestro had several popular pan tunes during the decade; finally Kitchener and Sparrow's grip on Panorama was broken when the Trinidad All Stars won in 1980 with an arrangement of Scrunter's "Woman on the Bass."

Holman's example helped pave the way for these calypsonians, by demonstrating that Kitchener and Sparrow were not the only ones who could write music for the steelband. His persistence in composing own tunes was also emulated by a young Starlift player named Len "Boogsie" Sharpe. It was Sharpe's new band, Phase II Pan Groove, that first succeeded, in 1987 and 1988, in winning Panorama with an own tune. Since that time the own tune has become commonplace—Desperadoes and Exodus have both won Panorama with own tunes, and many more bands have reached the competition finals playing their own tunes. The success of the own tune is further evidence, along with his many arranging innovations, of how Ray Holman's artistry and vision have impacted the steelband art form.

The first 15 years of Ray Holman's career as a steelband musician spanned an era of dramatic change in the steelband movement and his experiences exemplified important trends. As a Queens Royal College student from a modest but respectable Woodbrook family, Holman's participation with Invaders set a precedent for class integration of steelbands. Like many panmen in the 1950s, he learned to play pan in a relatively communal style—limited arrangement, improvisation, and audience participation—but later helped to define the greatly expanded role of the arranger in Panorama. The breadth of repertoire that he arranged for the steelband was typical for the 1950s and early 1960s, and at the same time his personal taste and arranging style were unique and helped condition the musical taste of a generation of steelband listeners. Holman's insistence on arranging his own compositions, or "own tunes," for Panorama have expanded the options for both steelband arrangers and calypsonians, and his success in this area has boosted the image of the "panman" as a complete musician.

Although I have made the case here that the aesthetic choices of one musician can influence the development of an entire art form, I do not mean to imply that larger social forces are less important. Clearly, Holman's involvement with the steelbands was part of trend during the 1950s in which many middle class people began to participate in steelbands, both as players and supporters. This middle class participation has, in a general sense, contributed to many profound changes in the steelbands, including increased hierarchy with the arranger at the top, an emphasis on arrangement over improvisation, orchestral rehearsal techniques, less exclusive neighborhood affiliations, a reduction in inter-band violence, and other things.

Just as clearly, however, Holman's personal contribution to the steelband cannot be adequately explained in terms of his social class. For example, while Holman's musical tastes were conditioned by listening to the classical music he heard on records in his home and the homes of friends, he never studied classical music formally. Moreover, steelband musicians from poorer neighborhoods where no-one owned phonographs or records have told me that they also heard classical music on Sunday morning radio broadcasts (e.g., Edwards 2000). On the question of repertoire, Holman's interest in playing a breadth of styles and genres was consistent with those of most lower class panmen, and at odds with middle class cultural pundits who railed against foreign influence. And to the extent that Holman's sensibilities and musical experiences did differ from those of the average panmen, this was welcomed and appreciated by Invaders' other members, as was the formal training of many middle class musicians whom the steelbands actively sought out (Dudley 1997:38–51; Stuempfle 1995:83–86). The difficulty of applying a class label to Ray Holman's outlook is not surprising when you consider that his "class conditioning" included thousands of hours spent in panyards[13] as well time spent with his family, in his neighborhood, in his school. Holman's music was influenced by the great diversity of people and sounds that were around him, as well as by certain personal gifts and sensibilities that people around him did not have.

Ray Holman continues to arrange for Panorama, though he has not stayed for long with one band since leaving Starlift. Some people believe that his romantic style is out of sync with the frenzy of modern Panorama; but in the same breath they might tell you that they love his music in other venues. Whether or not he wins Panorama again, Holman's music continues to provide an alternative sensibility, and his experience and knowledge are a living musical link to a time when steelbands were at the peak of their popularity in Trinidad, playing at fetes, concerts, and on the road. He has influenced younger arrangers both through his music and his personal example of artistic integrity. Most significantly, his tireless adherence to composing his own music for Panorama has made space for possibilities that have yet to be realized. This evolving potential, and the pride Ray Holman and other steelband musicians continue to feel for the unique beauty of their instrument and their music, are captured in Alvin Daniell's lyrics to "Pan on the Move":

> Pan beaters this year, in a dilemma
> Which tune to render—Sparrow, Kitchener?

The choices so limited,
Arrangers are restricted,
This year we decide to do we own thing

Don't doubt it,
we sit down and write we own song,
Arrange it,
we own self so we could rock town,
When you hear it, you go get in the groove,
Pardner, Pan on the Move

NOTES

1. The present study draws upon my Ph.D. dissertation research in Trinidad and Tobago between 1992 and 1994 (Dudley 1997), as well as interviews and numerous conversations I have had with Ray Holman during the two years (1998–2000) that he has been my colleague as Visiting Artist with the University of Washington School of Music.

2. These are some of the most influential tuners in the early history of the steelband: Neville Jules of the Trinidad All Stars and Spree Simon of Tokyo steelband were two of the very first to tune pans that could play melody in the early 1940s; Ellie Mannette of Invaders made important improvements to the tone of the instrument and developed several influential patterns for the layout of notes during the 1940s and 1950s; Allan Gervais tuned for bands like Cavaliers in the South from the 1960s and influenced a whole generation of tuners with his bright powerful sound; Bertie Marshall of Highlanders is credited with introducing "harmonic tuning" in the early 1960s, the addition of overtones that give the modern pan its bright sound.

3. See Goddard 1991 for a review of some of the most well-known origin stories.

4. As an indication of how popular Invaders were, Neville Jules explained that the famous rivalry between Trinidad All Stars and Invaders began because All Stars used to seek out Invaders in the streets in hopes of sharing the huge crowd that followed them (Jules 1999).

5. Round the world meant a repeating progression of I–vi–ii–V; syncopation was I–I7–IV–iv–I–vi–ii–V, like Rhythm Changes in jazz.

6. Errol Zephrine, Invaders' best seconds player

7. Neville Jules recalls that All Stars first resorted to the practice of secret rehearsals, and first played a classical piece on the road, with the express purpose of showing up Crossfire, who had outplayed them in public in the 1956 carnival (Jules 1999).

8. The Hallelujah chorus, from Handel's *Messiah,* was recognized as sacred music, making it a controversial piece for the Bomb; "Acceleration Waltz" is by Johann Strauss; Liebestraum is a piano piece by Franz Liszt.

9. This is the recollection of legislator Ronald Williams, a member of the CDC who helped plan the first Panorama (*Trinidad Guardian* 2/14/80).

10. In 1967 a test piece called "Paris is Burning" (or perhaps "Is Paris Burning?" which was the title of a popular 1966 war movie) in the style of a Bomb was also required, but this was not popular and was never again repeated.

11. The straight was the section of the race track where the bands paraded before the judges, as opposed to the "ground"—the open fields where Starlift stopped to play their bomb tune for supporters.

12. He was not alone in this—the Desperadoes steelband hired brass band arranger Beverly Griffith, whose winning arrangement of Mighty Sparrow's "Melda" in 1966 was also remembered as a landmark in the use of "jazz" in steelband arranging (Odingi 1993).

13. The vacant lots where steelbands store their instruments, rehearse, and socialize.

8. "Will Calypso Doom Rock'n'Roll?": The U.S. Calypso Craze of 1957

Ray Funk and Donald R. Hill

From late 1956 to the middle of 1957, the United States was awash in a "new" music phenomenon, the Calypso Craze. Following a two-decade presence in nightclubs and on record, suddenly calypso was all the rage. Fueled by the unprecedented success of Harry Belafonte's *Calypso* long-playing album on RCA Victor, the first million-selling record album in the history of the industry, the music market was temporarily transformed by a brief calypso mania. An incredible number of calypso records were rushed to the market, nightclubs around the country switched to an all-calypso policy, and many in the industry came to believe that rock'n'roll was dead and that calypso was taking over. This chapter traces the trajectory of this chimerical Calypso Craze and its subsequent crash only a few months after it began.

SETTING THE STAGE

In Trinidad, calypso dates from the turn of the twentieth century, where it developed as English-language Carnival music.[1] By the 1930s, calypso was wedded to a venue called the *tent,* a place where new calypsos were sung each year before the pre-Lenten Carnival. Calypsos were topical songs that aired the news of the day, gave a position on relations between men and women (usually from the male singer's point of view), or discussed other issues that were "in the air." Although musical styles and the instrumentation backing the singers changed, the function of calypso remained essentially the same throughout the 1950s and beyond. Calypso continued to be seasonal music and continued to be a cultural expression for the Creole (largely Afro-Trinidadian) segment of a multicultural society. Although different forms have been spawned over the years, calypso as a seasonal and topical music outlasted the U.S. Craze and continues into the present.

Early in its development in Trinidad, new issues were taken up every year in calypso, with mostly new lyrics. The melodies remained traditional and were reused over and over again. In the 1930s, new melodies were added to the kit so that each year both the lyrics and the tunes were sometimes newly composed. The increasing popularity of a calypsonian known as the Roaring Lion (Raphael De Leon) was the key to this development. Lion was enamored with American popular music, especially the Mills Brothers (the most popular group in the United States in the 1930s) and Bing Crosby (the most popular soloist). Others followed Lion's lead, and by the 1940s, Trinidadian calypso, while still functioning as a seasonal topical music of Carnival, began to develop in new ways by attending to "foreign" (American) styles.

A pioneer in expanding calypso outside of Trinidad was Lionel Belasco. Belasco was born in Barbados and raised in Trinidad. His rather was a tallyman and his mother a concert pianist. He learned to play European classical music on the piano in his youth but was drawn to the traditional music that was all around him, especially Afro-Trinidadian music. By 1900, he was leading his own band and by the mid-1910s he moved to New York City, which was to become his base of operations for much of the rest of his life. He died in 1967 in New York. He made his first records in 1914 in Trinidad and subsequently recorded many times in New York and elsewhere. By the late 1930s, Belasco had learned the Tin Pan Alley music business in Manhattan. In Trinidad there was no tradition of copyrighting popular music and Belasco became the first to copyright many tunes and lyrics in New York City that had circulated on the island. With calypsonian Wilmoth Houdini; New Orleans born jazz musician and entrepreneur Spencer Williams; and concert singers Leighla Whipper, Massie Patterson, and Gracitia Faulkner, Belasco jointly copyrighted or published music and lyrics of the songs he had adapted from West Indian sources. One song published in a booklet in 1943 was "L'Année Passée," which was the original tune to "Rum and Coca Cola." Through their joint efforts, these West Indian entertainers established a foothold in the North American music industry.

In the mid-1930s, calypsonians from Trinidad began making annual visits to New York City where they recorded their latest calypso hits. Decca was dominate in issuing calypso 78 rpm records for a decade following the mid-1930s, but RCA Victor also issued calypsos on their Bluebird label. Calypsonians also performed in nightclubs. At the time, interest in calypso was largely confined to Manhattan and a few East and West Coast cities. Records in these areas sold briskly to both West Indians and white Americans, the people who ventured into the Village Vanguard or the Cordon Bleu to hear the songs of the Roaring Lion, Atilla the Hun, King Radio, the Growling Tiger, or, in the 1940s, the Lord Invader. These calypsonians had made their names in the calypso tents in Trinidad and were now taking their singing talents "to the world," as Tiger once expressed it. Club goers and record buyers also liked songs performed by Trinidadians who had not made a reputation back home but who developed singing styles and stage presence to appeal to Americans not familiar with Trinidadian culture. In this group were the Duke of Iron, Macbeth the Great, and Sir Lancelot.

Meanwhile, the Allied presence in Trinidad during World War II increased sharply as the island became a major lend-lease base for outfitting the war effort. Although outdoor Carnival was banned during the war, calypso tents boomed. GIs were favored patrons (they had more money than Trinidadians), causing the prices of tickets to increase and fundamentally changing the tent clientele (through the 1950s). One American visitor, comedian Morey Amsterdam, in Trinidad on a USO tour, must have visited the tents and heard Invader's great calypso of 1943, "Rum and Coca Cola." Returning to New York, he copyrighted the song with his publisher and a vocalist and changed the lyrics somewhat. This song, as sung by the Andrews Sisters (the most popular female group of the war), became a million-seller. The sales of "Rum and Coca Cola" took the record business out of a prolonged slump and set the stage for a postwar explosion of many musical styles.

Invader sued Amsterdam et al. as the true composer of the lyrics to "Rum and Coca Cola." Lionel Belasco sued as the composer of the melody. Eventually both won their cases. Belasco accepted a share of the back royalties and Invader received a cash payment.[2]

In the late 1940s, two new record formats were perfected—long playing and 45 rpm. The quality of the sound on the recordings also improved. "Rum and Coca Cola," which was banned on the radio and later on television for its risqué lyrics and for its "free" advertisement of Coca Cola (John Cowley, personal communication to Don Hill, May 2000), made a reappearance during the Calypso Craze but did not make much of a splash:

> Calypso Craze or not, "Rum and Coca-Cola" still isn't considered proper programming material by the broadcast industry.
>
> Undismayed by the long-time radio restriction on the tune, Capitol and independent record label Aladdin Records were rushing their versions of the tune on the market. Capitol slice is by the Andrews Sisters, who originally had the hit Decca version of the tune in 1945.
>
> A check of the networks have revealed that ABC, CBS and NBC still have "Rum and Coca-Cola" on their restricted list. ("'Rum & Coke' Still Banned," Friedman, February 16, 1957)

Copyright problems continued in calypso, as this March 1957 article indicates:

> The calypso trend is driving home to publishers and record companies an important lesson, namely: There are a tremendous amount of calypsos which are copyrighted. It has generally been assumed in the trade that calypso material, which is often folk-based, is in public domain. ("Calypso Trend Spots Copyright Pitfalls for Unwary Disking," *Billboard*, March 23, 1957)

After World War II, interest in calypso remained strong in New York City, at the Catskill resorts where some New Yorkers vacationed, and in Boston. Concerts were held in the late forties in Manhattan at the Renaissance Ballroom, Carnegie Hall, and Town Hall. At least one performance has been preserved, from Town Hall in December 1946.[3] The emcee was Alan Lomax and the sponsoring group was People's Songs, a conglomeration of artists interested in promoting music and liberal causes. The performers were Macbeth the Great, the Duke of Iron—each of whom had built up a respectable clientele in the New York area—and Lord Invader, whose popular "Rum and Coca Cola" song was in litigation. They sang a range of calypsos and other folk songs from Trinidad. This helped establish a practice of combining various genres of West Indian music together, in this case, in a single concert. Calypso in the United States would come to be defined more widely than the Carnival music of Trinidad and would encompass many types of music from the English-speaking Caribbean, as well as new songs composed in the United States that mimicked West Indian styles. By the early 1950s, calypso developed a presence in Miami, Chicago, and California.

Calypso was broadcast over the radio, especially in New York but also on nationally syndicated shows such as the *Mercury Theater* and the *Rudy Vallee Show*. And calypso continued to be performed in bohemian clubs in Manhattan, especially the Village Vanguard where, in 1951, a young American of West Indian descent, Harry Belafonte, began his club career as a jazz singer.

Ross Russell, owner of Dial Records and a promoter of bop records, became interested in West Indian music, thinking that the records would sell well in the United States (phone interview of Ross Russell by Don Hill, August 12, 1996). On a visit to Trinidad in 1953, he met Aubrey "Bolo" Christopher, of Christopher Brothers Cycle and Radio Services in Port of Spain (phone interview of Aubrey Christopher by Don Hill, August 17, 1996). They decided to record calypsos, steelband music, and other Carnival and religious music in late February and early March 1953. The Dial 10" long-playing albums that resulted were the first LPs recorded in Trinidad. (Russell also recorded or released music from other West Indian islands.) Regrettably, their sales were marginal.

A more successful small label that marketed calypso long-playing recordings during and after the Calypso Craze was Cook, founded by High Fidelity pioneer Emory Cook (his "microfusion" process made possible one of the first commercially viable stereo recordings). The Cook label included calypsos, other West Indian music, classical music, and field recordings of rituals from various parts of the world. Beginning in the middle 1950s. Cook visited Trinidad on a regular basis and made both field and studio recordings of calypso and other carnival music. Cook marketed his records in the West Indies and in the United States. The records were moderately successful in the islands and are still sold in Trinidad today. However, in the United States, Cook's records seemed to appeal only to a few hard-core fanatics. The 1957 issues of *Billboard* scarcely mention the Cook label and none of his calypso recordings appear in the top popular LP list nor in the various singles' lists.

Throughout the 1940s and early 1950s, a few calypsos recorded in the United States were issued on different labels. Monogram, run by Manny Warner, issued calypso, Latin, and Haitian records. Little is known about the label, though several of the leading calypso singers in the United States (Duke of Iron, Macbeth the Great, and the Charmer aka Louis Farrakhan) recorded for Monogram. The label also leased calypso tracks from record labels in England, Trinidad, the Virgin Islands, the Bahamas, and Bermuda. Though Monogram records remain relatively scarce, more calypso recordings were issued on this label than on any other. The company's business appears to have been small and targeted to the expatriate West Indian and Latin communities.

Other than these three labels, record companies largely ignored calypso music, issuing occasional releases by artists who had recorded a calypso or two as a novelty. The presence of Harry Belafonte, not this ongoing low-level interest in the genre, pushed the general American public to listen to calypso.

HARRY BELAFONTE

The Calypso Craze of 1957 was a brief bubble that piggybacked onto Harry Belafonte's career. His skill as an entertainer and his honest portrayal of himself as a stylist of music from various parts of the world, and not as a calypso singer, allowed his own career to last beyond the Craze. He was dubbed the "Reluctant King of Calypso."[4] The Calypso Craze was launched and carried along by his million-selling album, *Calypso.*

Both of Belafonte's parents were from the West Indies. He studied acting at the New School for Social Research in New York and his earliest interest was in the theater (Smith 1988:56). After performing a song in a school play, he was asked by school chum Monte Kay to perform at his club, the Royal Roost. His first gig there was with legendary jazz musicians including Charlie Parker, Max Roach and Miles Davis (Smith 1988:57). But he was never comfortable as a jazz or pop singer. Kay became his first manager and when he started the Roost label, he recorded Belafonte's first record, issued in 1949.

Belafonte continued to sing and record several pop songs for Capitol but found that it was folk songs and not jazz or pop that interested him:

> I'd find myself going to these clubs. Well, when I saw people like Josh White, Pete Seeger, and Leadbelly, I was absolutely mesmerized. The songs these people were singing were different from Broadway, the Brill Building, Tin Pan Alley. I found a humanity in their songs. Fell in love with the stuff. . . . I began to see a place for myself in that world. As an actor, I could be a guy from the badlands, or a chain-gang singer, or a soul singer. . . . I ain't no Leadbelly and I certainly wasn't Seeger, but I decided I would mold the material and carve out a unique place as a conduit of all this rich music. (Smith 1988:57)

At his Village Vanguard debut in October 1951, Belafonte appeared as a balladeer doing British folk songs such as "Lord Randall," but already he could "vary [his repertoire] with a Calypso" (*Variety,* October 31, 1951:51; see also Gates 1997:163). He started touring nightclubs and his calypsos were regularly praised in reviews. Johnny Sippel, in a *Billboard* review of a February 12, 1953 appearance at the Cocoanut Grove in Los Angeles, praised Belafonte for his "great new act" of American folk material and his calypsos:

> These numbers are done in a realistic manner which would do credit to such famed islanders as [Wilmoth] Houdini and the Lion. Ditties are great pacers and won good laughs. "Hold 'Em Joe" is especially contagious and should be disked by Victor, for whom Belafonte tolls vocally. (Sippel 1957:27)

Time's reviewer noted that Belafonte was "packing them" in at the Cocoanut Grove for more than a month. Belafonte featured "an offbeat bit of calypso gibberish called 'Man Piaba'" ("Timber's Gotta Roll," *Time,* March 9, 1953). "Man Piaba" was a newly composed song evocative of Bill Roger's "West Indian Weed Woman," which was first recorded in 1934. Rogers was from British Guinea (now Guyana) and had performed in the West Indies and New York a decade earlier. Belafonte must have heard his record, or a folk variant, perhaps when he was growing up in Jamaica.

Commenting on a Belafonte performance in a Long Island nightclub, *Downbeat* noted that by the time he sang his third number, "Hold 'Em Joe," the audience "was joining in on the refrain on cue" (*Downbeat,* November 4, 1953:2). It was his "standard audience clincher" (*Downbeat,* March 23, 1953:4). RCA Victor recorded Belafonte's version of the song and used it in his first Broadway appearance. In March 1953, *Newsweek* noted that his recording of "Hold 'Em Joe" was "turning into a hit" ("Splash With Song," *Newsweek,* March 29, 1954:84).

In late 1953, Belafonte was part of John Murray Anderson's Broadway revue, *Almanac.* The show opened at the Imperial Theatre on December 28, 1953 (*Almanac* Playbill 1953). It was his popularity in this show that led to a Tony award and to his first appearance on the *Ed Sullivan Show* (Gates 1997: 164). In the Broadway show, he performed his popular "Mark Twain" and "Acorn in the Meadow." For his last number, he did "Hold 'Em Joe" (*Almanac* Playbill, 1953).

By early 1954, Belafonte was one of the most popular entertainers in the United States and received enormous press coverage. Cutting a strikingly handsome pose that no doubt contributed to his popularity in nightclubs and concerts, he said that he wore snug "'black silk trousers and colorful bullfighter shirts in all hues. . . . I can't see myself singing work songs or about chain gangs in a dinner jacket'" (Belafonte, quoted in *Island in the Sun* Exhibitor's Campaign Book, 1957:9). As to his singing of West Indian material, "He can do Calypso songs with a vivacity that is delightful. He has a good ear for the sound of the words and the rhythm of the music. He spent some of his early years in the West Indies, and this style is a vital part of his background" (Taubman 1954:2, 7).

Belafonte commented on these shaping years of his life in the introduction to one of his songbooks:

> I would say that the West Indian years, as far as my art was concerned, are probably the most significant of my life. Because there, as a boy, growing up in a colonial country, coming from a family that was a family of domestics, planters, workers, I was in a society that held on to the tradition of earlier years of singing and dancing. . . .
>
> When the people sold their wares in the street they sang about them. When the children got together and played games made out of their makeshift toys, they would sing their children's songs. When they went to a funeral, the people gathered and they sang. When they went into their church—there was never a choir as such—the group in the church sang. So that the West Indies and the time that I spent there, was the single greatest influence on me in terms of what I considered to be the real folk art—or the real meaning of the folk art. (Belafonte 1962:5)

Belafonte took part in another Broadway show in 1953, *Three for Tonight.* It was produced by Paul Gregory and was a vehicle for Belafonte and the dance team of Marge and Gower Champion. After ninety-four performances on the road, the show came to Broadway. Belafonte sang fourteen songs and won positive acclaim (Shaw 1960:161–162). Indeed, Brooks Atkinson of the *New York Times* commented:

> Why is Harry Belafonte so magnificent in *Three for Tonight?*
>
> Because he represents the fanaticism of a dedicated artist. Eliminating himself, he concentrates on the songs with fiery intensity. Although his man-

> ners are simple, his singing personality is vibrant and magnetic. (Brooks Atkinson, quoted in Shaw 1960:162)

It was during *Three for Tonight's* tour of the South that Belafonte was subjected to blatant racism of the kind that would shape his political activism for years to come (Shaw 1960:156–160).

A television version of *Three for Tonight* also proved popular (Shaw 1960: 172). But the idea for a whole album of Caribbean material came as an unanticipated by-product of another television show. On October 2, 1955, he starred in the first of five appearances on the *Colgate Comedy Hour* on NBC in a twenty-minute folklore segment called, "Holiday in Trinidad" (Shaw 1960:229–30). Originally this was to be an extended musical sketch constructed around the legendary hero, John Henry. Belafonte's old friend William Attaway was the music conductor and writer assigned to that segment and he helped develop its Caribbean theme (Shaw 1960:229).

Attaway was a staff writer for NBC who worked on various shows, including the *Colgate Comedy Hour* (Shaw 1960:230). He requested that Lord Burgess (Irving Burgie) work on the Belafonte segment. Burgess had already established himself as a performer of Caribbean folk music when he met Attaway.

> I was doing a lot of research into the folklore of the Caribbean when we went into the Village Vanguard with Max Gordon in 1954. Then I ran into a scriptwriter for Harry Belafonte. His sister had told him about me and he wanted to hear what I had, so I let him listen to my stuff, which by that point included "Day-O" and "Jamaica Farewell."
>
> When they heard the stuff, they were just getting ready to book the *Ed Sullivan Show/Colgate Comedy Hour* in the 8:00 time slot on Sunday. They hired Harry to do a John Henry show, and when they heard the material, they switched the whole thing to the Caribbean, around these songs. They did the program in October of 1955 and it was a smash. Harry was working at the Waldorf at the time, so we recorded the thing for RCA at Webster Hall. RCA originally made a couple hundred thousand copies, and the thing just went and went and went. (Burgess quoted in Philbrook 1997)

Lord Burgess had grown up in a West Indian community in Brooklyn and became serious about music while in the army, stationed in the Pacific during World War II. After the war, he studied classical music at Julliard and attended several other colleges after that. He started writing songs in the early 1950s while performing at the Village Vanguard. His discovery by Attaway marked the beginning of a very fruitful collaboration. Arnold Shaw noted:

> Jack Carson, the emcee of the *Colgate Comedy Hour*, was cast in the role of a tourist out on an island-hopping jaunt. Interpolated in the Attaway script were such calypso tunes as "Hosanna," "Come Back Liza," and "The Jack-Ass

> Song," on which Attaway collaborated with Burgess. Also heard for the first time by American audiences was the now-famous "Banana Boat Song" or "Day-O," as it was then known. (Shaw 1960:230)

With "Day-O," Belafonte was able to translate his original plan to celebrate black working men by singing about the steel-driving John Henry to its West Indian equivalent, the roustabout who worked all night at his trade.

In 1956 RCA Victor issued Harry Belafonte's second album, simply titled *Belafonte.* But it wasn't the *Belafonte* album, which only had one calypso track—"Matilda"—that triggered the Calypso Craze. A television show with West Indian vignettes proved to be the catalyst for the recording sessions that followed later that month resulting in Belafonte's third album, *Calypso.* The show also bonded Attaway, Belafonte, and Burgess in a relationship that lasted for many years.

William Attaway's notes on the back of the album proclaimed that the songs reached beyond calypso:

> Harry Belafonte in his selection of material for this album breaks through the stereotype which confines all calypso to a monotonous sameness. The result is not just another presentation of island songs—tired from being trotted out for the tourist on the twenty one day cruise . . . Here are the songs ranging in mood from brassy gaiety to wistful sadness, from tender love to heroic largeness. And through it all runs the irrepressible rhythm of a people who have not lost the ability to laugh at themselves. (1956)

Indeed, Belafonte never pretended that the album, despite its title, was filled only with calypsos:

> Two of my biggest records right now are not even calypso. "Jamaica Farewell" is a West Indian folk ballad and "Day-O" is a West Indian work song. (Belafonte, quoted in "The Calypso Craze," *Newsweek,* February 27, 1957:72)

Two songs by King Radio (Norman Span), "Brown Skinned Girl" and "Man Smart," are the only calypsos on the album.

"Day-O" was the first single from the album. In a different arrangement the Jamaican work song was released by the Terriers, a folk group, under the title "Banana Boat Song." Their version incorporated bits of another folk song, "Hill and Gully Rider." The combined popularity of the "Banana Boat Song" and "Day-O" led immediately to the tune(s) being covered by other artists. By January 1957, this hit song was recorded by Steve Lawrence on Coral, by the Fontaine Sisters on Dot, by jazz great Sarah Vaughan on Mercury and by country and western duo Johnnie and Jack on Victor (BMI advertisement in *Variety,* January 2, 1957:48). It was soon a track on several long playing records. By February not only were both Belafonte's and the Tarriers' versions in the top ten, but as *Newsweek* noted, "There was a Rheingold beer jingle to it, and even a zany little parody called the "Banana Boat Story" ("The Calypso Craze," *Newsweek,* February 27, 1957:72). By April, *Variety* reported that nine Japanese versions of "Banana Boat" were being planned.[5] Ultimately, Belafonte's single peaked at position #5 in 1957 (in *Billboard*) while the Tarriers reached #4. The other versions were quite respectable in the charts as well, with the Fontane Sisters (#13), Steve Lawrence (#18), Sarah Vaughan (#19), and Stan Freberg's comedy take off going to #25. It was the best-selling song for the year. Even more amazing were the sales of Belafonte's *Calypso* album, which was on the *Billboard's* charts for thirty-one weeks as number one, fifty-eight weeks in the top ten, and ninety-nine weeks on the U.S. charts—and became the first million-selling, long-playing record in the history of the recording industry.

The secret to the success of Belafonte's album was a subtle mix of several elements. The album features his attractive voice in a restrained, "minimalist" setting, accompanied by a prominent drum. The album emphasized the West African elements in West Indian music where voice and drums are paramount. Though there is a big band listed as accompaniment, the band is featured only on the last track. The lead instruments other than drums are the acoustic guitar and the penny whistle.

The songs are almost all celebrations of West Indian folk life and love. Bel-afonte affects a slight accent; otherwise, there is his precise, American diction singing high, ringing tones. Often his voice is set against a rich chorus, that features bass voices. The mood is one of celebration of work, love, singing, dancing, weddings, and village life. Side one starts with the famous echo-drenched shouts of "Day-O!" with the worker exhausted from a night of loading bananas on the boats. The listener is then carried to the slow-paced love song, "I Do Adore Her" with Belafonte's voice backed by guitarist Millard Thomas. The next song on the album is "Jamaica Farewell." It has become a Caribbean standard in its own right. Again, the gentle slow acoustic guitar leads have a mood of nostalgia for lost love and a simple, insular life. The pace picks up with "Is His Love Like Rum," a lighthearted wedding celebration with a penny whistle responding to the vocal lead. "Dolly Dawn" is a celebration of African roots, alluding to Dolly who sings and dances and "cause the rafters to ring." The song is carried by a long whistling solo that echoes the penny whistle but is simpler.

Side two starts with "Star-O," a reprise of "Day-O." The chorus celebrates the night sky, not the morning light. "The Jackass Song" is an adaptation of a traditional folk song about a donkey. A call and response between a mixed chorus and a West Indian penny whistle carries the melody, with Belafonte interjecting, "Juke me!" now and then. Next is "Hosanna," a spiritual about building one's faith on a strong foundation. "Come Back Liza," with its gentle message of longing, echoes "Jamaica Farewell." This time it is the loved one who leaves, not the singer as in the other song. The last two songs are real calypsos and are both compositions of King Radio (Norman Span). The lyrics of these calypsos carry messages of protest that may not have been so obvious to the American listener. Indeed, Trinidadian Geoffrey Holder does not mince words on the origins of "Brownskin Girl":

> "Brownskin Girl" too, is nothing more than a West Indian version of "Madame Butterfly," but here the words had to be changed since their meaning had to be changed since their meaning was all too shockingly apparent. The Americans came; they took over the island; there was lots of money; some of the islanders gave up their virtue easily for that money (some might have, anyway, I must admit) and found themselves with blue-eyed babies. The American soldiers had to go back on a battleship and cruelly, cruelly, they told the Brownskin Girl that if they didn't come back, why, throw away the baby, the damn baby. Those are the real words; in the American rendering, the Brownskin Girl is requested to stay home (kindly) and mind the baby! (Holder 1957: 60)

Clearly, the American version of the song to which Holder is referring is Belafonte's, even though Belafonte's lyrics do not hide the tale of white American service men abandoning their children to their brown-skinned mothers. The implications of "Brownskin Girl" and "Man Smart," Radio's other calypso on the album, seem never to have become an issue for Belafonte's innumerable fans. Perhaps the thrill of "exotic" sex trumps the issue of a father's responsibility in the mind of the American listener.

As *Calypso* etched its mark on the long-playing record market, Belafonte continued to be very well received:

> [As the] gent responsible for the Calypso Craze, Harry Belafonte's performance at the [Cocoanut] Grove [in Los Angeles] is without precedent. At his windup he will have established a new house record, shattering the mark previously held by Guy Lombardo in 1935. His off-beat calypso and folk music offerings were eagerly devoured by an enraptured audience, with the distaff sex particularly enamored. (Joel Friedman in "Personal Appearances" column, 1957)

Following the success of his calypso long-playing albums in the spring of 1957, Belafonte signed a new contract with RCA Victor:

> Harry Belafonte who in the past year has developed into RCA Victor's biggest album property, and a big singles seller as well, was finally snared to a new disk contract last week. He had been without a contract for the past month.
>
> Belafonte's deal reportedly is for a long term, and carries one of those fabulous gurantees [*sic*] reminiscent of the Golden Age of Record-Deals-which

> was the late 1940's. ("Victor Gets Belafonte Ink on New Pact," *Billboard,* April 27, 1957)

Belafonte released four more calypso albums, *Belafonte Sings of the Caribbean* in 1957, *Jump Up Calypso* in 1961, *Calypso in Brass* in 1966, and *Calypso Carnival* in 1971, all for RCA. He also recorded occasional calypsos on other albums, often as part of live medleys of his hits. He continued to be an immensely successful concert and recording artist for decades. While he performed such hits as "Day-O," "Jamaica Farewell," and "Matilda" in almost every concert, he succeeded in having calypso as a small aspect of a very wide repertoire.

When interviewed by a Caribbean journalist during the Craze about the fact that he was not a "real" calypso singer, Belafonte was blunt in response, distinguishing himself from what he perceived was the calypso scene:

> I find that most of the culture coming out of Trinidad among calypso singers is not in the best interest of the people of the Caribbean community. I think that it's racist, because you sing to our own denunciation on color. You sing about our sexual power, and our gift of drinking, and rape, and all the things we do to which I have, and want, no particular claim. What I sought to do with my art is take my understanding of the region and put it before people in a positive way. (Harry Belafonte, quoted in Gates 1997:168)

With this attitude, Belafonte avoided overly suggestive songs. At the same time he did not sugar coat the message of his calypsos. His political commitment compelled him to be interested in songs that emphasized struggles for freedom from racism and oppression. He tried not to sing calypsos that gave a negative image of West Indians, and he distanced himself from being king of that kind of calypso.

However, while he was not a calypsonian, Belafonte has done more to make calypso music known around the world than most calypsonians. Although a "reluctant king," he is still one with an enormous legacy.

THE CALYPSO RECORDING CRAZE OF 1957

The Calypso Craze of 1957 played out on two major fronts: on records and in nightclubs. Calypso over the radio, television, and on film was of lesser importance and calypso shows in theaters were not particularly successful. At the beginning of the Craze, it was difficult to see where calypso would have its greatest impact. As one newspaper article in January 1957 reported, "Suddenly, calypso is everywhere—in nightclubs, on radio and TV, in college auditoriums and concert halls" (Craft 1957:79).

Calypsonians, calypso singers, and other performers[6] had albums on major labels. RCA issued albums by the Duke of Iron and Zebra. Lord Christo came up from Trinidad to appear at the Blue Angel nightclub in Chicago and recorded an album for Mercury while he was there. Lord Flea recorded an album for Capitol and Columbia, and the Massie Patterson calypso troupe recorded one also. Calypso artists from the Caribbean who performed in hotels and nightclubs to tourists—the Eloise Trio from the Bahamas, the Talbot Brothers from Bermuda, and the Fabulous McClevertys from the Virgin Islands—suddenly had records on major labels. Black folk singers with a wide repertoire—Stan Wilson, Ted Browne, and Russell Daville—issued albums that focused on their calypso performances. All kinds of obscure labels issued calypso singles and albums. Latin artists—Candido and Joe Loco—recorded calypso-oriented albums. Others—Tito Puente and Prez Prado—recorded calypso singles. Jazz and popular female singers—Sarah Vaughan, Dinah Washington, June Christy, and Rosemary Clooney—followed Ella Fitzgerald in trying their hand at calypso. Various anthologies of calypso material were issued, many featuring songs recorded years earlier and released to take advantage of the projected sales boom. Columbia and Folkways even issue calypso albums for children.

Of the singles, the only West Indian songs to reach the top were "Day-O" or "Banana Boat Song" and "Marianne." The original title of "Marianne" was usually spelled *Mary Ann* and has been claimed by several calypsonians. "Mary Ann" was the most popular song for the carnivalesque celebrations in Trinidad for VJ ("Victory over Japan") Day at the end of World War II on August 15, 1945. The Roaring Lion (on Guild Records) and Lord Invader (Disc) recorded it in New York that year; in Invader's version he mentions that he was not in Trinidad for the "bacchanal." "Mary Ann" was picked up by two Latin bands and recorded in 1947 by Pupi Campo and by Armando Jack the next year (Salazar 1999:35). Terry Gilkyson and the Easy Riders, a trio of folk singers based in Los Angeles, recorded "Marianne" in March 1956. The Easy Riders augmented the Trinidadian original with a lilting three-guitar arrangement and new verses. The Hilltoppers, Burl Ives, and the Lane Brothers soon covered the Easy Riders' version (BMI ad in *Variety,* February 27, 1957:50).

Sales of calypso records never matched the industry's expectations. The Calypso Craze was largely a boom-and-bust phenomenon. Data from the weekly issues of *Billboard* tell the story. First, Belafonte's "Calypso" dominated the long-playing charts for many months. No other calypso album had any significant sales. Meanwhile, a handful of calypso records entered into the various single charts. Most of these were listed in the popular singles' charts, a few in the rhythm and blues charts, and a few made the country charts.

In the United States, 45 rpm singles sold to teenagers, while long-playing records tended to be sold to adults and middle-class ones at that. The hope in the industry that calypso would replace rock'n'roll was a misreading of the record-buying public. It was rock'n'roll that appealed to working and subsequently middle-class youth, the people who bought 45 rpm records; it was never calypso.

Calypso in Trinidad filled a different and complex role. It appealed to all ages but most of all to adults; it was a Creole medium of expression. It was music for the tents at Carnival time and music that was both topical and often political. Each year, the calypsonians sang new songs to capture the spirit of that year's Carnival celebration. That spirit, the essence of Trinidadian calypso, was lost in white America and songs that commented on political or social events were shed of their original meaning. For example, Invader's original version of "Rum and Coca Cola" is about Yankee soldiers and prostitutes working for the "Yankee dollar":

> When the Yankees first came to Trinidad
> Some of the young girls were more than glad
> They said that the Yankees treat them nice
> And they give them a better price. (Hill 1993:239)

The Andrews Sisters "clean up" the verse:

> If the Yankee come to Trinidad
> They got the young girls all going mad
> The young girls say they treat them nice
> Make Trinidad a paradise. (Canadian Decca 10205–A)

The Trinidadian calypsos that were part of the boom in the United States tended to be the ones about male–female relations and of a suggestive nature. Geoffrey Holder made this point in his article on calypso:

> As to the lyrics, My! my! . . . No one has ever stopped to ask what "Marianne" does, do you realize that? Here is how the lyrics say it: "All day, all night, Marianne / Down by the seaside siftin' sand." Marianne is a woman of the streets and she has been working all day and all night at her ancient trade. I want to get that point over. And the sand she sifts is men—men, like grains of sand, one or another doesn't make much difference. (Holder 1957:15)

Not so the "Marianne" of the Easy Riders where the verses focus on a woman (the singer) who is going to get married and who is loved by all the children! And "sifting sand" involves little kids playing with Marianne; she certainly isn't a prostitute! American sensibilities were secure.

The river of calypso releases, which swelled to a torrent during the first half of 1957, proved to be barely a trickle by the end of the year.

THE NIGHTCLUB SCENE

In the late 1930s, calypso singers performed at the Village Vanguard, an integrated Greenwich Village club (Hill 1993:161–163). After the war, calypso singers appeared at several nightclubs in New York and a few other places around the country. In nightclubs, calypso's adult nature could be appreciated. Art D'Lugoff, promoter and later impresario of the Village Gate in New York, presented a series of calypso concerts at Carnegie Hall's recital auditorium and packaged a calypso troupe for travel around the country (Schoenfeld, 1956:1). South Florida featured calypso on a regular basis from the early 1950s (telephone interview of Irvin Brown by Ray Funk, April 22, 2000). In the late 1930s, calypso singers performed at the Village Vanguard, an integrated Greenwich Village club (Hill 1993:161–163). In late 1956, *Variety* noted that calypso had been gaining momentum over the past couple months in nightclubs and was on rise across the country in other live venues:

> In addition to a flock of New York spots which are on a Caribbean kick, cafes in Chicago, Philadelphia and Miami Beach are now spotlighting calypso music and talent. Packaged shows are touring the top colleges, such as Yale and Princeton, and even hotels, such as the Sheraton chain, are featuring calypso talent via the Talbot Brothers, a sextet from the Bermudas. (Schoenfeld 1956:1)

Soon New York City had several night clubs devoted to calypso—the "Calypso Room," the "Trinidad Room" and what was regarded in New York as the most famous, the "Jamaica Room" on Third Avenue. *Time* noted,

> In upper Manhattan a saloonkeeper from County Cork recently had his ceiling strung with fishnet, his mirrors adorned with palm fronds, and proudly announced the conversion of the back room into the Ekim Calypso Dock. ("Calypsomania," *Time,* March 25, 1957, p. 55)

In February 1957, a Boston restaurant was revamped and opened as the "Calypso Room" with calypso bands and calypso dance instructors. Other nightspots followed. In Pittsburgh, Dore's restaurant closed for renovation as a calypso nightclub (*Variety,* "Calypso a La Chow Mein; Allegenies' Hold-'Em-Joe; Brit. Teaches Trinidad Terp" [April 3, 1957, p. 83]). The club dates were part of the folk song movement in the 1940s and 1950s and continued after the Craze. Johnny Barracuda spent thirteen years as the featured performer at the African Room on the East Side in New York, singing calypso almost exclusively (telephone interview of Johnny Barracuda by Ray Funk, April 3, 2000).

In the mid-1950s, the United States was beginning to integrate racially, especially youth who dominated the record market. The first development was reflected in Belafonte's presentation of calypso on stage, on television, and on records. Integration had been a favorite issue of the folk-song movement whose performers had joined singers in integrated clubs. This connection between calypso and liberalism was largely a white phenomenon, as was the folk-song movement itself. That is, the West Indians involved in calypso in the United States were largely presenting their music within a white American context.

A factor that made calypso more appealing as a nightclub rather than a recording phenomenon was its suggestive lyrics. As one reporter noted:

> [As to risqué lyrics, they're] there, all right. Some calypsonians get a little over enthusiastic when dealing with love and life, and a lot of their songs can't be put on records. There's one in particular, "The Big Bamboo," that can be heard in various interesting versions at adult dens around town. (Craft 1957:79)

Another aspect of calypso music that couldn't be recorded was live "extempo." Calypsonians had been known to have impromptu matches (calypso "wars") in the tents, trading insults with each other. This translated into a nightclub device where calypso singers would make up verses about members of the audience. The Mighty Panther noted that early in his career, he and other calypsonians would go out to meet tourists arriving on cruise boats and serenade them with extempo verses about themselves (telephone interview of Vernon Roberts by Ray Funk, February 2000). Extempo lyrics about tourists continues to be a tradition at Maracas Beach and the scenic observation overlook above Port of Spain in Trinidad to this day. This tradition was evident during the Calypso Craze in nightclubs:

> If you're ringside in a nightclub with your best girl, keep an eye on that singer in the bright striped shirt and the tight pants. If he moves in close and starts making small talk and asking casual questions between whacks on his guitar, take heed. You may find yourself the subject of a ditty like this:
>
> Here's a young man, the roving kind,
> You know what's in my mind,
> I won't have to tell you any more,
> Young lady, slap him down on the floor
> (a calypso singer, quoted in Craft 1957:79)

Yet even with all these elements that made calypso music appropriate as nightclub fare, the mad phase of switching decor and going for an all-calypso policy seemed to collapse with the other elements of the Craze. After six months, Manhattan's La Cupidon was ready to call it quits:

> With the engagement of Miss Louise, Le Cupidon is exiting its calypso policy. The holdover from that era is the décor which is serviceable under most policies, plus the King Flash Trio which makes like the Trinidaddies. (*Variety*, June 26, 1957, p. 55)

In November, the last of the nightclubs in Boston to feature a calypso motif and an all-calypso booking policy closed (*Variety,* November 20, 1957, p. 66). Even though "all-calypso" nightclubs were finished not all the calypso singers were out of work. Many continued to perform regularly into the 1960s.

Trinidadian calypso has been performed in the United States since 1912 when Lovey's Band traveled from its island home to record in New York City. Shortly after World War I, West Indian immigration to the East Coast of the United States increased to such an extent that approximately one-quarter of the black people in New York City were of West Indian descent by 1930. And with this population came their music, especially calypso. In the mid-1930s, the hottest singers from Trinidad began annual visits to the New York to record and play in local clubs. Within a decade, interest in calypso in the United States had spread to the West Coast by Sir Lancelot, Lionel Belasco, and others. Lancelot appeared in several important Hollywood films in the 1940s and 1950s. The most popular hit single during World War II—"Rum and Coca Cola"—as recorded by the American Andrew Sisters, is a calypso. Several others—"Run Joe" and "Stone Cold Dead in the Market"—were also popular.

Nightclub appearances and occasional recordings spread interest in calypso. By the middle of the 1950s, calypso music had a minor but persistent presence in the American entertainment scene. With the volcanic rise in popularity of Harry Belafonte in late 1956 and 1957, calypso became a "new" fad. For a few brief months everybody seemed to record a calypso or a newly written song in the calypso style. Then, as fast as it rose in popularity, calypso faded into the background, to be subsumed within the larger, growing "folk-song" scene. There it sat until 1964 when a new generation of West Indian immigrants reinvigorated interest in calypso within their own expatriate communities. But this time around, it was not calypso that was to engage America but Jamaican reggae.

What can one say about the Calypso Craze? Why did it not replace rock'n'roll as predicted? There are several answers to that question. First, calypso was an adult entertainment more at home in nightclubs than in teenager-packed auditoriums. rock'n'roll was a youth rebellion and pitch men were wrong in thinking that calypso would replace rock'n'roll. Calypso did not appeal to young people; it was not rebel music. Furthermore, calypso was not primarily a dance music as rock'n'roll was, although entrepreneurs and dance studios tried to make it so, as evidenced by this *Billboard* story of 1957: "Capitol Records will combine with the Arthur Murray Dance Studios to promote a new dance instruction disk tagged the 'Ray Anthony Calypso Dance'" ("Calypso Via Disk, Dance," in *Billboard,* March 9, 1957).

> Many have predicted the death knell of calypso because the kids can't dance to it. [Dick] Clark figures his kids have the answer to that, too, with a dance called "Calypso." According to the jockey, this is a modified cha cha step which the kids are doing to all the calypso songs. Reportedly, it's a strong fad in the Quaker City, which could help to keep calypso above water for a considerable time. ("Futures Spark DJ Attention," *Billboard,* March 23, 1957)

Dick Clark's prediction was wrong. Here too calypso failed to meet the teenagers' test. Calypso was Carnival music for contemplation (calypso in the tents) or for "dancing" ("road marching") in the streets, not for American theaters or dance halls.

Calypso made practically no impact on what was then called "Country and Western" music; one of the few country calypso songs beyond Johnny and Jack's version of the "Banana Boat Song" was Canadian-born Hank Snow's "Calypso Sweetheart."

Calypso made a small impact on rhythm and blues, then mostly a black American genre. But it did not do well in black communities, with the exception of those East Coast cities in which there was a substantial West Indian component within the black community. A *Billboard* reviewer had this to say about a calypso show at the Apollo Theater in Harlem, the premiere Black American venue in the United States:

> Another flop was a recent calypso outing at Harlem's Apollo. The show, which closed several weeks ago, was described by Frank Shiffman, manager of the theater, as "a minor debacle." No plans are in the works for an early repeat at the traditional show-place for rhythm and blues and jazz performers. (April 29, 1957, p. 61)

An important "problem" with calypso was the lyrics. As we have seen, the lyrics were commonly changed, both for clarity's sake and to make them less explicitly sexual. Some record companies went to great lengths to assist the listener in understanding lyrics:

> Columbia Records is jacketing three new calypso singles with a special jacket containing lyrics to the tunes.
>
> Diskery feels that many buyers throughout the country have had difficulty in understanding the lyrics to calypso songs. This sing-along idea, it's felt, will promote calypsos in many areas. ("Jacket Lyrics With Calypsos," in *Billboard,* April 6, 1957, p. 18)

The "Mitch Miller-style" sing-a-long to calypso records never caught on.

The greatest interest in calypso was in the northern urban centers, not in rural America and not in the South. And record sales of calypso recordings during the boom were higher and lasted longer in the long-playing album format than in the teen-oriented singles on 78s or 45s. No pundits noticed that all the hit calypso recordings in terms of sales were by folk artists—Harry Belafonte, the Terriers, and Easy Riders—none of whom saw themselves as calypsonians. For each of them, calypso was part of a much wider folk repertoire. The sales of these hit recordings are better seen as precursors of the huge sales that folk recordings by the Kingston Trio and Peter, Paul and Mary would have, rather than any widespread interest in calypso.

As fads go, the Calypso Craze was not particularly long lived. On May 22, 1957, *Variety* announced that "Calypso is Stone Cold Dead; Rock 'N Roll Still Swing" and noted that the flow of new calypso releases had dwindled from twenty to twenty-five a week to only a few releases. It was apparent by this date that calypso did not ring the death knell for rock'n'roll. By the end of the year, calypso was barely noticed in the industry.

Did calypso have any lasting impact on American popular music? Yes. It boosted the career of Harry Belafonte. After the Craze was over, calypso added a minor dimension to the folk music scene; songs such as "Ugly Woman," "Man Smart (Woman Smarter)," "Matilda," and "Marianne" became folk and pop standards. Harry Belafonte, who began as a jazz and folk singer, emerged from the folk revival as the first great world music star in the United States, a harbinger of Paul Simon and others. And if popular Hawaiian music won the Pacific, "Americanized" calypso continued as the music of choice in tropical hotels in the West Indies and elsewhere on the East Coast of the United States for decades to come. Finally, newer West Indian calypso, in its traditional form as well as other Trinidad music forms—soca, rapso, and chutney—gained their own spots in the World Music arena.

NOTES

Thanks to Kevin Burke, John Cowley, Michael Eldridge, and Steve Shapiro as well as to singers such as the Roaring Lion, the Mighty Panther, Johnny Baracuda, and Irvin Brown for their assistance over the years the authors have pursued calypso research directly related to his paper.

1. Calypso was also performed in theaters, on film, and on television but had less impact in those venues. That part of the story is beyond the scope of this paper. See Hill 1993, which details calypso in Trinidad and the United States prior to the 1950s.

2. For the details of the lawsuits over "Rum and Coca-Cola," see John Cowley (1993).

3. These recordings were reissued in 1999 on two compact discs, annotated by Donald R. Hill and John Cowley (1999).

4. This phrase is used in a great number of publications at the time including Hy Steinman, ed., *Harry Belafonte: His Complete Life Story* (New York: Hillman Publications, 1957).

5. "Japanese Boat," *Variety,* April 10, 1957:72. The only version confirmed as being issued is by Michiko Hamumura (RCA EP 4095), an eighteen-year-old teen sensation in Japan.

6. According to a convention established by the authors, "calypsonians" are singers who had experience performing in Carnival calypso tents in Trinidad. "Calypso singers" are West Indians who had no tent experience. Others were folk or popular singers or artists who sang an occasional calypso.

9. The Politics of Cultural Value and the Value of Cultural Politics: International Intellectual Property Legislation in Trinidad

Robin Balliger

Contemporary concerns with the "global" mark a shift in thinking about the nation-state as the "container of social life," and the central terrain on which to analyze the production of citizen-subjects, economic development, political sovereignty, and cultural distinctiveness (Appadurai 1990, 2003; Gupta and Ferguson 1992; Basch, Glick Schiller, Szanton Blanc 1994; Brenner 1997; Castells 1997; Comaroff and Comaroff 2000; Hardt and Negri 2000). A central concern for many "developing" nations has been the supranational control exercised by international lending agencies such as the International Monetary Fund (IMF). Structural adjustment policies and privatization undermine state sovereignty, and the imposition of austerity programs increases poverty and hardship among the most vulnerable populations (Hakkert and Goza 1989). Achille Mbembe (2001) argues that in addition to the direct economic impact of these policies, the "tutelary government" exercised by the IMF and World Bank in Africa not only undermines the material base of society, but also destroys specific relations of political legitimacy. Fractured social, political, and economic relations are largely responsible for increased violence, banditry, and witchcraft accusations, which ultimately threaten the very existence of the postcolonial state.

I draw on these analytic insights to address questions of sovereignty in the Caribbean, especially the area of international intellectual property (IP) law as another important arena of supranational control. During the course of multilateral negotiations of the General Agreement on Trade and Tariffs (GATT), 152 states agreed to revise and enforce intellectual property law with the goal of achieving global "harmonization" by the year 2000. Much of the worldwide debate on IP law focuses on "North–South" conflicts of interest and on unequal relations of power between metropolitan and "developing" nations. Through a situated analysis in Trinidad, however, I show how the implementation of intellectual property legislation must also be analyzed in relation to transnational class consolidation and deepening inequality and instability within nations. In Trinidad, IP laws are supported by national cultural producers (thereby disrupting reductive "North–South" analysis), but enforcement criminalizes underclass pirate cassette dealers, for example, and generates protestations from consumers. Moreover, the emphasis on individual authorship threatens to erase the social context of struggle from which Trinidadian expressive culture arose. When much of the population becomes excluded from "their" culture's expressions and profits, what then constitutes community? Exploring how intellectual property legislation is negotiated, accommodated, and resisted by various interests raises questions of social fragmentation as national subjects are repositioned by transnational forces (Balliger 2001).

Colonial and postcolonial analysis problematizes the concept of sovereignty because state formation has always been embedded in a global economic, political, and social context (Scott 1995; Chambers and Curti 1996; Stoler and Cooper 1997). This is especially true of the modern Caribbean, forged by the "world-encompassing processes" initiated by European expansion more than five hundred years ago, which eliminated the native population and created Creole societies (Mintz and Price 1985; Trouillot 1992; Gilroy 1993; Yelvington 2000). Spain first colonized Trinidad in 1498, it had a significant French population, and then became a British colony in 1797, with a substantial population of African slaves and free blacks. After emancipation in the 1830s, East Indian indentured laborers were brought to the colony, initiating the dual ethnic and cultural character of contemporary Trinidadian society (with 40.1 percent Indian descent, 39.3 percent African descent, 16 percent mixed, and 4 percent Chinese, white, Syrian and "other").[1] While national definitions of culture are often "imagined," Trinidad's colonial history and racial divisions make questions of national culture especially contentious, and the polarization of Afro- and Indo-Trinidad dominates sociohistorical debate (Singh 1988; Ryan 1996).

Music figures prominently in public discourse about culture, race, and place in Trinidad and has recently become central to debate on intellectual property, as music is Trinidad's primary "creative" product. Calypso music (songs of topical social commentary), which voiced opposition to British colonialism in Trinidad and after independence in 1962, exemplified national culture, along with the Afro-Trinidadian performance traditions of steelband and Carnival. Since the 1980s, Indo-Trinidadians have contested their exclusion from definitions of national culture through the popular Indo Trinidadian music of chutney (Ramnarine 2001), and in the 1990s through the first nationally broadcast "Indian" radio stations. The first Indian government (United National Congress; UNC) was elected in 1995. While racial divisiveness threatens to leap from public discourse and music to actual ethnic violence (Premdas 1993; Hayde 1997; Allahar 1999), much of the backdrop to this situation has been a severe economic decline after Trinidad's oil boom. The Ministry of Social Development reported that since the late 1980s, poverty levels have increased from 3 percent to 36 percent. In addition, there have been multiple currency devaluations and cuts in the public sector (Crichton and de Silva 1989; La Guerre 1994; World Bank 1995; Dookeran 1996).

Beyond their direct economic impact, privatization and commodification also affect definitions of culture. Much analysis of international IP law in the context of neoliberalism illustrates how the metropole maintains a West–Other binary, as "authors with intellect are distinguished from cultures with property" (Coombe 1997:90). However, public discourse on intellectual property in Trinidad produces subjects in contradictory ways—both as ahistorical autonomous subjects of capitalism who participate in culture through consumption, and as situated cultural subjects contributing a unique, nationally defined cultural experience to the global marketplace. While Trinidad has been coerced by metropolitan interests into adopting IP legislation designed to protect foreign technology and entertainment industries, parliamentary debate focused on the enhanced protection of "national culture," particularly the steel pan (considered the most important acoustic instrument of the twentieth century, arising from an urban, black underclass). By mobilizing legitimate historical charges of cultural imperialism, the government fosters cultural nationalism in a period of racial tension and economic decline, along with rhetorically salvaging national sovereignty. A definable cultural identity also promotes an attractive image of political stability for foreign investors.

While state discourses represent "culture" as historically shared by members of the nation, pressure from a globalizing economy leads to representations of cultural expression as the creation of an autonomous subject. Commercial interests attempt to redefine popular understandings of Trinidad's music as socially produced ("we 'ting"), into the valuing of music as an individually authored commodity. The move from social text to individual product undermines music's historical role in anticolonial struggle and its contemporary importance as a sphere of social critique. Recent revisions in copyright law also aim at eliminating cassette piracy and have led to a crackdown on sidewalk cassette dealers, who are often poor youth. But forms of petty production such as cassette piracy are important sources of income precisely for those segments of the population increasingly excluded from the workings of the global economy. In sum, national debates about music production and consumption exist in wider economic and ideological fields, and illustrate how globalization disrupts national culture, intensifies ethnic and class conflict, and produces new social–spatial formations.

AUTHORIZING CULTURE

Before analyzing the cultural politics of intellectual property legislation in Trinidad, I briefly historicize conceptions of authorship and culture that inform contemporary neoliberal discourse. Most critics of bourgeois ideology note the emergence of a modern subject concurrently with capitalist expansion and liberal humanism in Europe in the late Renaissance. In contrast to premodern Europe and understandings of God's universe as composed of nonequal elements, the modern individual is conceived as a "self-sufficient and self-contained monad." In 1690, John Locke articulated the "possessive" character of the modern individual in that man has property in his own person; the mixing of human labor in the transformation of nature not only creates value in "his" property, but "natural human acquisitiveness" separates the civilized from the savage (who exist in a state of nature). Although modern individuals are naturally autonomous and equal, they must freely give up their natural state to become members of civil society, in which the purpose of government is to protect and regulate property by law (Locke 1980).

Locke also argues that to protect "equality," hierarchy is necessarily reintroduced in the form of man over woman (facilitated by the ideology of a public and private sphere), parents over children, and master over slave. Kant extends this core contradiction of modernity not only to reason over emotion within a divided subject, but also to the nation over the individual, to relations among nations, and over time and succeeding generations (Kant 1963). In contrast, Marx argues that liberalism is neither natural nor universal, but an ideology serving dominant class interests. By declaring individuals equal as political subjects, the state depoliticizes inequalities based on birth, class, education, and profession (1990). Marx rejects the "Robinson Crusoe" model of the independent, "self-contained monad," by describing how capitalism disguises the social character of labor and its products (Marx 1976). Relating these ideas to art and cultural production, Janet Wolff (1992) describes how the idea of "aesthetic autonomy" and the concept of genius first appeared in the late Renaissance (as did copyright), and, by the nineteenth century, art was understood through the lens of Romanticism as an autonomous activity that transcends the social.

The anthropological concept of culture that emerged in the late nineteenth century transferred "possessive individualism"[2] onto groups by drawing on German Romantic ideas that a people had a distinctive character and spirit. Ethnic groups and nations are commonly understood as "collective individuals" whose most prized possessions are their culture and history (Handler 1991). While essentializing notions of culture have given way to understandings of difference as a discourse embedded in relations of power, the language of cultural diversity remains dominant in international relations. Kearney comments on how the concept of culture has entered into legal discourse just as anthropologists are debating the usefulness of the concept: "It is somewhat ironic that while the conditions of transnationalism are causing anthropologists to reconsider the validity of the culture concept, the growth of transnational communities is causing the legal system to pay more attention to it" (1995:556–557). The possessive concept of culture is a necessary component of globalization, as neoliberal assumptions frame international discourse on "culture"—its reification enabling cultural ownership, preservation, and exploitation. Non-Western peoples have employed the language of rights and ownership to make claims against dominant forces, but their arguments for particularity must be conducted within a broader conformity, as "the spread of bourgeois law around the world, backed by the weapons and wealth of overdeveloped nation-states, has made these ideas difficult for people anywhere to ignore" (Collier et al. 1995:14). Or, as Handler writes: "That putatively diverse national and ethnic groups understand one another well enough to fight about who 'owns' the past suggests that all of them have been assimilated into a global culture of the present" (1991:72).

Rosemary Coombe's essay, "The Properties of Culture and the Possession of Identity: Postcolonial Struggle and the Legal Imagination" (1997), addresses hegemonic constructions of authorship in the context of international law. Coombe argues that contemporary discourse on cultural appropriation is polarized in two positions that she labels Romanticism and Orientalism, both of which draw on the concepts of a universal Culture (capital "C") and cultural relativism (small "c"). Legal constructions of authorship are imagined in Romantic terms in which an autonomous subject freely creates from his imagination—transforming any "idea" into "expression," which then represents his work and property. Coombe contrasts this "imperialist" view with the "Orientalist" understanding of a univocal "voice" capable of transparently speaking for an authentic cultural tradition. While "Native Peoples" have made claims based on internationally recognized definitions of property, cultural claims are profoundly limited compared to the rights of individual authors (to whom royalties flow). While I agree with Coombe's contention, she tends to overlay this duality on Western and non-Western peoples:

> The law offers two possibilities of property that reflect two visions of culture. Intellectual property laws enable individual artists imagined as acultural Romantic authors to collect royalties for the reproduction of their personal expressions as reward for their contributions to a "human" cultural heritage. Cultural property laws enable collectivities to physically control objects that can be shown to embody the essential identity of a "culture" statically conceived. (1997:86)

However, these two visions of culture cannot always be mapped onto "white" artists and "Native" people. In Trinidad, defining individual or cultural ownership has become a contentious question among people with a *shared* national culture and reveals a conflict between national cultural producers and lower-class consumers. This illustrates that the international imposition of neoliberal concepts of property onto less powerful nations also fuels class antagonism within the cultural space of the nation-state.

INTELLECTUAL PROPERTY, INTERNATIONAL RELATIONS, AND THE STATE

In discussing the globalization of intellectual property legislation, I attend to the continuing power of the metropole to shape policy on a global scale, while developing a more nuanced analysis. Much of the critical scholarship on international intellectual property legislation emphasizes "North–South" conflicts of interest, and the superior power of the "North" to enforce its position over weaker states, thus eroding national sovereignty. However, this approach masks a more complex analysis of transnational class interests, an increase in inequalities within nations, and the re-territorializing of identities in transnational space. Stoler and Cooper's approach to globalization highlights the necessity of bringing the metropole and colony (or postcolony) into one analytic field, attending to different populations and agendas within those categories, and conjoining political economic and discursive analysis:

> The current focus on the cultural and representational features of colonial authority powerfully underscores that we can understand little about the political economy of colonialism without attending to the culturally constructed and historically specific notions of "labor," of "trade," of "freedom," and of the practices and perceptions in which relations of domination were lived. But the cultural work in which states engage and the moralizing missions in which they invest are discursive fields both grounded in and constitutive of specific relations of production and exchange. (1997:18)

Ronald Bettig's *Copyrighting Culture: The Political Economy of Intellectual Property* (1996) offers an overly structural approach to cultural production, but it raises important issues regarding the globalization of intellectual property legislation. Bettig points out that copyright appeared with the historical emergence of capitalism and that protection has always required the state. He argues that intellectual property legislation follows the expanding markets (such as in software and entertainment) of powerful nations, and that protecting IP internationally has been fueled by an emphasis in the U.S. economy on the production of services, along with new forms of protection necessitated by the international division of labor. The United States has dictated the terms of protection, and "Free Trade" areas have been a central method of advancing these interests:

> The global proliferation of communications technologies and the expansion of the realm of intellectual property is a process that clearly benefits the advanced economies of the United States, Europe, and Japan. The incorporation of intellectual property protection into the General Agreement on Tariffs and Trade (GATT) signaled the consolidation of control over intellectual and artistic creativity in the hands of transnational corporations based in rich countries. (1996:5)

In addition to "metropole–periphery" conflicts, Bettig addresses the issue of intellectual property for classes across and within nations. Since the 1980s, he cites increasing class consolidation (e.g., NAFTA was supported by "big capitalists" in all three countries); clashes within nations between more advanced export sectors and those industries involved in copyright infringement; and the widening gap between rich and poor (within industrialized countries as well). Economists trace these developments to the debt crisis of the 1970s and the power of nonaligned nations in this period. The structural crisis in transnational capital fueled efforts by international economic policy-planning organizations such as the IMF and World Bank to "reestablish the international unity of the capitalist class in the face of popular social movements" (Bettig 1996:190). Debt payments to the IMF have largely been serviced by reducing the "labor share" of income, so that international redistribution of income has been accompanied by a regressive redistribution on the domestic level. Because a significant portion of interest payments to international banks are "returned" to local elites as interest on stock of previous capital flight, "Popular classes are not only forced to undergo austerity to pay international debt, but also to fund their own upper classes" (Pastor 1989:99).

To summarize recent intellectual property law in Trinidad, I draw on the work of Taimoon Stewart and Keith Nurse from the University of the West Indies. Stewart's primary concern is the conflict of interests between North and South nations, not only in terms of their economies, but also with regard to value systems, morality, and community. South nations claim that the pirating of foreign technology is done on humanitarian grounds, or that their IP laws reflect greater access to food and medicine. But Stewart argues that cross-country differences matter little when the North establishes the "rules of the game." The World Intellectual Property Organization (WIPO) administered international agreements on intellectual property in a one-country, one-vote system (giving developing nations greater influence), until more powerful industrialized nations undercut this system by successfully including TRIPS (Trade-Related Aspects of Intellectual Property Rights) under the World Trade Organization in the Uruguay Round of GATT in 1994. Developing countries were given to the year 2000 to implement IP legislation, with the goal of achieving "global harmonization" ("harmonization" meaning upwards to EU and U.S. law).

In the Caribbean, Jamaica and Trinidad signed bilateral treaties with the United States to revise their domestic legislation in advance of the transitional deadline, and Trinidad instituted new laws in early 1997. In Stewart's analysis, the government's argument that strong IP laws will attract foreign investment is flawed, and "while some benefits can accrue to us in terms of protection for our artistes under copyrights, by far the bulk of the new intellectual property regime protects owners of foreign goods and technologies" (1996:20). Trinidad will receive little benefit from this legislation, but the state must absorb all administrative and enforcement costs, and is subject to cross-retaliation in areas other than IP to ensure compliance.

Writing on the music industry and Carnival, Keith Nurse summarizes the impact of international IP law on developing countries as follows:

(1) additional administrative and enforcement costs
(2) increased payment for foreigners' proprietary artistic work
(3) price increases associated with greater market power for copyright producers
(4) enhanced protection and collection of copyright royalties for developing countries. (1996:22)

Simply put, most benefits will flow to the international music industry, whose global losses from piracy in 2005 were estimated at $4.3 billion.

Nurse also critiques the economic inequalities of cultural production on an international level and with regard to race in Trinidad. In an interesting reversal of the cultural imperialism thesis, he favors privatizing Carnival and shifting it away from a festival to "seeing carnival as an industry" (personal correspondence 1997). He characterizes the dominant discourse on Carnival as modern Europe's "dialogue with itself," in which Western cultural critics romanticize Carnival as an authentic festival of liberation in danger of losing its meaning through commodification, as seen in Payson's description of Carnival's "evolution from sacred to commercial ritual" (1995:12). However, Carnival in the

Caribbean has been situated in the circuit of global capitalism for the last five hundred years. Nurse challenges the perception of Carnival as something only "black people do," as other races have always been involved—primarily as entrepreneurs—through the sponsoring of music and masquerade competitions, the selling of fabric and alcohol, the renting of sound systems, and so forth. While the question of "who benefits?" from cultural production in terms of race is an extremely important question, conflicts of interest within Afro-Trinidadian populations are an important issue I discuss below.

PARLIAMENTARY DEBATE ON INTELLECTUAL PROPERTY, THE POLITICAL USES OF PAN, AND THE SEARCH FOR AN AUTHOR

In Trinidad, constructions of culture and authorship have emerged as a field of contestation within the nation by different economic and political interests. Analyzing the articulation of spatial scales is useful for thinking through contradictory relationships between the state and transnational sphere, as well as that of the state and various national interests (Sassen 1996; Brenner 1997). Parliamentary debate on IP might be understood as *performing* state sovereignty (in the context of its erosion by supranational lending agencies, law, and trade policies), by shifting the IP debate towards the protection of national culture, especially the steel pan. However, with the dramatic increase in racial tension in Trinidad in recent years, national discourse about the steel pan becomes reframed by Afro-Trinidadian or Indo-Trinidadian interests. Beyond constructions of culture as shared by members of the nation, or by a national ethnic group, the redefinition of culture as individually authored is being promoted by the local copyright organization that represents national cultural producers, especially calypsonians. I discuss how these contradictory interests affect specific populations and popular understandings of cultural expression, beginning with parliamentary debate on IP legislation, which focused on protecting the steel pan as the ultimate image of national cultural achievement.

In accordance with a bilateral treaty signed with the United States, Trinidad had both to "rush" to enact intellectual property legislation in advance of the deadline for developing nations and to provide even greater IP protection than the TRIPS agreement. As a result, parliamentary debate on intellectual property was largely a matter of form over substance (but necessary for the staging of political sovereignty). The package of legislation was debated through early 1997 and included five bills in the following areas: Patents, Industrial Designs, Layout Designs of Integrated Circuits, Protection Against Unfair Competition, and Geographical Indications. While this legislation primarily protects multinational corporations and foreign investors, parliamentary debate focused on protecting the steel pan and was extensively covered by the major news media. Legislation that clearly represents a capitulation to foreign powers was recast as providing enhanced protection for national culture. Focusing on the steel pan not only constructed IP legislation as something Trinidadians would support, but also form part of a continuing political effort by the (Indian dominated) UNC government to foster "national unity."

Opening remarks in the House of Representatives by Kamla Persad-Bissessar, Minister of Legal Affairs, articulated a familiar discourse of modernization (naturalizing "development" and neoliberal interests), enhanced by contemporary Silicon Valley, techno-liberationist assumptions:

> Mr. Speaker, as we approach the year 2000; as we approach the 21st Century, we see unfolding before our eyes, a new age, a new era. We see the world shrinking before our eyes as we enter into the high tech electronic age: we see the Hon. Prime Minister with his laptop computer and so many others with computers. We see a shrinking world, as we speak in one place we can hear our words broadcast across the globe in a couple seconds; incidents as they occur in one place can be relayed in seconds across the entire continent as we are witnessing globalized economy.
>
> No more in Trinidad are we isolated; no more are we insulated from world events. Indeed, we cannot afford to be isolated and we cannot afford to be insulated from what is taking place in the rest of the world. Within this changing scenario, in the count down to the 21st Century, this Government has embarked on a progressive legislative agenda so as to facilitate the absorption of advanced technologies and the stimulation of domestic activity in order to contribute to the development of Trinidad and Tobago and so to place Trinidad and Tobago firmly on the world map.

One could argue that Trinidad was never insulated from world events, but was forged *by* world events (especially histories of conquest and colonization). However, it would simply be metropolitan arrogance to refute the statement that "we cannot afford to be isolated . . . from what is taking place in the world." While efforts to create a more equitable society on a national level have certainly not vanished, there is an increasing sense of powerlessness in the context of the triumph of capitalism, international class consolidation, and the economic and military power of the United States. Moreover, the invasion of Grenada in 1983 and remilitarization of the Caribbean during the Reagan era chilled radical politics in the region (Deere 1990; Payne and Sutton 1993), except for groups espousing martyrdom, such as the Jamaat-al-Muslimeen, who attempted a coup in Trinidad in 1990.

Later in her parliamentary statement, Persad-Bissesser describes forms of intellectual property such as artistic works: "We think of calypso and chutney as ready examples in this land of ours." While calypso is a world-renown form, the inclusion of "chutney" in her opening remarks reflects greater recognition of Indo-Trinidadian music and culture under the UNC. She admits that enacting intellectual property legislation is now a matter of meeting "international obligations," but argues that IP legislation will encourage "creative activity in this country, industrialization, investment and trade" designed to enhance the "quality of life for all of us in Trinidad and Tobago." Here, state political authority benefits from producing a unified narrative of national culture, or by addressing "Indian" or "African" contributions in a pluralist model. This encourages further analysis of the "political uses of ethnicity," as Kevin Yelvington argues that ethnic identity is fostered by post-independence politicians in the "anti-neo-colonial" struggle (1993). However, encouraging a racial identity also risks divisiveness because "race" encompasses historically divided geographies of power, resources, electoral support, and claims to artistic creation.

As the debate on IP legislation opened to members of parliament, the issue of the steel pan took center stage, initiated by Eulalie James, the opposition People's National Movement (PNM) representative from Laventille West (a poor, urban, Afro-Trinidadian community where pan is said to originate).

> Mr. Speaker, nowhere in this Bill does the legislation attempt to deal with the frightening situation of our national instrument, King Pan. Mr. Speaker, can we not protect the pan? . . . I am aware that the pan was discovered and it evolved. It continues to evolve. Its 1969 tone is much different from that of 1995, and much more refined is it not? Mr. Speaker, I am aware that it will be very difficult to identify the actual inventor or divisor of pan. I am aware that there are arguments as to whether the pan was discovered or invented. Without any doubt, what we know today is that the pan was either invented or discovered in Trinidad and Tobago. . . . could there not be an agreement as to who is the most likely person we can identify as the actual divisor? Does the Act not envisage one or more inventors, point inventors or co-inventors? (Minutes of the House of Representatives, Port of Spain, July 9, 1996)

James's statement, while claiming credit for her political constituency of Laventille, points to a central contradiction of authorship and cultural property. The fact that IP law protects individuals as "authors" negates the social contexts that fuel creative expression. Both calypso and pan emerged from a subordinate population over years of racial, class, and anticolonial conflict; indeed, one book on the history of the steelband recounts more than ten narratives on the invention of pan (Goddard 1991). Because the steel pan arose from an impoverished black district, being a "pan man" was associated with uncouth behavior and violence. While this stigma continues even today, it has largely been supplanted by a cautious pride brought about by the international recognition of pan, and steelbands come to perform in Trinidad's carnival from as far away as Japan and

Switzerland. In a small former colony like Trinidad, one cannot underestimate the power of international recognition in confronting persistent feelings of "secondclassness" (Lovelace 1996). At the same time, greater resources in nations such as Switzerland have enabled superior pan production. Some of Trinidad's best tuners have been lured abroad, so there is also the perception that Trinidad is "losing" pan to the world, a perception that the lack of patent reinforces. In parliament, the importance of pan in relation to cultural struggle was quickly subsumed by the rush to conform to internationally established definitions of invention. Ultimately, the search for an author appeared futile as the pan has likely passed into "public domain."

When the senate met to discuss intellectual property legislation, a more critical discourse emerged. The imbalance of power inherent in international agreements, North–South conflicts, and even the politics involved in the pan discussion were voiced:

> Sen. M. Daly: This is to protect certain interests . . . It also protects us because we will get foreign investment as a result of passing these laws, but it completely ignores indigenous concerns. So, not only do we have this situation where, in my opinion, superficial political credit is being claimed, but we are going to hear from every political contender, that the steelband is the greatest invention of the 20th Century. . . . I ask, what legislative support is there in this country for the steelband? What opportunities have we lost on this occasion to dialogue with these experts and interest groups, to tell us?
>
> Sen. Rev. D. Teelucksingh: . . . 73% of the homeless people, the vagrants, and so on, in the town, were former mas men. . . . 53% were former pan men. You speak about intellectual property rights and property protection. This is a result of our failure over the years to see the need to protect the property treasure of your people [applause]. The property treasure of their minds and their hands and culture have been exploited to the extent where, of all homeless people you see, 73% of them were former mas men and pan men. (Minutes of the House of Representatives, Port of Spain, July 12, 1996)

These statements highlight unequal power relations involved in IP legislation, while transforming state subordination into a nationalist cause. The "failure" to protect culture raises continuing questions of self-worth, and can also be read as a masculinist national politics easier to applaud in the Red House (Trinidad's House of Parliament), than to support in policy or daily practice. While it is common to hear complaints that "Trinidadians don't value their own," with the pressure to commodify culture from international and national locations, valuing one's culture is increasingly constructed as paying for it. In the next sections, I discuss the contradictory efforts to transform national subjects who conceive of themselves as embodying a rich cultural heritage, into ahistorical subjects who participate in culture through consumption.

UNLEARNING CULTURE AS "WE 'TING": THE ECONOMICS AND CULTURAL POLITICS OF COPYRIGHT

Trinidad enacted its first copyright act in 1985, and along with the "general overhaul" of intellectual property legislation, replaced it in 1997, increasing penalties for cassette piracy to up to ten years in jail and TT $100,000 (approx. US $17,000). While parliament emphasized the protection of Trinidad's "cultural property" for political reasons, pressure from a globalizing economy aligns with the interests of cultural producers on a national level to represent culture as the property of individuals. Educational efforts and police enforcement of antipiracy laws contribute to the recasting of culture as a commodity. However, popular memory works against the reification of calypso, soca, and steelband music, because these are thought of as "festival" music, and are associated with a history of mass participation and freedom. Cassette piracy is the dominant form of music distribution in Trinidad because most people simply cannot afford to buy new tapes or CDs. The crackdown on piracy sparked public debate on intellectual property and culture.

On the broadest level, the impetus for increased enforcement of copyright, patent, and all intellectual property law is pressure from foreign interests. However, discourse on cultural and economic imperialism must also be seen for its value in terms of cultural nationalism and in garnering support for the Government—especially in a period of heightened poverty and social tension. An article by senator and professor Ken Ramchand in one of the major newspapers articulates this view; in fact, Ramchand wrote this piece in the form of a letter to himself from a grassroots reader:

> Dear Kenos,
>
> . . . I am begging you to make the connection between the copyright laws other people forcing we to sign, and the laws of the oppressor that they throw down from the time they bring us here . . . Make people understand that copyright laws are designed to benefit not creators but businessmen. In our case, foreign businessmen. Tell them the International copyright laws we rushing to sign exist to serve the interests of the not so absent absentee landlords of our culture and society. Same old boots. Same old khaki pants. Old plantation, new crops. Carrying me back to old Virginny.
>
> What we fighting about is the art and endurance and soul of all who came as strangers to these blessed islands that we labour to make our home. That is the struggle and creativity our folklore and mas commemorate and mean . . . (Ramchand 1997)

Ramchand argues against American cultural imperialism while articulating a romantic view of Trinidadian culture. Ironically, while he contrasts oppressive images of the plantation to the art, soul, and struggle of the Trinidadian folk, his promotion of such an image of national culture serves the intensifying commodification of Trinidad's music and mas, as "Carnival" is identified as the export that will give Trinidad competitive advantage in the neoliberal marketplace (Nurse 1996b). The nostalgic discourse of "our culture" generates national solidarity to combat increasing economic, racial, and generational fragmentation in the context of globalization.

Popular discourse also illustrates a concern with exploitative international power relationships involved in cultural ownership and control. While Trinidad is famous for calypso music (Rohlehr 1990), the most popular calypso in history was "Rum and Coca Cola," recorded in the United States by the Andrews Sisters in 1943 and selling an estimated four million copies. Lord Invader (of Trinidad) successfully sued after proving he was the composer, but never received adequate compensation.[3] Similarly, Lord Melody penned many of the songs that made Harry Belafonte's career. Most artists in "underdeveloped" countries lack the power to effectively control and market their music internationally, but there have been some improvements in this situation. Although it's a sore spot among Trinidadians that the biggest selling soca song was also recorded by a foreigner, Arrow's "Hot Hot Hot" of 1983 not only sold three to five million copies, but he has reportedly earned royalties into six figures.

Along with the enhanced legal framework of copyright in Trinidad, the Copyright Organization of Trinidad and Tobago (COTT) was formed in 1985 to protect the rights of songwriters and collect money (for both foreign and local artists) from music sales, broadcasting, and licensing. In their *Annual Report* (1995), COTT reported distributions to local owners of approximately TT $215,000 and to foreign owners of TT $585,000. The amount of royalties distributed has increased steadily in recent years. Besides interfacing with international intellectual property organizations, COTT conducts workshops and advertises in the local media to educate the general public and local businesses about copyright law. They also collaborate with the government and police on enforcement.

COTT is actively reeducating the public about their relationship to Trinidadian music and culture—away from thinking of music as "we 'ting"—to conceptualizing music as an industry made up of individual authors. Alvin Daniell, composer and chairman of COTT, produces a weekly one-hour television program called *Calypso Showcase* that features interviews with calypsonians and issues related to music. Two segments on copyright featured entertainment lawyers, calypsonians, members of the police force, and a former pirate cassette dealer. These programs focused on the need to dislodge popular conceptions of music as shared national culture and to reconceptualize music as a commodity.

> In this country here . . . we like to believe that calypsonians and calypso belongs to everybody, and that attitude is what affects not only the artist but the society as well . . . People want to enjoy music and they have a right to . . . but they seldom see the *artist* in the excitement, they seldom see the *artist* in the enjoyment, they believe that to get a tape it is for *them* to enjoy at a minimum cost. (Watchman, calypsonian)

> I would hope that we move away from the concept that music is just anything . . . and that the people who produce this music do not really need the reward from their music. Just as we look at work . . . they have worked and expect payment, and that people cannot just tape the people's music . . . (Winston Cooper, Assistant Superintendent of Police; see Daniell n.d.)

Watchman's statement clearly articulates the popular perception of "Trinidadian music" as a cultural text that *belongs* to Trinidadians. Cooper's statement reiterates John Locke's theory on labor as the basis for property, and in this context, emphasizing the *work* in music is an excellent argument. Since his statements were spoken in a televised interview, I find the ambivalence of the words, "the people's," particularly interesting. Given the nature of Cooper's argument, I assume he meant "the people's music," describing the possessions of individuals, but the words might also be interpreted as "the peoples' music," or as music belonging to a group or culture. While both phrases are "possessive," this ambiguity is central to issues of ownership and articulates a persistent confrontation between use value and exchange value (Marx 1976).

COTT has succeeded in collecting licensing fees from major promoters. For many of its member composers, receiving even small amounts of money for royalties makes a difference on a subsistence level. However, there have also been complaints regarding the targets of antipiracy campaigns, as pirate cassette dealers are poor youth with few employment opportunities. COTT is certainly not responsible for arrests, but they have instigated police enforcement of copyright infringement.[4] One letter to the editor addresses the issue of affordability for consumers and argues that piracy is a way to make a few dollars.

> Dear Editor:
>
> The present action of copyright clean-up campaign of all those self-employed youths and others who sell recorded cassettes for a living has disrupted me greatly.
>
> Firstly music is everybody's and mostly everyone knows quality music. And secondly every person does not have a stereo or turntables to spin a record. And most certainly a person will not purchase a $30 original cassette which is not a quality recorded cassette, whereas a cassette sold by a trying youth will have a combination of singers which cost cheaper. Presently people have no money to spend stupidly. . . .

> . . . As a solution for more record or C.D. sales and a chance for those frustrated youths who are now unemployed, is it possible for copyright owners to grant a license for those people in the cassette selling business?
>
> Signed,
> Frustrated and Unemployed[5]

Another article discusses the arrest of a pirate cassette dealer and his incomprehension of guilt:

> In an obvious way of clamping down on persons selling pirated cassettes around the country, Magistrate Narine ordered Pacheco to pay the maximum fine for selling the cassette.
>
> Pacheco, 19, of La Horquetta, Arima, appeared dumbstruck as Magistrate Jai Narine imposed the fine in the Port of Spain Third Court.[6]

This statement illustrates the use of law in protecting class interests, and would probably be read by Trinidadians as "racial" as well.[7]

A columnist for the *Express* combines consumer concerns with a hyperbolic description of increased enforcement as follows:

> a "Kristallnacht" for creators, and it leaves me profoundly uneasy. I meet young men eager to enforce copyright infringement with a kind of brownshirt enthusiasm that seems to be entirely removed from the intent and practice of the law.
>
> When COTT cracked down on sidewalk music pirates, they made it impossible for people to buy cheaply priced compilations of calypso tapes. (Lyndersay 1997)

Some people claim that piracy is an organized industry having nothing to do with a "scrunting youth man."[8] Because of its illegal nature, accurate data is difficult to obtain, but my sources indicated there are groups involved who own about twelve music sets, in addition to smaller groups and individuals. However, enforcement has emphasized the endpoint of sale, and the majority of sidewalk cassette sellers are poor youth. The criminalizing of pirate cassette dealers vividly and tragically symbolizes the contradictory effects of transnationalism from "above" and "below," as the masses have been increasingly abandoned by the state and have been thrown into a globalized marketplace, where a "whole counterzone of informal transnationalization has also emerged" (Robotham 1998:319). Simply put, while neoliberal *ideology* condemns piracy, neoliberal *economic policy* actually fuels it—as global economic inequalities force people into informal or illegal activities to survive.

I have expanded North–South analysis of global power relations by examining the multiple affects of international intellectual property law in Trinidad.

Transnational forces fuel the reconceptualizing of state sovereignty, producing competing subjectivities within the nation-state as the interests of cultural producers clash with enduring popular understandings of cultural belonging. Fostering a sense of shared Trinidadian culture was politically useful during the anticolonial struggle and served the same classes who now, in the postcolonial era, seek to transform a politicized popular culture into an economically profitable one. Similarly, discourses on "cultural imperialism" may be "resisting" on the level of foreign domination while effacing inequalities and difference within the nation. Popular expression in Trinidad has always required resources and has been involved in the circuit of global capitalism—which negates teleological narratives of a pure culture of resistance becoming a purely commodified popular culture. What I find most important to examine are changing relationships to cultural expression for subjects differently positioned in society—indicative of new geographies of culture and power.

It may be inevitable under advanced capitalism that "culture" bares a reified and possessive character, whether it is constructed as the property of groups or individuals. While I have analyzed cultural ownership at several levels, important questions remain regarding contradictory discourses operating in the same space and how it is possible to foster both a sense of culture as historically shared and as a commodity. Finally, I suggest that we think beyond analyses of state discourses or the global trajectory of commodification—towards examining the "value" of competing discourses and the production of social instability.

NOTES

1. The 1991 census data is from a survey conducted by the Institute of Social and Economic Research, UWI, Trinidad.

2. C. B. Macpherson argues that the "possessive" character of individualism is central to modern liberal-democratic theory from the seventeenth to the nineteenth centuries. "Its possessive quality is found in its conception of the individual as essentially the proprietor of his own person or capacities, owing nothing to society for them. The individual was seen neither as a moral whole, nor as part of a larger social whole, but as an owner of himself. The relation of ownership, having become for more and more men the critically important relation determining their actual freedom and actual prospect of realizing their full potentialities, was read back into the nature of the individual. . . . Society consists of relations of exchange between proprietors. Political society becomes a calculated device for the protection of this property and for the maintenance of an orderly relation of exchange" (1975: 3).

3. Raising additional questions about autonomous authorship, Donald Hill argues that Lord Invader's "Rum and Coca Cola" was based on a Martiniquean folksong (1993: 234–40).

4. See, e.g., "COTT goes after 'free music,'" *Punch,* June 28, 1997; "Police for Pirates!: COTT flexes its legal muscle," *Punch,* August 24, 1997.

5. "Give licenses to cassette dealers." *Express,* November 21, 1992.

6. "'Pirate' fined $5,000 for cassette." *Guardian,* July 21, 1994.

7. " The conflict of interests between composers and pirate cassette dealers exists largely within the Afro-Trinidadian population as they are the majority of producers. However, in the polarized racial climate of late, this type of incident would probably be read through race as well. When describing an incident of domestic abuse, robbery, or any unusual occurrence, in popular discourse the next question is likely to be: "Was it an Indian or African?" In this piracy case—regardless of the "facts"—the newspaper article would probably be understood as an example of racism because "an Indian judge ordered the maximum fine against a plaintiff of mixed African and Spanish descent."

8. "Skulduggery and Crossbones." *Express,* August 13, 1995.

Afterword

Roger Abrahams

Scholarly interest in the West Indies, after a century of academic limbo, is now flourishing. The combination of the ease of access and the shrinking of support for ethnographic fieldwork in the more exotic areas of the world has sent many ethnographers, folklorists, and other social scientist into the area. More, Caribbeanists find themselves fighting academic battles alongside others flying the flag of postcolonial studies. The external colonialism of the ex-British Empire is further intensified by those studying Ireland, Wales, and Scotland as colonial experiments under the alternative name of Archipelagic Studies. Clearly the worm has turned, at least in the enclosed gardens at the seats of higher learning.

This abundant literature now being published begins to establish the centrality of creolized forms of expression, both within and outside the Greater Caribbean sphere of influence. The task for ethnographic fieldworkers in that area of the world is to establish the common features of the Carnival movement, taking matters far beyond Port of Spain and its satellite communities and well into the cognate activities found in other festivities as carried out in New Orleans, Rio, Havana, Port au Prince, Montevideo, as well as Trinidad. Because each of these cities has built a nationalistic rhetoric around its signature festivities, until now they have each been studied as if they were sui generis. But each has now developed satellite festivities wherever expatriate communities have established a beachhead. The features that all of them share are becoming ever clearer, and these too are worthy of scholarly notice. Anticipating just such a move, the Transatlantic Black World is being knit together with studies of healing and other religious practices that transcend any national boundaries on either side of the Atlantic.

The generation of the mid-twentieth century writing on the subject, whether or not they were West Indians, had the advantage of drawing on the vernacular knowledge and memories of local savants who had been publishing in newspapers and journals for some time, and gathering together at reunions to remember the past pleasures of playing. The encounter of mainland Americans and Trinidadians, which occurred after World War II as travel and communication between these areas improved, found their apotheosis in works by Trinidadian scholars such as Errol Hill and Gordon Rohlehr, along with the Tobagonian J. D. Elder. The late Jacob Elder, it must be said, was not only a scholar and a cultural minister, but a peripatetic enthusiast of all West Indian traditions, and he, along with his disciple Daniel Crowley, should be credited with preliminary studies of regional festivities. Their limitations were not, as Pamela Franco suggests in her essay in this collection, that they were masculinists, but that they were men who luxuriated in talking about their observations and their representative experiences more than to write about them. Never downplaying the importance of women in the development of Carnival today, they nevertheless were constrained by the journalistic conventions of their time in discussing sexual display.

The group that produced the issue of the *Caribbean Quarterly* referred to by many of these essays, still stands as the creators of a foundational document in Trinidad Carnival discussions. But now there have been a series of new groups who have come into being on the model of the Pearse, Crowley, and Jacob Elder bunch who launched such a lively address to past Carnivals, in which a group comes together to say things that none of them would have realized if writing from their own chambers. This becomes evident in comparisons of their work with the jottings of non-West Indians, who treated Carnival and other West Indian festive forms in terms of an annual catharsis, a letting-go licensed by the calendrical celebration characteristic of European seasonal rites. It is important to recognize how very different the Trinidad Carnival is from the seasonal rites emanating from the European traditions of the northlands.

These events emerge from the holidays associated with tropical agriculture of the sort practiced on the plantation. They seize upon the holiday season celebrated throughout the Catholic world before Lent. Even the adherence of the British colonies to the Anglican calendar, with its emphasis on Christmas as the major festive time, seems to have been overshadowed by the power of Carnival play as it was developed in places such as Port of Spain. Carnival emerged, as did Christmas in the Eastern Caribbean, as the slave holiday season. Now, throughout the Black Atlantic, it has become the major event around which the various African American communities plan their year.

The discourse on carnivalization hasn't quite caught up with these insights concerning the cultural continuities of the Greater Caribbean. Historical and literary studies continue to insist that Carnival represents a break from the routine world in which license is given for all to enter the reversible world of Cockaigne. Thus, the nineteenth-century fixation on distanced observation remains at the heart of those who write on the pervasiveness of carnivalization as a device of social and political resistance.

The description of what is being called "the new cosmopolitanism" still privileges the figure of the artist as flâneur, drawing on the brilliance of the Baudelaires and the James Joyces of the nineteenth-century city-wanderers. The critical community, lying in wait for the establishment of a new set of heroes, already has developed the terms in which the international movement will be described in this period of postcolonial musings: creolization and carnivalization join the postmodern thesaurus that used to be anchored in observations of *difference* and hegemony. Is not the new millennium witnessing an intellectual rearrangement in which the old cosmopolitans of Baudelaire, Joyce, Mann, Stein, Eliot, and Woolf, all of whom helped define the very concept of modernism, are now being nudged aside by the more recent ex-pats attempting to forge the conscience (or at least the consciousness) of their race, by figures such as Patrick Chamoiseaux, Edmund Glissant, V. S. Naipaul, Derek Walcott, Salman Rushdie, Edwige Danticat, and Anthony Appiah, all using local dialectal features for international audiences who cannot possibly understand their local meanings. Indeed, they seem to want to call all forms of ironic social commentary as emerging from carnivalesque motives, following the path blazed by the Russian language philosopher, Mikhail Bakhtin. When viewed from the perspective of the sporty fellows of real carnival play, Bakhtin himself comes under suspicion of being a romantic ironist, for his observations emerged at some remove from the actual experience of the festivity. His brilliant perceptions of such events were generated through his reading of Rabelais, and not from any event he might have experienced. The distance between the social theory of the Bahktinians and the actual experience itself, perhaps, was first discussed by Samuel Kinser in his book on contemporary Mardi Gras, where he records both the history of the event and the ways in which he actually experienced it as an outsider observer.

Perhaps a steam-valve explanation works effectively in the ways in which Carnival was played in the European cities in which it provided (and still provides) the beginning of the yearly cycle of celebrations. But it loses its explanatory vigor when applied to Trinidad Carnival, and for that matter, to any of bacchanals that emerged as Africans and Europeans encountered each other as slave and master. This power differential, even today, manifests itself in the way Carnival is produced and played by the players themselves. The event, in principle, brings everyone together, regardless of race, gender, and the remnants of class manifested in terms of social status; but once they are all brought together by the event, they find themselves celebrating separately, with an acute consciousness of just where the lines are customarily drawn. More than this, the traditional performances themselves continue to be coded with markers of historical and social distinction. Blowing off steam remains as experientially distinct as can be from the idea of liberation or emancipation. It would skew an understanding of both pre- and post-emancipation societies to regard Carnival mainly in terms of the way it marks the yearly passage. It would be equally fruitless to see the event in terms of class or race or gender concerns that build toward equality.

While the celebration of ole mas in Viey la Cou, as Garth Green describes it in this volume, elevates those eccentric performances, the players and their crew seem to neglect the fact that they were developed under conditions in which mumming players existed in contrast to a system of behavior in which they were tolerated because of the largesse of the planter class. Throughout the plantation world, slaves were occasionally permitted to demand the "Chrismus Gif'" or to live with the antics of the clowns and robbers and libelers of Carnival. The rites of deference, condescension, and displays of respect to the planters and their agents were maintained, even after emancipation. In fact, when I first began to do fieldwork in the West Indies, at the seasons of celebration I found the strong reminders of the master–slave relationship in the songs and the luck-visit practices of the performing and begging mummers. While sitting in the ruins of the Big House in which I was camped, the Christmas players coming into what was left of the yard still asked permission to enter in elaborate language, singing "A Merry Christmas to the master" and ending with "We beg you a penny to buy our Christmas bread."

The street figures that now are found mainly in Viey la Cou were vestiges of just such seasonal begging practices, even though they also served as some of the most delightful and threatening to the attending crowds. Green argues persuasively that the whole project is shot through with nostalgic impulses that are seldom acknowledged on the part of the players. One wonders what the response would be if these players were asked directly exactly what is being lost as these roles have dwindled in the street celebrations. Perhaps the impulse to preserve these old ways derives from a disgust with the commercialization of the rest of the big show, but to express this feeling by having another costume mas hardly seems to allay the fears of the antimodernists, or, as jazz people call them, "the moldy figs" in the crowd. (I am reminded of the times when some of the best contemporary New Orleans musicians walked by Preservation Hall and heard the music being made there: "Those guys just can't bleeping play.")

Many observers today discover again and again that the holiday moment is really a holiday season that, for the most ardent participants, lasts all year. This is not an event that serves as a point of discharge for the players, but more a culmination of a year's work of planning, sewing, rehearsing, tuning the instruments, and, for the calypsonians, finding that right note that will cause the muse to descend upon them for the song-combat to come. This anticipation is far from any catharsis for the participants; *emancipation* rather, even more than *carnivalization,* is the more appropriate analytic term for the sense of wild energy arising during the Carnival moment. The history of Carnival playing makes that clear: this is an event that celebrates not only the historical act of slave liberation, but uses the emancipation as a way of establishing and reinforcing a community of feelings and meanings.

Just at that historical moment when the most exportable product of the Caribbean, its music and dance and festive styles, bring this part of the creole world into the spotlight. So many sturdy studies have been produced that it has been difficult to stay abreast of the good work being done. But with the help of friends, especially former students, I am aware of the directions this work has taken, as represented in all its facets by this fine collection of essays. In the main, these and many other recent publications on Caribbean cultures encourage the view of the "new cosmopolitans"—who resemble the old cosmopolitans in the value they place on the idea of global residence and the observation of cultural flow from a distinctively removed and generally dispassionate position. They both lack much political bite, but that is for another day's argument.

Yet in important ways, the trained ethnographer, by making microcosmic observations of life in the big cities, marks a breakthrough for the profession. All of the participants here, including myself, have benefited from the ready willingness of the playful participants to explain things to outsiders. All I am saying is that there is a lively vernacular theory about how to perform which is found throughout this huge area of the world, and we ethnographers have profited greatly from the willingness of these native exegetes to talk to us and to try to teach us how to feel, as well as how to understand such play.

Once the ugly stepchild of the family of cultures, the Mondo Creole is being given ever-greater notice even among scholars. This collection of essays builds on the work of the last two decades written by folklorists and ethnographers. As in its European forebears, Carnival continues to reflect and refract political concerns on local, national, and international tropics. That is, the muse that descends often speaks in ironic tones, making fun of those who have proven themselves unreliable, whether locally, regionally, or in world affairs.

As mentioned in the introduction to this volume, Carnival has become an "industry" in Trinidad. Because of—or in spite of—its local anchoring, it has maintained its place in the political dynamic of the nation. It remains the vital reminder that the principle "All We Be One" has maintained its place of promise, even as the islands are as divided by racial and class distinctions in the everyday.

At the heart of the Trinidadian Carnival lies a paradox: the event remains a local production revealing local points of references and reflecting local political and economic concerns—most of which are far from clear to revelers from outside—yet the event travels well, and has created what Phil Scher cannily calls a "transnation." Its portability creates a sense of wonder wherever it travels. The introduction draws attention to how the transnation events have created a separate scholarly industry—the editors call attention to at least a dozen monographic publications, and, except for Scher's own book, the list ends at the turn of the century.

Accounting for this efflorescence of Trinidadian style celebrations must go far beyond the obvious: that Trinidadians have populated the cosmopolitan centers wherever they found employment and some degree of official acceptance; and that because of the growth of the tourist-driven economy, Carnival is just good business as well as good-time events.

Even though the most successful of these display events have drawn huge tourist spectatorship, they all have maintained a place for launching local, usually satiric statements. More, they all continue to mark both slavery times and emancipation. Beneath the glitzy front presentations lies a substrate of historical celebration of the moment of political emancipation, and they all continue to comment on the failure of everyone to achieve social and economic parity. This theme has remained at the imaginative center of the proceedings even when civic authorities and chambers of commerce would like to limit the local dimensions and especially those that maintain the tradition of resistance.

Indeed, such conditions often find their way into the thematic presentations that lie at the center of the parade as it goes by the judge's stand. What is discovered by ethnographers is this hard core of social commentary that confronts the frivolous aspects of the festival with the conditions that those in power would like to subordinate, at least while the bacchanal proceeds.

Trinidad Carnivals are hardly unique in making an attempt to keep ole mas or its equivalent alive. The nostalgic position of those using ole mas-type costumes and characters neglects to remember that these figures were tied to earlier sociopolitical forces that, if they have not disappeared, have been overtaken by the spectacular character of the festive presentations. The organizers of Viey la Cou, as both Garth Green and Pamela Franco point out, are an outgrowth of a politics of nostalgia that is not always self-evident, even to the performers themselves.

But this kind of nostalgic re-presentation is far from unique to Trinidad. Every Carnival in the Greater Caribbean has groups that attempt to keep the old forms alive for much the same political reason as the organizers of Viey la Cou. Indeed, even in the Eastern Caribbean where I began my field observations, there were events, called concerts, sponsored by Protestant churches, which called on old-timers to show and tell how they used to play.

Appropriately, they place the revivals in the social imaginary of the old yard, the area around which family activities merge at the gates, with the presence of *outbokers*. Submerged within *le court* of *le cou*, is *le coup*, the striking out or making the blow, perhaps most fully at *jouvay* or its opposite number in Rio or Port au Prince, Buenos Aires, Montevideo, or the Bahamas, anyplace that has history of the enslavement of Africans.

The very idea of Carnival in these many places brings alive Philip Scher's idea of transnation (perhaps *trance-nation* is appropriate as well, for the liminal enactments of deepest Carnival bring the participants to the state of high enjoyment that if not involving trancing, is very similar). The vigor of Black Atlantic Carnivals has been maintained in that first blowout of jouvay, that moment in which sudden liberation is felt by all, even sneaking up on the skeptics and others in resistant uptight mode. Every time one of the old contestive forms, like calypso or capoeira, samba or . . . is enacted, it reenacts the creative (and still, often, improvised) confrontations of the old style of celebration. More, these contestive forms remain a deep element of Black Carnival—that is, the dimension of the celebration that remembers the continuing split between the balls and masks of European style elites, held behind closed doors, as the more African elements take over on the streets.

It is surely not surprising that Carnival in Trinidad, as is true of all others within the Greater Caribbean, has a pulse-driven music and dance dimension that is a variation of what musicians often call the Congo rhythm. Each tradition exhibits a signature way of careering or marching as in jumping up, jamming, or wining in Trinidad. Each has a historically rooted musical style, usually with an accompanying dance, which are taken indoors, into jook joints and music halls, cabarets and night clubs. Witness, for instance, how the mazurka became the *zook* in Martinique, or the quadrille, now underlaid with congo rhythm, became the *kadri* throughout the francophonic Caribbean. Many other festive traditions, then, are involved in the dance crazes of now one, now another period of popular culture history. All associate the dance with wanton behaviors and wild people, such as Les Apaches in France and the Dirty Boogie in Shreveport. Street March, wining, pan: all are both ineluctably local by legend, rooted historically in one neighborhood such as Storyville or Laventille, usually a slum neighborhood, a barrio or favela. Each draws upon the most

African style of multi-metric apart playing and call and response singing and dancing, especially as the celebration proceeds in time and space. Again, the singing and marching and dancing is associated with slave holidays in that particular country.

Equally important: Carnival throughout this broad region is driven by pleasure clubs that are also dead serious, being the repositories of the ancient wisdom of religious instruction and healing to those strong enough to become an initiate. In the form of self-help groups, like the New Orleans groups of "social aid and pleasure societies," the clubs are best thought of as burial societies, and also as the extension of the principle of the African *susu* or savings groups. In Cuba as in many other Latin American places, these clubs, *cabildos,* and the *candombes* of Buenos Aires and Montevideo, are regarded as a connection to specific African nations. So long as the community imagines itself as a community during carnival, the idea of the enslaved past and the moment of emancipation will remain deeply embedded in the social imaginary of the Carnival world. Perhaps, as in many other places, the Trinidadian community exists only as Carnival is played.

As with the plays of the Moors and Christians found throughout Latin America in association with the feast of Corpus Christi, celebrations are held at many other times in one locale or another. Focusing on the *reconquista* by which the Moors were banished from Spain, the ritual combat at the center of the proceedings is overtly represented not only as a religious but a racial struggle. The ubiquity of the black–white contrast, underscored by the ways in which faces and bodies are painted on both sides of the color line, reveals this barely hidden history. With the addition of Indians in the New World setting, the racial coding becomes even more obvious, and more complex. When the primary message of Carnival maintains its denial of such distinctions in the face of the moment of celebration as experienced by everyone attending, even then apprehension of such difference on the ground level never leaves. This is all the more intensified by the centrality of those of lowest estate who are given the honor of providing the founding moment of the festival.

Dan Crowley, who attended Carnival in a great many places, and in fact died while attending one, maintained the continuities among and between them, giving them a sexual, racial, and class reading: Distinguishing European and African American events, he noted:

> Profanation is the specialty of European Carnivals, elements of which are specifically designed to be sacrilegious, as shocking as possible to the conservative and the religious. But in the New World Carnivals, such specific sacrilege is rather rare, and where it occurs it is a specialty of the upper classes who are usually relatively lighter-skinned than their lower-class countryman. Bahians

> and African-nationalist Cariocas (natives of Rio) often compare their increasingly race-conscious Afoxé and Bloco Afro parading organizations with Catholic religious street processions on Corpus Christi and other holy days. "This is our chance to display our culture and religious beliefs, just like the (white) Catholics of their festivals. . . . That's why they are down on Carnival, always trying to stop it or change it or limit it." For people of this orientation, coming out in Carnival is a political act as well as a cultural one. (Crowley 200)

Crowley and his colleague, the Tobagonian J. D. Elder, introduced me to these traditional activities. The West Indies that I came to know through their efforts and introductions was alive with artistic invention. The 1960s produced so many first-rate talents who had been educated to emigrate, that one only had to read their voluminous literary production to know that the culture was alive and well, even if no longer totally centered on Port of Spain or Kingston. The generation of V. S. Naipaul, Derek Walcott, and Kamau Brathwaite, Geoffrey Holder, and the many other artists, dancers, musicians, designers, choreographers who followed have achieved such exalted honors on the international arena that opportunities have been opened for many others who continue to allow themselves to speak out West Indian tonalities. Among them are Edna Brodber, Paule Marshall, Jamaica Kincaid, Earl Lovelace, and many others. And the satellite events in Toronto, or Brooklyn, or Notting Hill, now achieve a life of their own, and are featured in books, television documentaries, and films.

Indeed, in the 1960s when I first approached the multiple cultural practices of this region, other academics maintained their disinterest in the social and cultural questions arising from the mixed character of the population. This was before the new cosmopolitanism settled in, and Indian and Caribbean literary figures had ascended to Nobel heights. Even those most disenchanted with the villages or neighborhoods from which they had emerged saw in the festive life of the region a way of maintaining visceral connections while following through on the promise of their "education to emigrate." While this is called a *diaspora* now, it differs so greatly from its Jewish progenitor that it is difficult to recognize what is diasporic about it. For the region never appeared to be a holy land, and there was little sense of forced dispersal of its peoples in the Caribbean communities that have sprung up through the West. Rather, staying in touch with home, and returning whenever one wished is the rule rather than the exception, a rule made all the more powerful with the growing use of mobile telephones, e-mail, and the many other ways in which communication that is not face to face but very tied to older ideals of the extended family are used. The long and the short of it is that both the people and their cultural productions travel well. The creative sector of the various Antillean communities capitalize on the vitality and the adaptability of their festive forms, developing in the event an art that underscores its ideal of mobility. This is paralleled by the growth of tourism which has made the play of Carnival into a magnetic force field that not only attracts drop-in visitors but also those who become "addicted" (their word) and return year after year. In many ways, they have provided the model for the rest of the mobilized world for how to leave home and not suffer all of the feelings of dislocation experienced by past generations—or as cosmopolitanism of all sorts has it, how to make the embodiment of separation into a cash cow.

Without cultural intervention and mediation, traditional forms of expressive culture that developed within small communities will gently fade away except as operations of nostalgia. Those seeking entertainment and spiritual uplift are just out of ear-and-eye range in the more powerful, colorful, but less conflictual street activities going on during Carnival.

The widespread use of mobile phones alone has kept the various Caribbean communities connected on a more regular basis, giving promise of closer family relations, more reunions, and more competition between these communities as to who will have the lustiest and most vigorous Carnival. Ever since the apparatus of the state was able to make the airwaves available to record Carnival mayhem, and the women-winers took over, it was clear that ol' mas was forever doomed except among those hardy antiquarians who launched a self-conscious counterattack in one of the quieter corners of the energized Port of Spain.

As the authors of many of these articles demonstrate in general and in particular, Carnival Trinidad-style has become both a source of pride in the Trinidadian transnation and a model for other islands such as Aruba, as described by Razak. In fact, it has been so powerfully maintained that diasporic West Indians from any of the islands now draw on the transnation Carnival as a way of articulating Anglophonic Caribbean cultural difference. Not only the expatriates from the small islands include themselves in the celebration, but others come from larger post-colonies, those formerly in the sway of Jamaican and not Trinidadian cultural forms. Guyanese and Belizean expatriates wail away with their Trinidadian counterparts; they are part of the greater West Indian ethnic population, socializing with each other, playing trans-Caribbean music at their parties, and playing the games of "all fours" and dominoes, and generally disdaining identification with other African American groups.

Because the most entrepreneurial of this transnational community have profited from of the mobility of so many Carnival mas types, it would be easy enough to simply argue that Carnival has been kept alive because of commercialization, international communication, and the commoditization arising with the sales of videos from each year's celebration in Port of Spain.

But as these articles testify, that is only a part of the story, and a small part at that. Carnival has become a way of celebrating an identity that differs from that of other ethnic Americans, including African Americans from the mainland. Playing Carnival someplace, whether back in Trinidad or in one of the satellite events, becomes one of the most important ways of asserting ethnic identity.

To return to my opening remarks, then, these papers articulate the many ways in which Carnival has adapted to contemporary conditions. The historical bent of the scholarship on the event has been superceded by close attention to the protean capacities of those who play every year, and if they are not able to do so, feel the lack in their very bones.

Glossary of Terms

Baby Doll: A costume somewhat similar to the **Dame Lorraine,** accompanied by a drama in which passersby are accosted by the masquerader who accuses them of fathering an illegitimate child (a doll). The Baby Doll threatens to call a policeman if the accused does not give some money for "child support."

Bacchanal: A key term in Trinidad and Tobago. Although most usage carries with it the general sense of confusion, uproar, and disorder, it can be both good and bad. Thus it can be used to describe a noisy and joyous occasion as well as extremely disreputable and scandalous conduct.

Bad John: An outlaw, a man of violent behavior and criminal reputation.

Band: A group of masqueraders, organized around a theme and divided into **sections** that participates in Carnival. The band is organized by a **bandleader** and competes against other bands for the Band of the Year title. Historically, the term was used to designate groups of stickfighters, or the associated female singing and dancing societies.

Bandleader: The organizer and (sometimes) designer of a Carnival **band.**

Barataria: An eastern suburb of Port of Spain, Barataria has a rich Carnival tradition; two of the best-known wirebenders, Cito Velasquez and Geraldo Veiera, come from there.

Barrack Yard: The yards created by the formation of barracks around central space. Such barracks provided housing for laborers in and around Port of Spain and consisted of a long, low building with small rooms divided from one another but under the same roof. The barrack yards were communal and often held the one, shared water source. Barrack yards became associated with rough language and behavior and have also been cited as the source and performance center for many masquerade types, especially the **Dame Lorraine.**

Beast: Many-headed ferocious character often at the center of Devil bands, chained and barely kept under control by his minions of imps and devils.

Belmont: A working-class neighborhood in Port of Spain, Belmont is home to one of the last Fancy sailor bands, that of Jason Griffith.

Blue Devil: A masquerade figure dressed in shorts and painted blue. The blue devils travel in bands and make an eerie, high-pitched whooping noise. They often have one of their number in chains who must be forcibly restrained. They gather money from spectators in return for keeping the dangerous devil away.

Borokeete: (also: Burroquite; Borokeet; Boroquite, among others) A masquerade costume in which a man or woman appears to be riding on a donkey. The donkey costume is worn around the waist and the masquerader's torso rises up from the middle of the donkey's back. This masquerade is very popular with Indian masqueraders.

Brass Band: Term used to describe musical band at Carnival and to distinguish it from a Carnival **band.** There need not be any brass instruments in the band, but horns are frequently used.

Buljol and Bake: Traditional Carnival breakfast food often served with coffee. Buljol is made from salt fish that has been soaked and shredded and made into a salad with hot peppers, tomatoes, cucumbers, and other ingredients. The word comes from the French brule-gueule, or burn-mouth. Bake is a deep-fried bread.

Calypso Monarch: Awarded at a competition held at the **Savannah,** the Calypso Monarch (formerly Calypso King) is the performer judged to have the best new calypsos of the year.

Calypso: (Also kaiso, cariso) A popular song marked, traditionally, by clever rhyming and social commentary. Calypsos may be either written or extemporaneous and are generally topical.

Caribana: Toronto's annual West Indian Carnival and the largest Carnival in Canada, rivaling Brooklyn as the largest one in North America.

Carnival King: The largest and fanciest male costume of any band. The winner of a competition of such costumes held during **Dimanche Gras** is crowned Carnival King for that year.

Carnival Queen: The largest and fanciest female costume of any band. (See **Carnival King**). Not to be confused with the **Queen of Carnival,** who was the winner of the prestigious beauty pageant (now defunct) of the same name.

Chipping, Chip: A light easy, shuffling dance used as both rhythmic locomotion and a way to rest while marching in a band or following a steelband.

Dame Lorraine: A Carnival figure of a man dressed as a woman with exaggerated buttocks and oversized breasts. The buttocks sway in a comical fashion when the masquerader walks.

Devil: Essentially a class of Carnival characters under which many specific characters may be found, including Red, White, Blue, and Black Devils; Imps, Jab Jabs; Jab Molassis; Beasts; Book Men; and others.

Dimanche Gras: From the French, meaning fat Sunday, or meat Sunday; this is the Sunday before Ash Wednesday and the beginning of Lent. In Trinidad, Dimanche Gras is marked by Carnival competitions including the **Calypso Monarch** competition and the King and Queen of Carnival costume contest.

Dragon: Carnival character representing a dragon with scales, tail, and often wings.

Fancy Indian: A subset of the class of masquerade known as Indian, these costumes represent the height of splendor and skill in Indian regalia. Often taken from images of Native North American attire, the costume might include war bonnets, feathers, mock quill work, and other features of Indian garb that are enhanced and embellished. Other kinds of Indian masquerade include Black Indians, Red Indians, or Warrahoons, and Blue Indians.

Fancy Sailor: A version of the sailor costume characterized by elaborate decoration and intricate, often humorous headpieces. (See also **sailor; king sailor**)

Fatigue: To bother or pester verbally; to tease.

Grand Stand: Area of seating on the south side of the **Savannah** stage where the judges and the quieter audiences sit. One can generally hear better in the Grand Stand; this is where **pan** aficionados sit during **Panorama.**

Headpiece: That part of the Carnival costume worn on the head.

Imp: A Carnival masquerade form depicting a kind of devil or minion of the beast in Devil bands. (See **beast** and **devil**)

Jamette: A bad woman, possibly derived from the French *diametre* for the imaginary line dividing the social circle into upper and lower halves. The word may also come from the French slang for a whore, *jeanette.* The **jamettes** constituted the "obscene" element in Carnival in the nineteenth century and were the focus of middle-class reform.

J'ouvert (jouvay, jouvert, etc.): From the French *jour ouvert* (open day, or day-break). J'ouvert is the beginning of Carnival, at which time King Carnival is given the keys to the city and the revelry begins. In Trinidad, J'ouvert begins around two o'clock in the morning when people come out into the street to celebrate. There are a wide variety of costumes associated almost exclusively with J'ouvert, many of which include covering oneself with paint, mud, or oil.

Jab Jab: From the French (*diable*=devil), a Carnival costume in which the masqueraders dress as devils. Now associated primarily with **j'ouvert,** the jab jabs were the "fancy" devils dressed in satin knickers or knee breeches.

Jab Molassi: Molasses Devil. This character covers himself with molasses or some sticky substance such as oil or pitch and dresses in shorts, horns, and a tail. Traditionally, the jab molassi would threaten to rub the offending substance on onlookers unless they gave him money.

Jagabat: (origin unknown, probably Hindi). A loose woman; a woman of questionable morals. Also used for a woman chasing a wealthy man.

John John: A poor neighborhood in Port of Spain, also known as "behind the bridge." It shares a Carnival tradition and deep rivalry with other neighborhoods both in the immediate area and across town. (See **Belmont, Woodbrook, Laventille**)

Kaiso: See **calypso.**

Land Ship: A Friendly Society that developed in Barbados, modeled on the British navy. Land Ship groups were identified by a ship's name and had a hierarchy of officers from Lord High Admiral on down. At selected times, the Land Ship societies parade, performing drills and coordinated dances.

Las Lap: The final period in Carnival, taking place in the hours before midnight on Shrove Tuesday after the **Parade of the Bands.**

Laventille: The neighborhood just a little further east of **John John** and further up into the hills overlooking the city. Laventille is home to one of most famous steel-bands, Desperadoes.

Lime: As a verb, the term means to hang around with friends, pass the time, and talk. The word seems to have reappeared in Trinidad during World War II with the arrival of American sailors to Trinidad. Liming drives from the word for English sailors—limeys—so-called because of their habit of carrying citrus on long ocean voyages to avoid scurvy. In Trinidad, limey came to be used to describe any low-class white. The socializing and loafing about of sailors in Port of Spain and their often rude and disorderly behavior inspired the new usage. The term survived the departure of the Americans and has lost its derogatory connotation. As a noun, the word is used to describe loosely organized social gathering. The gathering may be around an event or some kind of purpose (a beach lime, a movie lime). In this sense, too, a lime may be the group of friends that hang around with each other, even if they are not together at that moment. Thus, a cohort, a group of companions.

Mas Camp: The headquarters of a masquerade band, where the costumes are assembled. This is often, too, where registration for the band takes place, but it need not be. The site may be temporary or permanent. In Brooklyn, many of the mas camps are temporary, while in Trinidad some camps run all year from the same location, constructing costumes for carnivals around the world.

Mas: Short for masquerade, the term usually refers to the costume of an individual or to the whole costume theme of a band. The term also, however, is used to mean a confusion, a trouble. In this latter sense it is often expressed as **Ole Mas.**

Masman (men): This term is primarily used to designate someone who constructs masquerade costumes. It is most commonly associated with either the person in charge of the band (see **Bandleader**) or someone who is an expert at one of the higher skilled crafts such as **wirebending,** papier-mâché, etc., or someone who designs the band itself. These roles may be embodied in one person, or they may be separate.

Midnight Robber: Masquerader whose costume consists of a broad-brimmed hat fringed with tassels, an elaborate cape, baggy trousers, and a tunic generally bearing a skull and crossbones and who carries a dagger and pistol. The midnight robber gives elaborate and terrifying speeches in which he boasts of his destructive power and evil reputation. He demands money to spare the onlooker's life.

Moko Jumbie: A masquerader who stalks about on very high stilts. The moko jumbie used to collect money from people on second-story balconies. The name is a compound derived from distinct Africa sources; *moko* most likely being derived from Hausa for "ugly" and *jumbie* deriving from Kongo sources for "spirit."

Monday Mas: Period of Carnival on Monday night before Shrove Tuesday. This **mas** is generally more mellow and is played with steelbands and with only parts of costumes or tee-shirts.

North Stands: The temporary bleacher-style seating erected across from the **Grand Stand** in the **Savannah** at Carnival time. The North Stands are where the more riotous audiences sit, especially during **Panorama.**

Ole Mas: (Ol' Mas). Refers to a type of masquerade portrayed during **J'ouvert** and typified by masquerade costumes lampooning public officials and current events. The term is also used, much in the same way *bacchanal* is used in its negative sense, to mean a confusion or a disorganized and unpredictable situation.

Pan Yard: Open lot or space where **pans** are stored and where steelband rehearsals are carried out. They are a chief **liming** spot during Carnival.

Pan: The Trinidadian term for steel drum and by extension, steelband music.

Panorama: Panorama is the national steelband competition and the largest steelband competition in the country. It takes place on the Saturday before Carnival in the **Queen's Park Savannah.**

Panorama: Trinidadian national steel band competition held in the Queen's Park Savannah in Port of Spain every Carnival season. Panorama is also the name given to several other steelband competitions, for instance, that held during Brooklyn's Caribbean Carnival every Labor Day.

Picong: Competitive, spontaneous verbal battle between calypsonians or others. Also utilized for teasing in general (see **fatigue**).

Pissenlit: An old masquerade, made illegal, in which men dressed in rags stained with fake menstrual blood.

Play(ing) Mas: To participate in Carnival. To join a band, or to masquerade in general.

Road March: The song played by Carnival bands on Carnival Tuesday. It is also a competition; the winning song is played most frequently by bands as they march during **the Parade of the Bands.** Each masquerade band is accompanied by a sound system and often by a live band as well (see **brass band**). As the masqueraders move through the streets, various popular **soca** hits are played. The one played by the most bands the most often is judged the winning road march.

Roti: Specifically the round, unleavened bread made from yellow split pea flour, salt, and water, into which is wrapped a serving of curry. Roti is used generically to describe the whole meal together. Roti may be a serving of curried potatoes (Hindi: *aloo* or *alu*) along with goat, chicken, beef, shrimp, or other meats, and various vegetables such as pumpkin, green beans (bodi), and spinach. Roti was brought to Trinidad by East Indians.

Soca: Trinidadian musical style originating in the 1970s as an evolution of calypso incorporating electronic music, and geared primarily to dancing at fetes or during Carnival parades.

Savannah/Big Yard: The vast park in Port of Spain where Carnival competitions are held. (See **Grand Stand** and **North Stand**).

Standard: A long pole atop of which is fixed an emblematic representation of a band's "section" or thematic subdivision. Standards may take the form of an addition to the costume, such as a spear for a warrior, or may be a more abstract, symbolic form such as a banner, geometric design, and so on.

Tent: Location where calypsos are sung and calypso competitions held. Admission is generally charged.

Track: The pathway leading up to the **Savannah** stage. This is the area where steelbands (also known as pan sides) wait and rehearse before performing during **Panorama.** The Track is also used during the King and Queen of Carnival competitions.

Viey La Cou: Literally "The Old Yard," it is a competition begun in 1987 to promote the preservation and continued performance of Old Time Carnival Characters.

Wine/Wining: A dance performed at fetes, at Carnival time, at discos, and so on. Wining is marked by the erotic gyration of hips, slightly bent knees, and rotation of the buttocks.

Wirebender: Carnival craftsman responsible for shaping the wire structures upon which costumes are created.

Woodbrook: A working- to middle-class residential area just west of downtown Port of Spain. Woodbrook has produced a number of famous **masmen,** including George Bailey and Stephen Derek as well as a number of steelbands.

Works Cited

Abrahams, Roger. 1983. *The Man-of-Words in the West Indies: Performance and the Emergence of Creole Culture.* Baltimore, Md.: Johns Hopkins University Press.

Abu-Lughod, Lila. 1991. "Writing Against Culture." Pp. 137–162 in *Recapturing Anthropology: Working in the Present,* ed. Richard G. Fox. Santa Fe, N.M.: School of American Research Press.

Aho, William. 1987. "Steelband Music in Trinidad and Tobago." *Latin American Music Review* 8 (1):26–58.

Ahye, Molly. 1991. "Carnival, the Manipulative Polymorph: An Interplay of Social Stratification." Pp. 399–416 in *Social and Occupational Stratification in Contemporary Trinidad and Tobago,* ed. Selwyn Ryan. St. Augustine, Trinidad and Tobago: Institute for Social and Economic Research and the University of the West Indies.

Allahar, Anton. 1999. "Popular Culture and Racialisation of Political Consciousness in Trinidad and Tobago." Pp. 246–281 in *Identity, Ethnicity, and Culture in the Caribbean,* ed. Ralph Premdas. St. Augustine, Trinidad and Tobago: University of the West Indies.

Alleyne, Doddridge H. N. 1988. Petroleum and Development (1962–1987). Pp. 19–26 in *Trinidad and Tobago: The Independence Experience 1962–1987,* ed. Selwyn Ryan. St. Augustine, Trinidad and Tobago: Institute for Social and Economic Research and the University of the West Indies.

Allong, Genevieve. 1984. "Changes in Carnival and in Popular Attitudes towards it between 1970 and the Present Day." Thesis, Caribbean Studies Program, University of the West Indies: St. Augustine.

Alofs, Luc, and Leontine Meirkes. 1990. *Ken ta Arubiano?* Leiden, Holland: University of Leiden.

Alonso, Ana Maria. 1990. "Men in Rags and the Devil on the Throne: A Study of Protest and Inversion in the Carnival of Post-Emancipation Trinidad." *Plantation Society in the Americas* 3 (1):73–120.

Altorki, Soraya, and Camillia El Sohl. 1988. *Arab Women in the Field: Studying Your Own Society.* Syracuse, N.Y.: Syracuse University Press.

Anderson, Benedict. 1983. *Imagined Communities: Reflections on the Origin and Spread of Nationalism.* London: Verso.

Anderson, Wosley W. 1993. *Caribbean Immigrants: A Socio-Demographic Profile.* Toronto: Canadian Scholars Press.

Anthony, Michael. 1989. *Parade of the Carnivals of Trinidad 1839–1989.* Port of Spain, Trinidad and Tobago: Circle Press.

Appadurai, Arjun. 1990. "Disjuncture and Difference in the Global Economy." *Public Culture* 2 (2):1–24.

———. 1993. "Patriotism and Its Futures." *Public Culture* 5 (3):411–429.

———. 1997. *Modernity at Large.* Minneapolis: University of Minnesota Press.

———. 2003. "Sovereignty Without Territory: Notes for a Postnational Geography." Pp. 335–350 in *The Anthropology of Space and Place,* ed. Setha M. Low and Denise Lawrence-Zúñiga. Oxford: Blackwell.

Aruba Esso News. Archived in the Biblioteca Nacional, Aruba.

Asad, Talal. 1982. "A Comment on the Idea of Non-Western Anthropology." Pp. 284–287 in *Indigenous Anthropology in Non-Western Countries,* ed. Hussein Fahim. Durham, N.C.: Carolina Academic Press.

Attaway, William. 1956. Calypso, liner notes to one long-playing record album, RCA Victor LPM-1248.

Bakhtin, Mikhail. 1984. *Rabelais and His World.* Trans. H. Iswolsky. [1968]. Bloomington: Indiana University Press.

Balliger, Robin. 2001. "Noisy Spaces: Popular Music Consumption, Social Fragmentation, and the Cultural Politics of Globalization in Trinidad." Ph.D. dissertation, Department of Cultural and Social Anthropology, Stanford University.

Baptiste, Owen, ed. 1988. *Women in Mas'.* Port of Spain, Trinidad and Tobago: Key Imprint.

Basch, Linda, Nina Glick Schiller, and Cristina Szanton Blanc. 1994. *Nations Unbound: Transnational Projects, Postcolonial Predicaments, and Deterritorialized Nation-States.* Basel: Gordon and Breach.

Belafonte, Harry. 1962. *The Belafonte Folk Song Book.* New York: Consolidated Music Publishers.

Bellour, Hellene, and Kinser, Samuel. 1998. "Amerindian Masking in Trinidad Carnival: The House of Black Elk in San Fernando." *The Drama Review* 42 (3):147–169.

Bettig, Ronald V. 1996. *Copyrighting Culture: The Political Economy of Intellectual Property.* Boulder, Colo.: Westview.

Bishop, Patricia. 1994. "Carnival as Export Commodity?" Address to Conference "Carnival: The Export Potential," University of the West Indies.

BMI advertisement. 1957. *Variety.* February 27.

Brand, Dionne. 2000. *In Another Place, Not Here.* New York: Grove Press.

Brennan, Timothy. 1993. "The National Longing for Form." Pp. 47–49 in *Nation and Narration,* ed. Homi Bhabha. London: Routledge.

Brenner, Neil. 1997. "Global, Fragmented, Hierarchical: Henri Lefebvre's Geographies of Globalization." *Public Culture* 10 (1):135–167.

Brereton, Bridget. 1975. "The Trinidad Carnival 1870–1900." *Savacou: Journal of Caribbean Studies* 11–12:46–57.

———. 1979. *Race Relations in Colonial Trinidad, 1870–1900.* Cambridge: Cambridge University Press.

———. 1981. *A History of Modern Trinidad and Tobago, 1783–1962.* Kingston, Jamaica: Heinemann.

Briggs, Charles. 1996. "The Politics of Discursive Authority in Research on the Invention of Tradition." *Cultural Anthropology* 11 (4):435–469.

Bryce-Laporte, Roy S., and Delores S. Mortimer. 1983. *Caribbean Immigration to the United States.* Washington, D.C.: The Smithsonian Institution.

Buff, Rachel. 1997. "'Mas' in Brooklyn: Immigration, Race and the Cultural Politics of Carnival." Pp. 221–240 in *Language, Rhythm and Sound: Black Popular Cultures into the Twenty-first Century,* ed. J. Adjaye and A. Andrews. Pittsburgh, Pa.: University of Pittsburgh.

Burton, Richard D. E. 1997. *Afro-Creole: Power, Opposition and Play in the Caribbean.* Ithaca, N.Y.: Cornell University Press.

"The Calypso Craze." 1957. *Newsweek.* February 27.

"Calypsomania." 1957. *Time.* March 25.

"Calypso Via Disk, Dance." 1957. *Billboard.* March 9.

Campbell, Stuart. 1988. "Carnival, Calypso, and Class Struggle in 19th century Trinidad." *History Workshop Journal* 26:1–27.

"Caribana '68." 1968. *West Indian Observer.* July 3.

"Caribana Ball." 1968. *West Indian Observer.* August 5.

"Caribana House Soon to Be Reality." *West Indian Observer* 2 (4):4.

"Caribana in Retrospect." 1968. *West Indian Observer.* August 2.

"Caribana Island Entertainment." 1968. *West Indian Observer.* August 11.

Caribana Official Web Site. 1997.

"The Caribana Story." 1968. *West Indian Observer.* July 4.

Castells, Manuel. 1997. *The Power of Identity.* Oxford: Blackwell.

Central Statistical Office. 1984. *Annual Statistical Digest No. 29* (1982). Port of Spain, Trinidad and Tobago: The Central Statistical Office.

———. 1993. *1990 Population and Housing Census.* Vol. II. Port of Spain, Trinidad and Tobago: Office of the Prime Minister, Central Statistical Office.

Chambers, Iain, and Lidia Curti, eds. 1996. *The Post-Colonial Question: Common Skies, Divided Horizons.* London: Routledge.

Clarke, Austin. 1996. *The Austin Clarke Reader.* Toronto: Exile Editions.

Cohen, Abner. 1980. "Drama and Politics in the Development of a London Carnival." *Man* 15 (1):65–86.

———. 1982. "A Polyethnic London Carnival as a Contested Cultural Performance." *Racial and Ethnic Studies* 5 (1):23–41.

———. 1993. *Masquerade Politics.* Berkeley: University of California Press.

Cole, Sam. 1994. "Cultural Accounting: An Example from a Small Caribbean Island." *Contemporary Economic Policy,* October: 92–103.

Collier, Jane, Bill Maurer, and Liliana Suarez-Navaz. 1995. "Sanctioned Identities: Legal Constructions of Modern Personhood." *Identities* 2 (1–2):1–27.

Comaroff, Jean, and John L. Comaroff. 2000. "Millennial Capitalism: First Thoughts on a Second Coming." *Public Culture* 12 (2):291–343.

Constantine, Carleton Zigilee. 1993. Personal interview. Port of Spain, Trinidad and Tobago. March 31.

Coombe, Rosemary. 1997. "The Properties of Culture and the Possession of Identity: Postcolonial Struggle and the Legal Imagination." Pp. 74–96 in *Borrowed Power: Essays on Cultural Appropriation,* ed. Bruce Ziff and Pratima V. Rao. New Brunswick, N.J.: Rutgers University Press.

———. 1998. *The Cultural Life of Intellectual Properties.* Durham, N.C.: Duke University Press.

Cooper, Frederick, and Ann Laura Stoler. 1997. "Between Metropole and Colony: Rethinking a Research Agenda." Pp. 1–56 in *Tensions of Empire: Colonial Cultures in a Bourgeois World,* ed. Frederick Cooper and Ann Laura Stoler. Berkeley: University of California Press.

Copyright Organisation of Trinidad and Tobago Limited. Annual Report 1995.

Costain, Brandi. 2002. *Toronto Talks: Featuring the Slang of the GTA's Black Youth.* Toronto.

"COTT Goes after 'Free Music.'" 1997. *Punch.* June 28.

Cowley, John. 1993. "*L'Année Pasée:* Selected Repetoire in English-Speaking West Indian Music 1900–1960." *Keskidee* 3:2–42.

———. 1996. *Carnival, Canboulay, and Calypso.* Cambridge: Cambridge University Press.

Craft, Loren. 1957. "Mad Fad from Trinidad," p. 79 in *Sunday News.*

Crichton, Noel, and Charles de Silva. 1989. "Financial Development and Economic Growth: Trinidad and Tobago, 1973–1987." *Social and Economic Studies* 38 (4):131–157.

Cross, Malcolm. 1980. *East Indians of Trinidad and Guyana.* Cambridge, Mass.: Cultural Survival.

Crowley, Daniel J. 1956. "The Traditional Masques of Carnival." *Caribbean Quarterly* 4 (3–4):42–90. Reprinted by Paria Press in 1982.

Cudjoe, Selwyn, ed. 1993. *Eric E. Williams Speaks.* Wellesley, Mass.: Calaloux Publications.

Daniell, Alvin. n.d. *Calypso Showcase*—Copyright #1 (video).

Day, Charles. 1852. *Five Year's Residence in The West Indies.* 2 vols. London.

DECO and NU/DCTD. 1984. *The Termination of Operations of Lago Oil and Transport Co. Ltd: Consequences and Search for Solutions.* Oranjestad, Aruba: DECO.

Deere, Carmen Diana (coordinator), Peggy Antrobus, Lynn Bolles, Edwin Melendez, Peter Phillips, Marcia Rivera, and Helen Safa. 1990. *The Shadows of the Sun: Caribbean Development Alternatives and U.S. Policy.* Boulder, Colo.: Westview Press.

De Freitas, Patricia A. 1994. "'Playing Mas': The Construction and Deconstruction of National Identity in the Trinidad Carnival." Ph.D. dissertation, Department of Anthropology, McMaster University, Hamilton, Ontario, Canada.

———. 1999. "Disrupting the Nation: Gender Transformations in the Trinidad Carnival." *NWIG* 73 (1&2):5–34.

Deosaran, Ramesh. 1978. "Work Ethic or Carnival Mentality?" Pp. 28–50 in *Carnival: Working Papers on Caribbean Society.* St. Augustine, Trinidad: Department of Sociology, University of the West Indies, St. Augustine.

De Verteuil, Anthony. 1984. *The Years of Revolt: Trinidad 1881–1988.* Newton, Port of Spain, Trinidad: Paria Pub. Co.

Diehl, Keila. 1992. "Tempered Steel: The Steelband as a Site for Social, Political, and Aesthetic Negotiation in Trinidad." Masters thesis, Department of Anthropology, University of Texas.

Dookeran, Winston C., ed. 1996. *Choices and Change: Reflections on the Caribbean.* New York: Inter-American Development Bank.

Downbeat. 1953. March 23.

———. 1953. November 4.

Dudley, Shannon. 1997. "Making Music for the Nation: Competing Identities and Esthetics in Trinidad and Tobago's Panorama Steelband Competition." Ph.D. dissertation, Department of Music, University of California–Berkeley.

Edmondson, Belinda J. 1999. "Trinidad Romance: The Invention of Jamaican Carnival." Pp. 56–75 in *Caribbean Romances: The Politics of Regional Representation,* ed. Belinda J. Edmondson. Charlottesville: University Press of Virginia.

Edwards, Leon Smooth. 2000. Personal interview. Port of Spain, Trinidad and Tobago, March 4.

Elder, Jacob. 1966. "Evolution of the Traditional Calypso of Trinidad and Tobago: A Socio-historical Analysis of Song Change." Ph.D. dissertation, Department of Anthropology and Folklore, University of Pennsylvania.

———. 1969. *From Congo Drum to Steelband: A Socio-historical Account of the Emergence and Evolution of the Trinidad Steel Orchestra.* St. Augustine, Trinidad: University of the West Indies.

Emerencia, Lydia. 1998. "The Struggle for Recognition of Papiamento in the Aruban School: A Long Story coming to an End?" Unpublished paper.

Enloe, Cynthia. 1990. *Bananas, Beaches and Bases: Making Feminist Sense of International Politics.* Berkeley: University of California Press.

Espinet, Charles S., and Harry Pitts. 1944. *Land of the Calypso: The Origin and Development of Trinidad's Folk Song.* Port of Spain, Trinidad and Tobago: Guardian Commercial Printery.

Express. 1988. February 5.

———. 1988. February 28.

Fabian, Johannes. 1990. "Presence and Representation: The Other and Anthropological Writing." *Critical Inquiry* 16:753–772.

Fahim, Hussein, ed. 1982. *Indigenous Anthropology in Non-Western Countries.* Durham, N.C.: Carolina Academic Press.

Figaroa et al. n.d."Carnival on Aruba." Mimeo, Archives of the Biblioteca Nacional, Aruba.

Foner, Nancy. 2001. *Islands in The City: West Indian Migration to New York.* Berkeley: University of California Press.

Foster, Cecil. 1995. *Caribana: The Greatest Celebration.* Toronto: Ballantine Books.

Fox, Richard G. 1990. Introduction. Pp. 1–14 in *National Ideologies and the Production of National Cultures,* ed. Richard G. Fox. American Ethnological Society Monograph Series (2). Washington: American Anthropological Association.

Franco, Pamela. 1998. "'Dressing Up and Looking Good': Afro-Creole Female Maskers in Trinidad Carnival." *African Arts* 31 (2):62–67, 91, 95.

Frazer, James G. 1959. *The New Golden Bough.* New York: Criterion Books.

Freedman, Joel. 1957. "Personal Appearances." *Billboard.* February 16.

Friedman, Jonathan. 1987. "Beyond Otherness of the Spectacularization of Anthropology." *Telos* 71:161–170.

Frow, John. 1991. "Tourism and the Semiotics of Nostalgia." *October* 57:123–151.

"Futures Spark DJ Attention." 1957. *Billboard.* March 23.

Gallaugher, Annemarie. 1995. "Constructing Caribbean Culture in Toronto: The Representation of Caribana. Pp. 397–407 in *The Reordering of Culture in the Hood: Latin America, the Caribbean, and Canada.* Ottawa: Carleton University Press.

Gates, Henry Louis. 1997. *Thirteen Ways of Looking at a Black Man.* New York: Random House.

Gilroy, Paul. 1992. *The Black Atlantic: Modernity and Double Consciousness.* Cambridge, Mass.: Harvard University Press.

———. 1996. "Route Work: The Black Atlantic and the Politics of Exile." Pp. 17–30 in *The Post-colonial Question: Common Skies Divided Horizons,* ed. I. Chamber and L. Curti. New York: Routledge.

"Give Licenses to Cassette Dealers." 1992. *Express.* November 21.

Glick Schiller, Nina, Linda Basch, and Cristina Blanc-Szanton. 1992. *Towards a Transnational Perspective on Migration: Race, Class, Ethnicity, and Nationalism Reconsidered.* Vol. 645. New York: Annals of the New York Academy of Sciences.

Gmelch, George. 1992. *Double Passage: The Lives of Caribbean Migrants Abroad and Back Home.* Ann Arbor: University of Michigan Press.

Goddard, George. 1991. *Forty Years in the Steelbands: 1939–1979,* ed. Roy D. Thomas. London: Karia Press.

Gotfrit, Leslie. 1991. "Women Dancing Back: Disruption and the Politics of Pleasure." Pp. 174–195 in *Postmodernism, Feminism and Cultural Politics: Redrawing Educational Boundaries,* ed. Henry Giroux. Albany: State University of New York Press.

Green, Garth L. 1998. "Carnival and the Politics of National Identity in Trinidad and Tobago." Ph.D. dissertation, Department of Anthropology, New School for Social Research, New York, N.Y.

———. 1999. "Blasphemy, Sacrilege, and Moral Degradation in the Trinidad Carnival: The Hallelujah Controversy of 1995." Pp. 189–213 in *Religion, Diaspora, and Cultural Identity: A Reader in the Anglophone Caribbean,* ed. John Pulis. New York: Gordon and Breach.

———. 2005. "'Authenticity' and the Construction of Identity in Trinidad Carnival." Pp. 297–323 in *Globalisation, Diaspora, and Caribbean Popular Culture,* ed. Christine G. T. Ho and Keith Nurse. Kingston: Ian Randle.

Green, Vera. 1974. *Migrants in Aruba.* Assen: Van Gorcum.

Greenblatt, Stephen. 1980. *Renaissance Self-Fashioning: From More to Shakespeare.* Chicago: University of Chicago Press.

Griffith, Jason. 1993. Interview. Belmont, Trinidad and Tobago. November 27.

Grugel, Jean. 1995. *Politics and Development in the Caribbean Basin: Central America and the Caribbean in the New World Order.* Bloomington: Indiana University Press.

Gupta, Akhil, and James Ferguson. 1992. "Beyond Culture: Space, Identity and the Politics of Difference." *Cultural Anthropology* 7 (1):6–23.

Hakkert, Ralph, and Franklin W. Goza. 1989. "The Demographic Consequences of Austerity in Latin America." Pp. 69–97 in *Lost Promises: Debt, Austerity, and Development in Latin America,* ed. William L. Canak. Boulder, Colo.: Westview Press.

Hall, Stuart. 1990. "Cultural Identity and Diaspora." Pp. 222–237 in *Identity: Community, Culture, Difference,* ed. Jonathan Rutherford. London: Lawrence and Wishart.

———. 1991. "Negotiating Caribbean Identities." *New Left Review* 209:3–14.

———. 1992. "New Ethnicities." Pp. 252–260 in *Race, Culture, and Difference,* ed. J. Donald and A. Rattansi. London: Sage.

Handler, Richard. 1991. "Who Owns the Past? History, Cultural Property, and the Logic of Possessive Individualism." Pp. 63–74 in *The Politics of Culture,* ed. Brett Williams. Washington: Smithsonian Institution Press.

Handler, Richard, and Jocelyn Linnekin. 1984. "Tradition, Genuine or Spurious." *Journal of American Folklore* 97 (385):273–290.

Hannerz, Ulf. 1996. *Transnational Connections.* London: Routledge.

Hardt, Michael, and Antonio Negri. 2000. *Empire.* Cambridge, Mass.: Harvard University Press.

Harris, Max. 1998. "The Impotence of Dragons: Playing Devil in the Trinidad Carnival." *The Drama Review* 42 (3):108–123.

Hartog, Johan. 1961. *Aruba Past and Present.* Oranjestad, Aruba: De Wit, NV.

Harvey, Claudia. 1984. "Carnival as an Instrument of Education II." Pp. 226–236 in *Seminar Papers. The Social and Economic Impact of Carnival,* ed. Jack Harewood. St. Augustine, Trinidad: Institute of Social and Economic Research.

Hayde, Wayne. 1997. "Lurching Towards a Race War." *Caribbean Dialogue: A Journal of Contemporary Caribbean Policy Issues* 3 (4):43–44.

Hebdige, Dick. 1987. *Cut'n'Mix: Culture Identity and Caribbean Music.* London: Routledge.

Henry, Frances. 1994. *The Caribbean Diaspora in Toronto: Learning to Live with Racism.* Toronto: University of Toronto Press.

Hill, Donald R. 1993. *Calypso Calaloo: Early Carnival Music in Trinidad.* Gainesville: University of Florida Press.

———. 1994. "West Indian Carnival in New York." *New York Folklore* 20 (1–2):47–66.

———. 1998. "'I Am Happy Just to Be in This Sweet Land of Liberty': The New York City Calypso Craze of the 1930s and 1940s." Pp.74–92 in *Island Sounds in the Global City,* ed. Ray Allen and Lois Wilcken. New York: Institute for Studies in American Music and the New York Folklore Society.

Hill, Donald R., and John H. Cowley. 1999. "Calypso after Midnight." Notes for one CD, Rounder 11661–1842–2. Cambridge, Mass.: Rounder Records.

Hill, Errol. 1972. *Carnival: Mandate for a National Theater.* Austin: University of Texas Press.

———. 1976. "The Trinidad Carnival: Cultural Change and Synthesis." *Culture* 3 (1): 54–85.

———. 1984. "The History of Carnival." Pp. 6–39 in *Seminar Papers. The Social and Economic Impact of Carnival,* ed. Jack Harewood. UWI, St. Augustine, Trinidad: Institute of Social and Economic Research.

———. 1985. "Traditional Figures in Carnival: Their Preservation, Development, and Interpretation." *Caribbean Quarterly* 31 (2):14–34. Special Issue on Carnival, Calypso, and the Music of Confrontation.

Hill, Lawrence. 1996. *Women of Vision: The Story of the Canadian Negro Women's Association.* Toronto: Umbrella Press.

Hobsbawm, Eric. 1983. Introduction: Inventing Traditions. Pp. 1–14 in *The Invention of Traditions,* ed. Eric Hobsbawm and Terence Ranger. Cambridge: Cambridge University Press.

Holder, Geoffrey. 1957. "That Fad from Trinidad." *The New York Times Magazine.* April 21:14.

Holman, Ray. 1991. Personal interview. Arcata, Calif., July 14.

———. 1993. Personal interview. St. Anne's, Trinidad and Tobago, July 7.

———. 1999. Personal interview. Seattle, August 8.

Honore, Brian. 1998. "The Midnight Robber: Masterpiece of Metaphor, Baron of Bombast." *The Drama Review* 42 (3):124–131.

Hoyer, W. M. 1945. *A Brief Historical Description of the Island of Aruba in English and Papiamento.* Curacao.

Inniss, Nicky. 2000. Personal interview. Port of Spain, Trinidad and Tobago, February 10.
Island in the Sun. 1957. 20th Century Fox Exhibitor's Campaign Book.
Ivy, Marilyn. 1995. *Discourses of the Vanishing: Modernity, Phantasm, Japan.* Chicago: University of Chicago Press.
Jackson, Anthony, ed. 1987. *Anthropology at Home.* London: Tavistock.
Jackson, Peter. 1992. "The Politics of the Streets: A Geography of Caribana." *Political Geography* 2:130–151.
James, C. L. R. 1963. *Beyond a Boundary.* London: Stanley Paul.
James, Carl E. 1989. *Seeing Ourselves: Exploring Race, Ethnicity and Culture.* Oakville, Ontario: Sheridan College.
Jameson, Fredric. 1989. "Nostalgia for the Present." *South Atlantic Quarterly* 88 (2):517–537.
———. 1991. *Post-modernism, Or, the Cultural Logic of Late Capitalism.* Durham, N.C.: Duke University Press.
John Murray Anderson's Almanac. 1953. Playbill for Imperial Theatre.
Johnson, Kim. 1984. "The Social Impact of Carnival." Pp. 171–207 in *Carnival: Working Papers on Caribbean Society,* ed. Jack Harewood. Department of Sociology, University of the West Indies, St. Augustine.
———. 1988. "Carnival in Trinidad." *Insight Guide to Trinidad.* APA Publications.
———. 1996. Tin Pan Alley, Part 1: The Soul in Iron: Considerations in Steelband Historiography. *Pan Lime* (Akron, Ohio), 3 (11, 12).
Joseph, Clifton. 1996. "Jump Up and Beg." *Toronto Life.* 30 (11):46–54.
Jules, Neville. 1999. Personal interview by telephone. October 28.
Juteram, Gillian. 1989. "Cultural Controversy in the Trinidad and Tobago Carnival." Thesis, Caribbean Studies Program, University of the West Indies—St. Augustine, Trinidad and Tobago.
Kalm, Florence. 1974. "The Dispersive and Reintegrating Nature of Population Segments of a Third World Society: Aruba, Netherlands Antilles." Ph.D. dissertation, City University of New York.
Kant, Immanuel. 1963 [1784]. "Idea for a Universal History from a Cosmopolitan Point of View." Pp. 11–26 in *On History,* ed. Lewis White Beck. Indianapolis: Bobbs-Merrill.
Kardinal Offishall. 2002. *Firestarter Vol. 1 Quest for Fire.* Figure IV: MCA Records.
Kasfir, Sidney Littlefield. 1998. "Elephant Women, Furious and Majestic." *African Arts* 31 (2):18–28.
Kasinitz, Philip. 1992. *Caribbean New York: Black Immigrants and the Politics of Race.* Ithaca, N.Y.: Cornell University Press.
———, and Judith Freidenberg-Herbstein. 1987. "The Puerto Rican Parade and West Indian Carnival: Public Celebrations in New York City." Pp. 305–325 in *Caribbean Life in New York City,* ed. Constance R. Sutton and Elsa M. Chaney. New York: Center for Migration Studies.
Kearney, Michael. 1995. "The Local and the Global: The Anthropology of Globalization and Transnationalism." *Annual Review of Anthropology* 24:547–565.
Kinser, Samuel. 1990. *Carnival American Style: Mardi Gras at New Orleans and Mobile.* Chicago: University of Chicago Press.
Klass, Morton. 1991. Singing with Sai Baba: The Politics of Revitalization in Trinidad. Boulder, Colo.: Westview Press.

Kondo, Dorinne. 1996. "The Narrative Production of Home, Community, and Political Identity in Asian American Theater." Pp. 97–117 in *Displacement, Diaspora, and Geographies of Identity,* ed. Smadar Lavie and Ted Swedenburg. Durham, N.C.: Duke University Press.

La Guerre, John, ed. 1994. *Structural Adjustment: Public Policy and Administration in the Caribbean.* St. Augustine: University of the West Indies.

Lee, Ann. 1991. "Class, Race, Color and the Trinidad Carnival." Pp. 417–433 in *Social and Occupational Stratification in Contemporary Trinidad,* ed. Selwyn Ryan. St. Augustine: Institute of Social and Economic Research, University of the West Indies.

Lewis, Gordon K. 1968. *The Growth of the Modern West Indies.* New York: Monthly Review Press.

Limon, Jose E. 1991. "Representation, Ethnicity and the Precursory Ethnography: Notes of a Native Anthropologist." Pp. 115–135 in *Recapturing Anthropology: Working in the Present,* ed. Richard G. Fox. Santa Fe, N.M.: School of American Research Press.

Liverpool, Hollis. 1986. *Kaiso and Society.* Diego Martin, Trinidad: Juba Publications.

———. 1990. *Culture and Education: Carnival in Trinidad and Tobago, Implications for Education in Secondary Schools.* London: Karia.

———. 1993. "Rituals of Power and Rebellion: The Carnival Tradition in Trinidad and Tobago." Ph.D. dissertation, Department of History, University of Michigan.

———. 1998. "Origins of Rituals and Customs in the Trinidad Carnival: African or European?" *The Drama Review* 42 (3):24–37.

———. 2001. *Rituals of Power and Rebellion: The Carnival Tradition in Trinidad and Tobago 1763–1962.* Chicago: Research Associates School Times Publications.

Locke, John. 1980 [1690]. *Second Treatise of Government.* Indianapolis: Hackett Publishing.

Lovelace, Earl. 1996. *Salt.* London: Faber and Faber.

Lowenthal, David. 1985. *The Past is a Foreign Country.* Cambridge: Cambridge University Press.

Lyndersay, Mark. 1997. "The Nature of Copyright." *Sunday Express.* April 20.

MacCannell, Dean. 1992. *Empty Meeting Grounds: The Tourist Papers.* London. Routledge.

Macpherson, C. B. 1975. *The Political Theory of Possessive Individualism: Hobbes to Locke.* Oxford: Oxford University Press.

Mahabir, Ashar. 1988/1989. "A Comparative Study of Carnival in Rio de Janiero and Trinidad's Carnival." Thesis, Caribbean Studies Program, University of the West Indies.

Manning, Frank E. 1977. "Cup Match and Carnival: Secular Rites of Revitalization in Decolonizing, Tourist-Oriented Societies." Pp. 262–282 in *Secular Ritual,* ed. Sally Moore and Barbara Myerhoff. Amsterdam: Van Gorcum.

———. 1978. "Carnival in Antigua: An Indigenous Festival in a Tourist Economy." *Anthropos* 73:191–204.

———. 1983. "Carnival and the West Indian Diaspora." *Round Table* 286:186–196.

———. 1984. "Carnival in Canada: The Politics of Celebration." Pp. 25–33 in *The Masks of Play,* ed. Brian Sutton-Smith and Diana Kelly-Byrne. New York: Leisure Press.

———. 1990. "Overseas Caribbean Carnivals: The Art and Politics of a Transnational Celebration." *Plantation Society in the Americas* 3 (1):47–62.

Manuel, Peter. 1995. *Caribbean Currents: Caribbean Music from Rumba to Reggae.* Philadelphia: Temple University Press.

Marx, Karl. 1976. *Capital.* Vol. 1. London: Penguin Books.

———. 1990. *On the Jewish Question. Karl Marx: Selected Writings,* ed. David McLellan. Oxford: Oxford University Press.

Mbembe, Achille. 2001. *On the Postcolony.* Berkeley: University of California Press.

McClean, Daisy, and John Murray. 1993. Personal interview. July 15.

McClintock, Anne. 1995. *Imperial Leather: Race, Gender and Sexuality in the Colonial Contest.* London: Routledge.

———, Aamir Mufti, and Ella Shohat (Social Text Collective). 1997. *Dangerous Liaisons: Gender, Nation, and Postcolonial Perspectives (Cultural Politics).* Minneapolis: University of Minnesota Press.

McGrane, Bernard. 1989. *Beyond Anthropology: Society and the Other.* New York: Columbia University Press.

McIntosh, Ronnie. 1998. *X: A Perfect Ten.* LP Arranged by Ossie Gurley, Clinton Crawford and Robert Greenidge, VP Records.

Mercer, Kobena. 1994. *Welcome to the Jungle: New Positions in Black Cultural Studies.* London: Routledge.

Miller, Daniel. 1991. "Absolute Freedom in Trinidad." *Man* 26 (2):323–341.

———. 1994. *Modernity: An Ethnographic Approach.* Oxford: Berg.

Minh-ha, Trinh. 1989. *Woman, Native, Other: Writing Post-Coloniality and Feminism.* Bloomington: Indiana University Press.

Mintz, Sidney. 1986. *Sweetness and Power: The Place of Sugar in Modern History.* New York: Penguin Books.

Mintz, Sidney, and Sally Price, eds. 1985. *Caribbean Contours.* Baltimore, Md.: Johns Hopkins University Press.

Minutes of the House of Representatives. 1996. Port of Spain, Trinidad and Tobago, July 9.

Minutes of the Senate. 1996. Port of Spain, Trinidad and Tobago, July 12.

Nakhleh, Khalil. 1979. "On Being a Native Anthropologist." Pp. 343–352 in *The Politics of Anthropology: From Colonialism and Sexism Toward a View from Below,* ed. G. Huizer and B. Mannheim. The Hague: Mouton.

Narayan, Kirin. 1989. *Storytellers, Saints and Scoundrels.* Philadelphia: University of Pennsylvania Press.

———. 1993. "How Native is a Native Anthropologist?" *American Anthropologist* 95(3): 671–686.

Nunley, John, and Judith Bettelheim. 1988. *Caribbean Festival Arts: Each and Every Bit of Difference.* St. Louis and Seattle: Saint Louis Art Museum and the University of Washington Press.

Nurse, Keith. 1996a. "International Copyright Regulation and the Music Industry." *Caribbean Dialogue* 2/4 (April/June):21–22.

———. 1996b. "The Trinidad and Tobago Carnival: Towards an Export Strategy." *Caribbean Labour Journal* 5(3):5–7.

———. 1997. Personal communication. May 8.

———. 1999. "Globalization and Trinidad Carnival: Diaspora, Hybridity and Identity in Global Culture." *Cultural Studies* 13 (4):661–690.

Odingi, Eddie. 1993. Personal interview. Port of Spain, Trinidad and Tobago, July 21.

Ohnuki-Tierney, Emiko. 1984. "Native Anthropologists." *American Ethnologist* 11 (3): 584–586.

Orloff, Alexander. 1981. *Carnival: Myth and Cult.* Wörgl, Austria: Perlinger.

Ortner, Sherry. 1984. "Theory in Anthropology since the 1960s." *Contemporary Studies in Society and History* 26 (1):126–166.

Oxaal, Ivar. 1968. *Black Intellectuals Come to Power*. Cambridge, Mass.: Schenkman.

Pan Aruban Newsletter. Archived in the Biblioteca Nacional, Aruba.

Pastor, Manuel. 1989. "Latin America, the Debt Crisis, and the International Monetary Fund." *Latin American Perspectives* 16 (1):79–109.

Payne, Anthony, and Paul Sutton, eds. 1993. *Modern Caribbean Politics.* Kingston: Ian Randle Publishers.

Payne, Nellie. 1990. "Grenada Mas' 1928–1988." *Caribbean Quarterly* 36 (3–4):54–64.

Payson, David. 1995. "Electrifying Carnival: Commercialization and Cultural Ritual." *Bulletin of Eastern Caribbean Affairs* 20 (2):12–17.

Pearse, Andrew. 1956. "Carnival in Nineteenth Century Trinidad." *Caribbean Quarterly* 4 (3–4):4–42. Reprinted by Paria Press, Port of Spain, Trinidad and Tobago in 1988.

Phalen, John H. 1977. "Kinship, Color, and Ethnicity: Integrative Ideologies in Aruba, Netherlands Antilles." Ph.D. dissertation, State University of New York State at Stony Brook.

Philbrook, Erik. 1997. *Sunny Side Up in Playback,* http://www.google.com/search?q=cache:qcCzUAzAYOMJ:web.telia.com/~u87125994/sunnysideup.htm+%22Irving+Burgie%22+Ed+Sullivan&hl=en&lr=&strip=1 (retrieved June 30, 2005).

Philippi, Desa, 1987. "The Conjuncture of Race and Gender in Anthropology and Art History: A Critique of Nancy Spero's Work." n1 (Autumn):34–54.

"'Pirate' Fined $5,000 for Cassette." 1994. *Guardian.* July 21.

"Police for Pirates! COTT Flexes Its Legal Muscle." 1997. *Punch.* August 24.

Pouchet, Edwin. 1993. Personal interview. Port of Spain, Trinidad and Tobago, July 29.

Powrie, Barbara. 1956. "The Changing Attitude of the Coloured Middle Class Towards Carnival." *Caribbean Quarterly* 4 (3–4):91–107. Reprinted by Paria Press, Port of Spain, Trinidad and Tobago in 1988.

Premdas, Ralph. 1993. "Ethnic Conflict in Trinidad and Tobago: Domination and Reconciliation." Pp. 136–160 in *Trinidad Ethnicity,* ed. Kevin Yelvington. Knoxville: University of Tennessee Press.

Price, Richard, and Sally Price. 1997. "Shadowboxing in the Mangrove." *Cultural Anthropology* 12 (1):3–36.

Pryce, Everton. 1985. "The Notting Hill Gate Carnival: Black Politics, Resistance, and Leadership, 1976–1978." *Caribbean Quarterly* 31 (2):35–52.

Pujadas, L. C., and M. Rampersand. 1987. "The National Income of Trinidad and Tobago, 1966–1985." Reproduced as Appendix 3 in *Trinidad and Tobago: The Independence Experience 1962–1987,*" ed. Selwyn Ryan. St. Augustine, Trinidad and Tobago: Institute of Social and Economic Research, UWI, 557–592.

Ramchand, Ken. 1997. "Making Mas with Copyright Laws." *Trinidad Guardian.* February 26.

Ramnarine, Tina K. 2001. *Creating Their Own Space: The Development of an Indian-Caribbean Musical Tradition.* Kingston: University of the West Indies Press.

Razak, Victoria. 1998(a). "Issues of Identity in Festival, Song, and Social Discourse on Aruba, Dutch Caribbean." Ph.D. dissertation, Department of Anthropology, State University of New York at Buffalo.

———. 1998(b). *Carnival in Aruba.* New York: Cenda.

Reddock, Rhoda E. 1994. *Women, Labour and Politics in Trinidad and Tobago: A History.* Kingston, Jamaica: Ian Randle Publishers.

Rickards, Colin. 1997. "The Caribana Parade: Is It Dead?" *Pride.* August 7–13.

Rife, David. 1972. "Genetic Variability among Peoples of Aruba and Curacao." *American Journal of Physical Anthropology* 36:1.

Riggio, Milla C., ed. 1998. "Trinidad and Tobago Carnival." Special expanded issue. *The Drama Review* 42 (3).

Robotham, Don. 1998. "Transnationalism in the Caribbean: Formal and Informal." *American Ethnologist* 25 (2):307–321.

Rohlehr, Gordon. 1985. "Man Talking to Man: Calypso and Social Confrontation in Trinidad from 1970–1984." *Caribbean Quarterly* 31 (2):1–13. Special Issue on Carnival, Calypso, and the Music of Confrontation.

———. 1990. *Calypso and Society in Pre-Independence Trinidad.* Tunapuna, Trinidad: Gordon Rohlehr.

Rose, Tricia. 1994. *Black Noise: Rap Music and Black Culture in Contemporary America.* Middleton, Conn.: Wesleyan University Press.

Roseberry, William C. 1988. "Political Economy." *Annual Review of Anthropology* 17: 161–185.

Rouse, Ewart. 1966. "The Steelband: Classics vs. Folk." *Trinidad Guardian.* Port of Spain, Trinidad and Tobago, November 23:18.

Ryan, Selwyn, ed. 1988. *Trinidad and Tobago: The Independence Experience 1962–1987.* St. Augustine, Trinidad and Tobago: Institute of Social and Economic Research, University of the West Indies.

———. 1991. *Social and Occupational Stratification in Contemporary Trinidad and Tobago.* St. Augustine, Trinidad and Tobago: University of the West Indies.

———. 1996. *Pathways to Power: Indians and the Politics of National Unity in Trinidad and Tobago.* St. Augustine, Trinidad and Tobago: University of the West Indies.

Salazar, Max. 1999. "Willie Torres: A Retired Musician's Fate." *Latin Beat Magazine* September:35.

Sassen, Saskia. 1996. *Losing Control? Sovereignty in an Age of Globalization.* New York: Columbia University Press.

Satzewich, Vic. 1989. "Racism and Canadian Immigration Policy: The Government's View of Caribbean Migration, 1962–1966." *Canadian Ethnic Studies* 21 (1):77–93.

Schechner, Richard. 1985. *Between Theater and Anthropology.* Philadelphia: University of Pennsylvania Press.

Scher, Philip W. 1999. "West Indian American Day: Becoming a Tile in the Gorgeous Mosaic: West Indian American Day in Brooklyn." Pp. 45–66 in *Religion, Diaspora, and Cultural Identity: A Reader in the Anglophone Caribbean,* ed. John Pulis. New York: Gordon and Breach.

———. 2003. *Carnival and the Formation of a Caribbean Transnation.* Gainesville: University Press of Florida.

Schoenfeld, Herm. 1956. "Trend: Trinidad Tunes, Calypso-Caribe 'Takeover' Kick." *Variety,* December 26:1, 42.
Scott, David. 1991. "That Event, This Memory: Notes on the Anthropology of African Diasporas in the New World." *Diaspora* 1 (3):261–284.
———. 1995. "Colonial Governmentality." *Social Text* 43:191–220.
Sebeok, Thomas A. 1984. *Carnival!* Berlin: Mouton Publishers.
Segal, Daniel. 1995. "Living Ancestors: Nationalism and the Past in Postcolonial Trinidad and Tobago." Pp. 221–239 in *Remapping Memory: The Politics of TimeSpace,* ed. Jonathan Boyarin. Minneapolis: University of Minnesota Press.
———, ed. 1996. "Resisting Identities: Theme Issue." *Cultural Anthropology* 11 (4).
———. 1993. Race and Colour in Pre-Independence Trinidad and Tobago. Pp. 81–115 in *Trinidad Ethnicity,* ed. Kevin Yelvington. New York: Macmillan.
Sharrif, Ali. 1997. "Calypso Hangs on by a Thread as New Rhythms and Hard Times Hit Caribana." *Now Magazine,* July 31–August 6. Accessed at http://www.nowtoronto.com/issues/16/48/news/feature2.html.
Shaw, Arnold. 1960. *Belafonte: An Unauthorized Biography.* New York: Chilton Co.
Shepperd, Patrick. 1984. "Caribana." *Polyphony* 6:135–139.
Simmonds, Austin. 1964. Calypsoes vs. Classics, *Trinidad Guardian,* Port of Spain, Trinidad and Tobago, February 9:9.
Simon, Pete. 1970. *Trinidad Guardian.* Port of Spain, February 1:5.
Singh, Kelvin. 1988. *Bloodstained Tombs: The Muharram Massacre 1884.* London: Macmillan Caribbean.
Sippel, Johnny. 1957. "Cocoanut Grove, Ambassador Hotel, Los Angeles." *Billboard,* February 21:27.
"Skulduggery and Crossbones." 1995. *Express.* August 13.
Smith, Joe. 1988. *Off the Record: An Oral History of Popular Music.* New York: Warner Books.
Smith, Maria. 1986. "Children in Carnival: A Moral Appraisal." Thesis, Caribbean Studies Program, University of the West Indies.
"Splash With Song." 1954. *Newsweek.* March 29.
Springer, Pearl, and Val Rogers. 1993. *The Viey La Cou Traditional Carnival Characters.* Port of Spain, Trinidad and Tobago: Queen's Hall Board.
Srinivas, M. N. 1967. "The Study of One's Own Society." Pp. 147–163 in *Social Change in Modern India.* Berkeley: University of California Press.
Stallybrass, Peter, and Allon White. 1986. *The Politics and Poetics of Transgression.* Ithaca, N.Y.: Cornell University Press.
Steinman, Howard, ed. 1957. *Harry Belafonte: His Complete Life Story.* New York: Hillman Publications.
Stewart, John. 1986. "Patronage and Control in the Trinidad Carnival." Pp. 289–315 in *The Anthropology of Experience,* ed. Victor Turner and Edward Bruner. Champaign-Urbana: University of Illinois Press.
———. 1989. *Drinkers, Drummers and Decent Folk: Ethnographic Narratives in Village Trinidad.* Albany: State University of New York Press.
Stewart, Kathleen. 1988. "Nostalgia—A Polemic." *Cultural Anthropology* 3 (3):227–241.
———. 1996. *A Space on the Side of the Road: Cultural Poetics in an Other America.* Princeton, N.J.: Princeton University Press.

Stewart, Susan. 1984. *On Longing: Narratives of the Miniature, the Gigantic, the Souvenir, the Collection.* Baltimore: Johns Hopkins University Press.

Stewart, Taimoon. 1996. "The Political-Economy of Reform of Intellectual Property Protection." *Caribbean Dialogue* 2/4 (April/June):19–20.

———. 1997. "The Marrakesh Agreement on Trade-Related Intellectual Property Rights: Implications for CARICOM Countries." Pp. 256–597 in *The New World Trade Order: Uruguay Round Agreements and Implications for CARICOM States,* ed. Frank Rampersad. Mona: Ian Randle and Institute for Social and Economic Research, University of the West Indies.

Stuempfle, Stephen. 1995. *The Steelband Movement: The Forging of a National Art in Trinidad and Tobago.* Philadelphia: University of Pennsylvania Press.

Sutton, Constance, and Susan R. Makiesky-Barrow. 1987. "Migration and West Indian Racial and Ethnic Consciousness." Pp. 86–107 in *Caribbean Life in New York City,* ed. Constance Sutton and Elsa Chaney. New York: Center for Migration Studies.

Taubman, Howard. 1954. "A Folk Singer's Style: Personality and Integrity Worth More Than Cultivated Voice to Belafonte." *New York Times,* February 7:2, 7.

Thomas, Jeffrey. 1986. "The Changing Role of the Steel Band in Trinidad and Tobago: Panorama and the Carnival Tradition." *Studies in Popular Culture* 9(2):96–108.

"Timber's Gotta Roll." 1953. *Time.* March 9.

Toren, Christine. 1988. "Making the Present, Revealing the Past: The Mutability and Continuity of Tradition as Process." *Man* (NS) 23 (4):697.

Trinidad Express. 1988. February 22.

Trinidad Guardian. 1957. January 3.

———. 1988. February 12.

Trotman, David V. 1986. *Crime in Trinidad.* Knoxville: University of Tennessee Press.

———. 1991. "The Image of Indians in Calypso 1946–1986." Pp. 385–398 in *Social and Occupational Stratification in Contemporary Trinidad and Tobago,* ed. Selwyn Ryan. St. Augustine, Trinidad and Tobago: University of the West Indies.

Trouillot, Michel-Rolph. 1992. "The Caribbean Region: An Open Frontier in Anthropological Theory." *Annual Review of Anthropology* 21:19–42.

Turner, Bryan. 1987. "A Note on Nostalgia." *Theory, Culture, and Society* 4 (1):147–156.

Van Koningsbruggen, Peter. 1997. *Trinidad Carnival: A Quest for Identity.* London: Macmillan.

Variety. 1951. October 31:51.

———. 1957. April 3:83.

———. 1957. May 22.

———. 1957. June 26.

———. 1957. November 20.

"Victor Gets Belafonte Ink on New Pact." 1957. *Billboard.* April 27.

Walcott, Derek. 1970. "What the Twilight Says: An Overture." Pp. 3–40 in *Dream on Monkey Mountain and Other Plays.* New York: Farrar, Strauss and Giroux.

———. 1992. "The Antilles: Fragments of Epic Memory." Nobel lecture. Oslo: The Nobel Foundation.

Walcott, Rinaldo. 2001. *Rude: Black Canadian Contemporary Culture.* Toronto: Insomniac Press.

Walsh, Martin. 1998. "Jouvay Mornin' with the Merry Darceuils: A Small Neighborhood Band on Carnival Morning." *The Drama Review* 42 (3):132–146.

Watson, Graham. 1991. "Rewriting Culture." Pp. 73–92 in *Recapturing Anthropology: Working in the Present,* ed. Richard G. Fox. Santa Fe, N. M.: School of American Research Press.

"West Indian Festivities Invade Canada." *West Indian Observer* 2(7):1.

West Indian News Observer. December 1967–January 1, 1969.

Wolff, Janet. 1992. "Foreword: The Ideology of Autonomous Art." Pp. 1–12 in *Music and Society: The Politics of Composition,* ed. Richard Leppart and Susan McClary. Cambridge: Cambridge University Press.

World Bank. 1995. "Trinidad and Tobago: Poverty and Unemployment in an Oil-Based Economy." Report 1482-TF.

Wuest, Ruth. 1990. "The Robber in the Trinidad Carnival." *Caribbean Quarterly* 36 (3–4):42–53.

Yelvington, Kevin. 1993. "Introduction: Trinidad Ethnicity." Pp. 1–32 in *Trinidad Ethnicity,* ed. Kevin Yelvington. Knoxville: University of Tennessee Press.

———, ed. 1993. *Trinidad Ethnicity.* Knoxville: University of Tennessee Press.

———. 2000. "Caribbean Crucible: History, Culture, and Globalization." *Social Education* 64 (2):70–77.

———. 2001. "The Anthropology of Afro-Latin America and the Caribbean: Diasporic Dimensions." *Annual Review of Anthropology* 30:227–260.

Yon, Daniel. 1995. "Identity and Difference in the Caribbean Diaspora." Pp. 479–499 in *Reordering of Culture: Latin America The Caribbean and Canada in The Hood,* ed. A. Ruprecht and C. Taiana. Ottawa: Carleton University Press.

Ziff, Bruce, and Pratima Rao, eds. 1997. *Borrowed Power: Essays on Cultural Appropriation.* New Brunswick, N.J.: Rutgers University Press.

Contributors

Roger Abrahams is Hum Rosen Professor Emeritus of Folklore and Folklife at the University of Pennsylvania.

Robin Balliger is a resident faculty member in the Liberal Arts Department at the San Francisco Art Institute.

Shannon Dudley is Assistant Professor of Ethnomusicology at the University of Washington.

Pamela R. Franco is Assistant Professor of Art at Tulane University.

Patricia A. De Freitas is Associate Professor in the Ethnic and Women's Studies De-partment at California State Polytechnic University, Pomona.

Ray Funk is a trial court judge in Fairbanks, Alaska, who produces a weekly world music radio show.

Garth L. Green is a lecturer in the Department of Sociology and Anthropology and Program in International Studies at the University of North Carolina, Charlotte.

Donald R. Hill is Professor of Anthropology at SUNY–Oneonta.

Lyndon Phillip is a Ph.D. candidate in Sociology and Equity Studies at the OISE/University of Toronto.

Victoria Razak is Visiting Assistant Professor in the Department of Urban and Regional Planning at the University of Buffalo.

Philip Scher is Associate Professor of Anthropology at the University of Oregon. He is author of *Carnival and the Formation of a Caribbean Transnation* and editor of a forthcoming textbook, *Perspectives on the Caribbean: A Reader in Culture and Representation.*

Index